The *The* TWO FACES *of the* CHURCH... GET RIGHT *with* GOD

ZAMORA GONZALEZ

WESTBOW
PRESS®
A DIVISION OF THOMAS NELSON
& ZONDERVAN

WestBow Press books may be ordered through booksellers or by contacting:

WestBow Press
A Division of Thomas Nelson & Zondervan
1663 Liberty Drive
Bloomington, IN 47403
www.westbowpress.com
1 (866) 928-1240

THE HOLY BIBLE, NEW INTERNATIONAL VERSION®,
NIV® Copyright © 1973, 1978, 1984, 2011 by Biblica, Inc.®
Used by permission. All rights reserved worldwide.

Scripture taken from The Message. Copyright © 1993, 1994, 1995, 1996,
2000, 2001, 2002. Used by permission of NavPress Publishing Group.

ISBN: 978-1-9736-4562-7 (sc)
ISBN: 978-1-9736-4561-0 (hc)
ISBN: 978-1-9736-4563-4 (e)

Library of Congress Control Number: 2018913674

Print information available on the last page.

WestBow Press rev. date: 2/6/2019

TABLE OF CONTENTS

PART THREE
LOOKING AHEAD

DEDICATION

This book would not have been written had it not been for my God who inspired me to write it. God has been my inspiration and only fan through it all. God gave me the strength, the boldness, and the wisdom to bring this book to fruition. If it had not been for God, who loves me, I would have died in my sin and I am forever grateful. I look forward to eternity when I can see my Father, ABBA, in the heavenly realm.

I also want to dedicate this book to you. It's because of you that I had to write this book, to let you know that you are not alone in your Christian journey. There are countless others who have had to struggle but have stayed the course and served God. God wants you to know that your struggles have not been in vain and that your crown of glory awaits you in heaven. "Let the peace of Christ rule in your hearts" (Colossians 3:15, NIV).

> "So, Satan went out from the presence of the Lord and afflicted Job with painful sores from the soles of his feet to the crown of his head. Then Job took a piece of broken pottery and scraped himself with it as he sat among the ashes. His wife said to him, "Are you still maintaining your integrity? Curse God and die!" He replied, "You are talking like a foolish woman. Shall we accept good from God, and not trouble?" (Job 2:7-10, NIV)

ACKNOWLEDGMENT

I want to thank the Pastors and ALL the individuals for their contributions as a source for the content of my book. And, I am also grateful to everyone for the permission to use the excerpts from their sermons, Bible study groups, books, and songs.

I want to offer my deep appreciation for those who allowed me to write about their experiences.

I am especially grateful to my family for being so understanding and patient while I was writing this book. I love each one of you.

INTRODUCTION

I have written this book because it needs to be told. I, like some people, can't handle the truth but I will welcome it if it's going to help me improve something that's lacking in me or stop a habit that's disturbing to others. I can truly assure you that it's not to cause contention or insult the church leadership nor its members in any way. But to encourage awareness and discussion into the matter and find a resolution. For those of you who have been hurt, I believe you may find healing and be encouraged to finish the race God has set before you. My story is to help create a root in the heart of the reader of what it truly means to live a righteous life. To live righteous means to have a moral compass that reflects Christ Jesus, the son of God. I will share first-hand accounts of how rude and indifferent church people can actually be. I will share the pain and sufferings I went through and the times that I thought that I would leave the church and go back into the world. But because of my love for God and my calling into His kingdom I endured. Not everyone in church is cantankerous and indifferent but believe it or not many do reflect the love of God.

I realize there is still hope for the church and I plan to do something about it. I apologize to the readers if the content of this book offends you but 'truth be told.' "For we must all appear before the judgment seat of Christ, so that each of us may receive what is due us for the things done while in the body, whether good or bad" (2 Corinthians 5:10, NIV). I gave this book a lot of thought before making the decision to write it. I honestly can tell you that it's not my intent to judge anyone, it's not my job, I leave that up to God.

Judgments are very difficult to stray from when making distinctions about certain people, places, and things. Especially when used in rare instances where the intent is not to offend people but to call attention to certain behaviors unbecoming that individual and one can't escape making that judgment. For the point I am trying to make in this book judgment may appear a bit too harsh but only if the reader sees himself or herself requiring a mirror into their behaviors and attitudes and can appreciate some "constructive criticism." Author of the book, *Road Less Travelled* and Psychiatrist Scott Peck explains the use of judgment as such,

> "…We will see that it is both impossible and itself evil to totally refrain from making moral judgments. An attitude of "I'm OK; you're OK" may have a certain place in facilitating our social relationship, but only a place. Was Hitler OK? Jim Jones? …The fact of the matter is that we cannot lead decent lives without making judgments in general and moral judgments in particular." [1]

I would rather have my own Christian family judge me now then to be judged by God on the 'Day of Judgment,' (2 Corinthians 5:10) because it would be too late to make amends.

God chose me to live a Christian life and to have an intimate relationship with him. I was serious about my salvation and feared going back to my sinful old life. I wanted to be effective in serving God. God had saved my soul, and I was grateful and looked forward to doing His will; and what he had purposed for my life. I was willing to do what I was called to do for the kingdom and grow in the knowledge of God. I felt my faith was strengthening day by day. I was totally dependent on God. I was attending Sunday school and Bible study. I read my Bible daily. I fasted on times when I needed to and when the pastor called the church to fast. I made prayer a priority. My home life was peaceful, and my family members were safe. I took the scripture verse very serious and wanted to be a 'light to the world' (Matthew 5:14-16, NIV). I wanted others to know that I was a servant of the Lord as I shared my excitement of having been born again. We are to let our salvation be a germ that infects the world.

However, but for several years I had been concerned and questioned my walk with God, and it had been a frightening and trying time for me. In recent years, I have noticed that some of the church members have made a shifted from holiness to carnality. I have observe a number of those once faith-believing people drifting away from the doctrines of the Bible. They are living semi-godly life if there's such a thing and are listening to the dictates of their own conscience. What they believe is all right behavior is changing the way Christianity is truly about. Upon listening to R.C. Sproul one day, I found it very interesting what he had to say about the matter of the conscience, and it alarmed me.

> "Thirty-one times the word for conscience appears in the New Testament, and it seems to have a twofold dimension to it. There is this idea of accusing and excusing when we sin the conscience is troubled. It is the tool that God, the Holy Spirit uses to bring us under conviction to drive us to repentance and to the healing of forgiveness that flows from that but also there is a sense in which this moral voice that is activated in our mind and in our hearts can also tell us what is right and give approval. … [However] the conscience is not the final ethical authority for human conduct. The reason being is that the conscience is capable of change. Where God's principles do not change, our conscience may undergo change and development. And that change can be in more than one direction. The hardness of the heart had set in the conscience can be seared, and the conscience becomes callous. …But we see an erosion of the power of the conscience that comes through repeated sins. If you do a sin often enough you built that callous on your conscience so that it becomes a faint voice in the deepest recess of your brain." [2]

R.C. Sproul is an American Theologian and Pastor whom I listened to on WFIF radio for over twenty years. I continue to listen even after his coming home on December 14, 2017. At first, I found him to be boring, but as I continued to tune in to his program, I began to take heed to what he was saying because he made me think about my own commitment in my walk with God. He made so much sense when he touched the topic of the conscience and the principles of God. R.C. expounded more on the subject further to include the following statement,

> "Acting according to conscience may be a sin because if the conscience is misinformed than the question we have to ask, is it misinformed? Is it misinformed because the person has been negligent of studying and reading the word of God? …If your conscience merely echoes the standards of the society in which you live, and your conscience is not informed by the word of God…then you better not let your conscience be your guide because your conscience can guide you to hell." [3]

Religiosity and the culture have come into the church and has created confusion in the minds of the people, and they have become unsure of who to serve, the Christ or the world. In the day of judgment, people will be held accountable for their decisions. Christians have, but one choice and that is to live holy or go to Hades. We have to make a shift to serve only God and get off the fence.

It was my personal experiences that prompted me to write this book. I will share personal situations about my own frailties as a Christian as well as my experiences with people in the church, and my own observations on their treatment toward one another. I could not stop my thoughts from calling out, "You hypocrites! You are all going to burn in Hades." It started to disturb me to think that church people were going to Hades and I felt very uncomfortable about that. I don't want my Christian brothers and sisters, or myself to spend eternity in Hades because of our callous behavior. I thought that if I wrote my story, we can all learn how the conscience if not supported by Scripture and God's truth can guide us into a secular way of thinking that will only lead us into the inferno fire of Hades.

Should I be concerned that you may think of me as being imprudent for writing on a problem that expands Thousands of centuries? There are numerous Biblical accounts of Christians bickering with one another and church falling out, as well as stories of Christians behaving like heathens as written by the Apostle Paul in his Epistle's to the churches. I understand that there have been ungodly Christian behaviors documented since the beginning of time. It may just as well continue to exist but like the historians of centuries ago, I also have something to say about the 21st Century church and their breaking away, and lack of love for one another.

We all expect to suffer personal losses and tragedies in our lives there's no doubt about it. What's not expected is to be treated with such callous and indifference by members in your own church. I will walk you through tears of disappointments, brokenness and personal losses experienced throughout the years in the church as a new convert as well as a veteran Christian. Through my own experiences, you will understand the different characteristics and behaviors that I was confronted with in the churches. T.D. Jakes admonishes us to be free of everything that is toxic in us through the redeeming Blood of Jesus,

> "The world doesn't care about what you say but what you do. The church should be known for love and compassion. Some of us have been in a spiritual prison. God is in the business of redeeming, restoring, and renewing. Our God is a liberator." [4]

When Christ Jesus went looking for followers, He looked for those that would deny themselves, take up their cross, and follow Him. We need to ask Jesus to operate on us and clean out those things that hinder our walk with Him. We need to make some changes in our attitudes and behaviors and be transformed to reflect Christ's love toward everyone.

My concern is that the church is going in the wrong direction. I am not here to judge the church or the members, but in writing my observations, it may appear as such. However, it's the only way to get the message across to the readers. This book is totally Christian based, and I don't apologize for that.

I have come to know that church people are multifaceted in their personalities. Some will put on a church face during church service, and then they switch and put on a worldly face on the outside. The truth as I witnessed it throughout the years is that the church had begun to lose its vision and purpose in the midst of the changing ideology from the polluted minds of the secular culture. Unfortunate for the new converts, the members are allowing this pollution to enter the church. In my translation, the church is acting indifferent and callous due to their long-standing affair with the world. They have one foot in the church and one in the world. I was listening to Pastor John Hagee give this sermon one Sunday, as he preached on the anti-Christ,

> "The establishment of a one-man government, and new world order. That the immorality infiltrating the church today is to oppose the doctrines of the Bible inclusively Jesus Christ. The Church of Christ must be careful because they are the target of this mass-movement to create a new heathen nation. So, Christ-followers, take note if you are not for Christ and all His teaching then you are for the anti-Christ." [5]

God gave His children 'free will,' and they are not forced to do anything they don't want. When God chooses us for His purpose, we can either reject His offer or follow Him. The followers of God hide their desire to sin from the God who gave them a choice. The Christian believer will either serve God in every sense of the Biblical word or choose to serve the world. But don't pretend to serve and continue to sin because the only one you are lying to is yourself.

Writing my church experience is in no way to cause anyone to stop going to church nor that you take sides as to what religious denomination is better. I in no way will try to encourage you to choose the church you should attend. People experience things differently, and I will not imply that every church member has had the same experience as I have. I am here to say that together we can make a difference. Not every experience I had in the church was negative. But for the sake of what I am trying to point out in my book about the Church of Christ, I will reflect on some of those negative occurrences with the hope that you and I will make a difference in bringing about a change in the church's attitude that will reflect God's love. I will share the good times that I was fortunate to enjoy with some of the most beautiful, gracious, loving and kind members this side of heaven. Those were life-changing moments that inspired me to continue to stay the course that God had outlined for me.

I have to admit that there were times I was very skeptic about inviting anyone to church with me for fear that they would be turned off by some of the member's unkind behavior. It scared me to think that someone may have a negative experience in my church and decide never to attend church again.

I learn the hard way that not every church has members that are completely delivered from their old self, and thus they carry their ungodly behaviors and attitudes into the church contaminating others to think like them. Consequently, the church is given the reputation of being a "Church full of hypocrites and two-faced people."

I have heard from people in the community, non-believers as well as believers who have left the church, and don't want to involve themselves with the church any longer, "because the church lacks compassion and it is very judgmental."

The converts who are coming into Christianity in today's culture will be faced with many challenges in which their faith will be put to the test, not just by the secular world but by their church family.

They will be faced with the church that will show them compassion, demonstrate a commitment to the things of God and outwardly show love towards their fellow members. In contrast, they may be confronted with a church that is non-responsive to the needs of their members, perceived to be callous as well as cantankerous.

Season Christians may not have a problem with this, but I would highly recommend that new converts stay away from those in the church who doubt the Bible and the existence of God. If we are to be effective ministers of the gospel of Christ Jesus, it will do us good to stay away from Scripture critics. You and I should have a strong desire to see the new millennium generation serve God wholeheartedly so that they will see that we love them and that Christ Jesus is for real.

Everything we read in the Bible is specifically designed for what we are dealing with. All Jesus wants is to see you happy and living like He wants you to live. Tell the self to empty itself of you and fill it with more of Christ Jesus. For you to be more effective in ministry, you must change and grow more spiritual. The more you grow in your spiritual life, the less vulnerable you will be to this world's evil culture. We all must work out our 'own salvation', but not alone, with Jesus (Philippians 2:12, NIV).

During my journey in an attempt to find my home church, God remained faithful. There were many times that I questioned God as to why I was to remain in a church where the members treated me with such indifference and caused me to hurt deeply.

I hope that you will stay the course with me and see that through all my pains and sorrows I survived and so can you. My experience is the reason that I am writing this book, and I don't believe in coincidences in life. If I had not experienced what I did in church how else will the leadership of the church and the members know what some of their members are experiencing that can be detrimental to their spiritual growth; and that it hinders the blessings God has for that church and their members. I am not the first, but I hope to put an end to it. What I have to say will make a difference. My hope is that when you read this book, you also will be made whole and will again enjoy church the way it was meant to be enjoyed.

I want to share this excerpt from a movie I watch portraying the story of a real-life 19th century Methodist Evangelist and circuit-rider in the Appalachians named Robert Sayers Sheffey and what he had to say about the church and the path it took, and how it speaks to where we are right now in the 21st century,

> "God never forces His will on man. He calls them unto Himself, but if they will not follow Him, then they have to go their own way. Every time we give up part of our faith to try to fit in the ways of the world, we lose it forever. We lose a precious part of God's promise sacrifice to the world, and the world will never give it back. And someday when the world tells us, we can no longer have our religion except where they say. And, God is driven from our schools, and our government, and our homes then God's people can look back and know that our religion was not taken from us it was given up. Handed over bit by bit until there was nothing left." [6]

I pray that the church leadership will wake up and take notice. I hope that open panel discussions with the membership and other church leaders will happen to discuss how they can better meet all the needs of its veteran members and new converts. It starts with the shepherd of the house. The church has to change to reflect the love of Jesus Christ. The world is looking toward the church, and we are supposed to be the beacon of light. We have turned that light off with our ungodly behavior toward one another. God can't be in the midst of such strife.

Although I have written in my book real events and occasions to keep it accurate and as close to the book's main objective, I changed the names of people and characteristics to protect the innocent, and any resemblance to anyone you know is purely coincidental. If you recognize anything, it would be the persons whom you have seen exhibit the ungodly characteristic and behaviors mentioned in the book.

I now feel comfortable being a child of God and do not mind the antics of those professing to be Christ-like but are acting like Satan's offspring. I have been made whole; I have God the Father, the Son and the Holy Spirit to guide me. We must trust and move with God and let him operate in our lives. With our heart, soul, and mind we will affirm with God that he can control us and do His will. I have told God, yes and I pray that you will do the same in this season and the seasons to come. When we say yes to God, it is then that He begins to reconstruct us. So, let us release ourselves to God, accept His rebuke for our past negative behaviors so He can fix us and make all things right with him. God still needs people who are Spirit-filled. God says that he has to step in and attack the church because the church is a mess and will continue to birth hypocrites, backstabbers, gossipers, whore-mongers, fornicators, and lazy worshippers.

Jim Caviezel shares a perfect observation referring to the Christians of today that relates to my point of Christians not desiring to live holy,

> "The problem I see right now is that many, many Christians have emerged themselves in paganism. They want to be cool to their pagan friends by being a little pagan so they can be cool. There is nothing cool in this. The only thing lacking in you is you don't want to be holy." [7]

The devil has put out a contract on the church. He is trying to stop the vision and dreams that God has for us. But God will let us know that the attacks of the devil are only a test. Still, God's love covers a multitude of sins, and He brings us out of our sins when we call upon His name. He is always covering us and gives us an early release from our bondage to Satan. The church will survive the onslaught of Satan's attacks. "But as for you, you meant evil against me; but God meant it for good, in order to bring it about as it is this day, to save many people alive" (Genesis 50:20, NIV). You and I must keep hope alive and continue to love our brothers and sisters in the church.

You and I will stand up and do what we must do for the church and for our church members. God will move us to where He needs us and will speak to us when He brings us there. You and I will not allow the problems of this world and the ungodly behaviors of the church members affect us anymore. We will encounter many trials and tribulations, but we will also remember the lesson that man is frail and undependable. But God through it all remains faithful and true to His word. Blessed be His name.

> "Hear, O Israèl: The LORD our God, the LORD is one. Love the LORD your God with all your heart and with all your soul and with all your strength. These commandments that I give you today are to be on your hearts. Impress them on your children. Talk about them when you sit at home and when you walk along the road, when you lie down and when you get up. Tie them as symbols on your hands and bind them on your foreheads. Write them on the doorframes of your houses and on your gates" (Deuteronomy 6:4-9, NIV).

Don't lose hope all is not lost. Let us believe in the saving grace of Christ Jesus our Lord and Savior who will never leave us nor forsake us. When God calls us, He does not walk away and leave us. You and I were saved not by our own volition but by God's pursuit to save a wretch like you and me. Take my word for it I am still here and so will you when it's all said and done. Together we will hold on and not give up. But let us continue to pray for one another. I love you, my brother, I love you my sister and know that God loves you more. We are here because God has extended our lives.

PART ONE

CHURCH

"Those of us who are strong and able in the faith need to step in and lend a hand to those who falter, and not just do what is most convenient for us. Strength is for service, not status. Each one of us needs to look after the good of the people around us, asking ourselves, "How can I help?" That's exactly what Jesus did. He didn't make it easy for himself by avoiding people's troubles but waded right in and helped out. "I took on the troubles of the troubled," is the way Scripture puts it.

Even if it was written in Scripture long ago, you can be sure it's written for us. God wants the combination of his steady, constant calling and warm, personal counsel in Scripture to come to characterize us, keeping us alert for whatever he will do next. May our dependably steady and warmly personal God develop maturity in you so that you get along with each other as well as Jesus gets along with us all. Then we'll be a choir—not our voices only, but our very lives are singing in harmony in a stunning anthem to the God and Father of our Master Jesus!

So reach out and welcome one another to God's glory. Jesus did it; now you do it! Jesus, staying true to God's purposes, reached out in a special way to the Jewish insiders so that the old ancestral promises would come true for them. As a result, the non-Jewish outsiders have been able to experience mercy and to show appreciation to God. Just think of all the Scriptures that will come true in what we do!

For instance: Then I'll join outsiders in a hymn sing; I'll sing to your name! And this one: Outsiders and insiders, rejoice together! And again: People of all nations, celebrate God! All colors and races, give hearty praise! And Isaiah's word: There's the root of our ancestor Jesse, breaking through the earth and growing tree tall, Tall enough for everyone to see and take hope!

Oh! May the God of green hope fill you up with joy, fill you up with peace, so that your believing lives, filled with the life-giving energy of the Holy Spirit, will brim over with hope!

Personally, I've been completely satisfied with who you are and what you are doing. You seem to me to be well-motivated and well-instructed, quite capable of guiding and advising one another. So, my dear friends, don't take my rather bold and blunt language as criticism.

Romans 15:1-16 (MSG)

Chapter One

In the Beginning...

It is late Fall 1999, and it is after nine o'clock on a Wednesday night. In the northeast, the nights get colder early as the temperature continues to drop. I am driving home after spending two hours there. I start to cry uncontrollably, with warm tears running down my cheeks and into my mouth. My nose is swelling up with mucus, and I'm banging on the steering wheel with my right hand while screaming to myself, "Why are you coming here? They don't want you there. They don't love you. They hurt you."

Suddenly, I hear a faint voice that comes from within my head, (my temples are pounding with pain due to so much crying) and I hear it say to me, "Because this is where I want you." This is the worst I have ever felt, and it hurt to the core of my being. I couldn't stand it anymore. I have had enough of their rejection and making me feel like I was an intruder. They ignore me when I greet them but greet everyone else around me. Week after week and month after month, for the past two years. I have left crying my eyes out and feeling the pain in my heart caused by their indifference.

Please indulge me for a moment as I share this scene below with you to prove the point about people who behave with such indifference that can hinder relationships within the body of Christ.

In the 1960s series Star Trek, there was an episode titled, 'The Arena' that featured Captain Kirk, (William Shatner) being transported to an alien planet and the alien called Gorn. The aliens who transported them both to this planet were called Metron. Captain Kirk and the Gorn were to battle it out until one of them was dead in order to leave the planet. The Gorns were considered a race of butchers. The Metrons were sort of neutral aliens. Kirk wins the fight because he used what he learned by using certain natural materials found on the planet with the purpose of killing the enemy, but he refuses to kill the Gorn. The Metron then decide to return the Gorn back to his ship.

If I were to put this scene into a Christian perspective I would say that the Metron represent the love and peace expected in God's kingdom, the Gorn symbolize the ungodly and Kirk symbolize the Christian. The scene symbolizes a fight between good and evil but the viewer cannot tell them apart because they both are looking to kill each other. They are indistinguishable at one point. If it were not for God and the Bible as a guide on godly living, we would all be butchers. Look around at those nations who are anti-Christianity. We are not far from becoming like the rest of the world. At the end of the episode, the Metron makes this observation to Captain Kirk, "You are still half savage, but there is hope" [8]

Indifference is a sin. Never would I have imagined that this could happen in the twentieth-first century and in this place of all places…church.

> St. Maximilian was quoted as saying, "Indifference is the greatest sin of the Twentieth Century." St. Maximilian Maria Kolbe was a Polish Conventual Franciscan friar who volunteered to die in place of a stranger in the German death camp of Auschwitz, which was located in German-occupied Poland during World War II. John Paul II declared him "the patron saint of our difficult century."[9]

Angels without Wings

I was a stay-at-home-mom of three children living in the suburbs, in a common-law relationship with a good man who provided very well for the family. I didn't grow up in the church. I was a pagan from birth until my conversion in my thirties. But if I was ever going to attend church, I would have preferred it be the Pentecostal church. There are several reasons why I was more inclined to seek out a Pentecostal church.

I think it had to do with my first experience when I was a child back in the 1960s. My mom took me to this place that I never forgot. That image would stay in mind throughout the years.

My mom didn't go to church, except when there was a baptism for one of the babies in the family. When I got older, I saw this baptism ritual as a reason to have a party with her sisters and their families, to get drunk and to have sibling fights.

It must have been summer because I had on only a dress and no sweater. I remember walking with her down this street. I lived in New York City, in the borough of Manhattan. My mom was a tall woman – five feet, nine inches and I remember looking up at her as we walked. She looked like a giant next to me.

Earlier that day I remember feeling like I was about to get one of my asthma attacks. I remember while I'm walking with her I am having difficulty breathing and was gasping for air. My chest felt tight. I already knew I would end up in this place (hospital) lying on a bed with a plastic tent over me to help me breath better. I saw that my mom stopped us in front of what looked like a store with curtains on the huge windows covering the inside and we walked in. It was small and quite crowded with people on both sides of the aisle sitting on folding chairs. There was a man standing on a platform talking to the people who were sitting down. Some of them glanced back at us and smiled and then turned back to listen to the man talking. Apparently, we had walked in during their church service that had been already in progress. I can hardly remember what the people looked like, except for the man standing. He had a light complexion and spoke Spanish.

The place was a store (I figured it out when I got older) that had been converted into a Pentecostal church. After walking into the church my mom and I sat in the chairs next to the door. I don't know how long we were there. I remember we sat down. Then I found myself standing on the platform with this man, my mom, and some other person. I am not sure if it was a male or a female. This man was holding my hand and speaking in Spanish as he is looked to the ceiling. He prayed for me, and I was breathing normally. I was healed of my asthma that day in the Pentecostal church.

I also like the praise and worship music in the Pentecostal church. I was watching this movie back in 1986, "The Color Purple" on cable television, and I got goosebumps when the daughter (Shug), played by Margaret Avery, was singing in her club across the river at the same time church service was going on at her father's (Papa Harris played by Leonard Jackson) church. He was trying to preach, but the music from the other side was too loud. The church members couldn't hear the preaching, so he signaled to the choir to start singing, "Maybe God is Trying to Tell You Something," (written by Tata Vega). The daughter was still singing when she heard the choir's words coming across the river. She stopped dead in her tracks and couldn't continue her own song. But after a quick reflection, she started singing the church hymn. She crossed over to where the church was, and the same people who were at the clubhouse were following her. When she reached the church, she swung open the doors and entered while singing. Like Shug, I was a sinner living the crazy life and doing whatever I wanted. At that moment, I wanted to be in that scene singing with the church. That scene really touched me.

At that moment I thought that if I ever decided to attend church, it would be an all-black Pentecostal church where I could sing songs like the one, she was singing. I thought that only blacks could sing that way. It's apparent that I had not traveled much to know that people from the South and the Mid-west have a different way of talking from those in the northeast where I grew up.

My spiritual conversion began at an unexpected time in my life. Let me say that it never entered my mind nor was I interested in going to church or becoming a Christian. It was in the summer of 1987 when I ran into my dear friend Meg in the downtown area as we were crossing the street in the opposite direction. We were both so excited to see each other we embrace for a long time. We talked about how we were both doing and what we were doing at the present time. Then she invited me to her church. My friend Meg had been my neighbor for several years when we lived in the same apartment building, (I was on the first floor and her on the second) in the west end of the city of Eastport back in 1976. Our families would come together for drinks, listen to music and have a wonderful quiet evening just talking, while the kids (my daughter and her son who were both four years old) played in the room. Meg and her family moved away, and we lost all contact with one another for more than ten years.

Meg was the first African American friend I ever had. Our friendship has spanned more than forty years. After our first encounter in the street, I kept running into her at the same place. I would always make up some excuse as to why I could not stop and talk to her much. In hindsight, I felt bad about lying to her and walking away, leaving her with the words in her mouth and wave goodbye from a distance.

I guess God was calling me, but I wasn't listening at the time. God had a plan, and no matter how hard I tried to get away from Him, He would put her in my path. She eventually invited me to attend a Sunday service, and it didn't take me long before I took her up on the invitation. Something strange happened that scared me so much that it made me think maybe I should go to church.

As a young adult, I had visited several Psychic (Santeria) places to have the Tarot cards read and to buy a few bottles of potion to keep evil spirits away and for medicinal reasons. I didn't know the truth about those places I was visiting or the negative impact that it would have on my soul later in life.

I grew up around my mother's family who practiced Santeria. They would come over the house and I would listen to their conversations about someone being cursed by some evil spell put on them and their belief in the dead spirits having special powers to heal or to take a person's soul from them. I grew up believing that it was all right to visit the Santeria Centers. Because of my family's involvement with the occult I would see dark shadows and sense evil spirits around me. For many years, I couldn't sleep with the lights off, and had to keep a nightlight on.

It was September of 1987 when I decided to visit a (Santera) High Priestess to have the Tarot cards read. The Santera did some type of ungodly spiritual ritual that day. She put a blindfold over my eyes and turn me around several times while she chanted. The rest was a blur to me. A few weeks after that visit strange things began to happen to me. I felt like my body joints (knees, arms, feet), were disconnected because I couldn't feel and I thought I was dying. The doctors couldn't find anything medically wrong with me. I was scared and didn't know what to do.

One day as I was walking from the street to my front door the thought that I was going to die made me feel lost and sad, but then I heard a faint voice say to me "Go to Ms. Maria's home and ask her to pray for you."

Ms. Maria was my next-door neighbor. I went to her home, and told her about my visit to the Santera. She invited me into her room and asked me sit down in a chair and she began to pray for me. I remember it was one in the afternoon and she didn't stop praying until around eight that night (her daughter walked in from work at four and relieved her, and she prayed with me.)

Ms. Maria was an elderly woman in her seventies, very graceful and sociable. Her smile would light up a room, and those around her had no other choice but to have fun in her presence. She was a devout Roman Catholic who attended church regularly. I was very grateful to her for taking the time to pray for me. I thank God for sending me to her.

Later that week, God brought to my remembrance my friend Meg's invitation to visit her church and so I called and told her that I was coming to her church the coming Sunday. I was so excited to be in a church because I felt that I had been given a second chance at life and I wanted to know this God my friend talked about. When I started to write this book, I researched the numbers one, four, and eight and what they symbolized. I remembered those were the hours that I had been with Ms. Maria and her daughter praying for me.

I don't know why they are important, but I thought it merit mentioning.

> The number one symbolizes the unity and primacy (Deuteronomy 6:4.) And that Jesus is our Intercessor and Shepherd (John 10:30.)
> About the number four, I found out that it originated in the creation (Genesis 1.)
> I found out that the number eight represents the number of New Beginnings. [10]

Meg's church was located in the inner city of Eastport in a neighborhood that is predominately Latino and was known to have a bad reputation for drugs and gang fights, and several homicides had occurred back in the eighties and nineties in that area. I knew the area very well since I had lived only a few blocks from the church many years before. The church was of the Pentecostal denomination and predominately African American. The once beautiful Greek architect building was now a sight for sore eyes with its faded patches of blue and gold paint and the mosaic stained windows were cracked and falling apart. The ceiling with its once beautiful art paintings was peeling off.

One Sunday after I had been attending church faithfully for several months my friend asked me to go downstairs with my children to the fellowship hall. When we got downstairs, she asked us to undress and change into some white gowns they supplied us with. We were to be baptized in their pool. I was excited that I was going to be baptized that I didn't bother to ask any questions. We were all asked to go into the pool together the pastor said a few quick words, and we were dunked into the lukewarm water. We got dressed and then were escorted out of the church. I felt it was done in such haste and almost secretively that I can't remember what was said. The only words I remember hearing was Meg saying to me, "change into these garments the Pastor is going to baptize you and the children." I didn't think anything at that time of how baptism should be conducted until after I went to another church and saw how it was actually done.

I Want Out of the Sin Business

When believers are baptized, they have been made free through their faith in the blood of Jesus that cleanses us from all unrighteousness. Baptism should cause us to die to sin and in our lust for the things of this world. In baptism, we have been resurrected by the death and resurrection of the Messiah, Christ Jesus. When we are baptized, we come out of the "Sin business."

I was coming out of my sin business and wanted out for good. Sin dragged me down to the deepest parts of the darkest pit. And my hope was staying connected to a church that would help me stay safe and grow in the things of the Lord.

If we aren't careful and protected sin will pop its ugly head again because we humans have been born with the propensity to sin and it comes upon us unexpectantly.

As I began to read the Bible and hear pastors preached, I learned that sin comes from the hardening of the heart. I learned that sin brings separation from God. We become weak to the sin, and the sin speaks to us. Even before we sin, we have a desire for that sin. We have to ask the Lord to help us with our desires. We need to keep our life sanctified and filled with the Holy Spirit, and always confess our sins. We must keep in mind that we can't hide our sins from God. We will never be able to be righteous on our own – but through Christ Jesus. Christ Jesus came so that He might take away our sins. He who abides in Him does not keep on sinning. If we continue to sin, then we don't know Christ Jesus.

I remember one pastor explain the points by which sin enters into the human mind. First, we are enticed by our cravings for the sin, whatever it is. Second, we are deceived into believing the sin is all right in our sight, and mind, so we commit it. Third, we enjoy the sin, and have made a choice to indulge in it even further. But given that we have freedom of choice we continue in the sin; and lastly, if we don't repent and ask for forgiveness, we die in our sins. We must not make 'Sin' a doctrine because it separates us from God because it can't live in the same place as holiness. We can't be righteous and unrighteous at the same time. And, we can't be clean, and unclean at the same time. This is why baptism is so important in the church when done correctly, it helps the new believer understand the sin, disobedience, and repentance factors. I had to do it over and over again. Repenting is receiving the first anointing of the Holy Spirit. We can't be a witness to the Lord until we repent.

I had made up my mind that the world couldn't have me anymore and I was no longer interested in living (La Vida Loca) the crazy life. The material stuff and the things I liked to follow had no control over me anymore. At least that was what I thought at that time. But it is so easy to fall back into the world if you are not strong in your faith and you don't have people who will hold you accountable. When we are weak converts, we begin to question God's laws, and we end up lost again living in the wilderness of our own doing. But, when we come out of the wilderness, we will walk with the Lord. The word of God is here to teach us and guide us in the ways that we must go, and the pastors are there in the pulpit to "drive that point home."

Meg's pastor was a petite soft-spoken (southern accent) middle-aged African-American female who dressed very elegantly, and who reminded me of my mother in her facial features. She could have been her sister they looked so much alike. I spoke to her several times because she was approachable and never made me feel intrusive. She would greet me with a genuine hug which again made me feel like my mom was hugging me. On one occasion I told her, "you remind me of my mom" she smiled and said, "oh I do" and gave me that big beautiful smile.

One Sunday she asked the church members to come up to the pulpit and stand in the presence of the Holy Spirit. I decided to go because I wanted to bathe in His presence. As I'm standing there, praising God with my eyes closed, I felt myself going down to the floor in slow-motion. I ended on the floor lying face-up. I was laid out on the floor, and my right arm and left arms began to stretch out slowly at the same time, and then I crossed my legs at the ankle and stood there unable to move. Then the strangest thing happened, I felt a piercing sensation going through the palms of both hands, and I moan faintly as if in pain but I'm not actually hurting. Again, the piercing sensation, but this time it was on both my feet and I moan again. After a while, I felt another piercing sensation going through the lower part of my hip, and I moan again ever so faintly. I still couldn't open my eyes, I couldn't move, and I wasn't sure what was taking place. The next thing that occurred was that my arms started moving straight up to the ceiling as I'm still lying on the floor, and I can't open my eyes as if they were glued shut; and I see a very bright light above me when I hear myself say these words, "God help me." I'm not sure if anyone heard me. But I heard a voice whisper to me "It is finished." Eventually, I was able to open my eyes and was assisted up from the floor. I went back to my seat. The Pastor said a closing prayer and dismissed the members. I knew that God had saved a sinner like me on that day. I would become an advent churchgoer from that point on.

Every Sunday, I would spend hours in church praising and worshipping my God. I loved every minute of it. I was on fire for this man named Jesus. God had saved me time and time again from the grips of the devil even when I did not know Him. He was my Savior, the One who had saved me from my destructive self and from dying in my sins. God loved me even when I was doing drugs, and He kept me from dying of an overdose. This God who would bring me safely home every time I went out to the clubs because I had gotten so drunk, I couldn't remember how I got there. "God saved a wretch like me."

Christians sometimes don't know what it is they are doing in the church in terms of their calling and ministry. Sometimes it is a mystery. But I suppose that part of our ministry is to share with people how God saved us from our sins.

I had refused to be entangled with the yoke of bondage, and I denounce Satan. I threw away the old me and put on the new me. At that point in my life, I wanted what Christ Jesus wanted from me. When we keep our minds on Jesus Christ, we will pursue peace with all people. Then we will know the word of God and know His voice. Stay in the presence of the Lord.

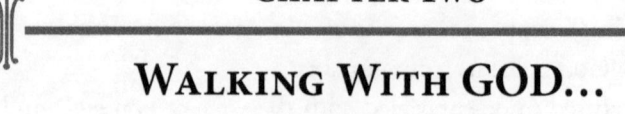

CHAPTER TWO

WALKING WITH GOD...
LIVING WITH MAN

God made a difference in my life, and I became an agent for the Lord. I was on a mission for the Lord. I was made free from all kinds of past sins. I believe that where the presence of the Lord is there is liberty. I had the liberty to take authority in Jesus name and get free from other people's agenda. Christians should never let people's agenda tie us up and burden us. We should be different from those in the world. God has called us to be free from the bondage of this world and to have a relationship with Him.

"Be completely humble and gentle; be patient, bearing with one another in love. Make every effort to keep the unity of the Spirit through the bond of peace. There is one body and one Spirit, just as you were called to one hope when you were called..." (Ephesian 4:2-4, NIV).

We the people are the church. We should be encouraging and edifying one another. We should be prepared and ready by helping others to turn from the darkness to the light which is Christ Jesus. We should warn the lazy, encourage the feeble-minded, help the weak, and be patient with everyone.

The church is made up of people with good and bad attitudes. When the members are in the church, they should all be the maximum reflection of God's kingdom. God desires that we do away with our negative attitude. Unfortunate, the problem in the church has always been the same in that when a member wants to be a good saint, there are bad saints in the church trying to distract and cause them to stumble. As the church works toward becoming the light of the world, then that is when hades itself comes against the good members. This problem is not new to the modern church. It's historical.

Show Others the Goodness of God

The true followers of Christ should always minister to all who walk into their church. Love as Jesus Christ did without prejudices. The church should be a family of holy living people the way it was intended from the beginning. To deal with holiness is to deal with our own weaknesses and it starts with our mind. The mind of the believer must be discipline in holy living with every breathing second of our lives. To accomplish living holy, the Christian must begin by mortifying the self (the flesh in us) and thus receive the Holy Spirit who will guide us into all truth. The church shouldn't give place to the devil. Holy living is doing things right as instructed to us in the word of God. It is a witness to the Lord at all times.

There are certain attitudes that don't belong in the church such as popularity. It's a bad attitude to have because the person tends to ignore what is going on in the church and believe it's all about who likes them. Denial is another bad attitude because the person will not address the problem him/her are facing. Church members should all have the Christ attitude that promotes Christian spiritual growth in the believer. There will always be sin in the church, and it's up to the leadership of the church to encourage those who have fallen by the wayside to attend individual discipleship classes. All the scripture is God breath and useful for teaching, rebuking, correcting, and training in righteousness.

"If your brother and sister sin against you," (Matthew 18:15, NIV). The method is to take the matter privately first and then publicly. The person must be warned in private and then a second time and after that have nothing to do with such a person. God is asking us to stand firm and know that He has our back. So, keep in mind that when we find ourselves in a crisis situation, all we need to do is change our negative thoughts and watch the situation change. To get there, we begin by getting on our knees to seek God with our "effectual fervent" prayers until we get a breakthrough. Know that the devil is relentless and therefore we must be more persistent.

In the parables, Jesus Christ tells us about the farmer who planted seeds and where those seeds fell. Church pastors constantly remind us of that parable, and they compare it to the folks in the church. Some of the seeds fell by the wayside ground, and these are the folks who hear the word but never receive it and remain unmoved by it. The message never sinks in. They can't remember a hymn. They are attendees but are not worshippers. They have a low resistance to the devil. Then there are the stony ground folks who are new and hear the word but they look like they will come around but no real change ever takes place in them. Everything they hear goes into one ear and out the other. They want a position and a promotion in the church – but their old habits never change. They are spoiled roots. The thorny ground folks receive and obey the word of God, and they really get saved and give up all the old habits that were offensive to God. They rely on God. But they become weary and faint when things go bad, and so Satan moves in on them. They become fearful of their circumstances. They doubt that God will fix their problem, and they sin. Their backsliding is dramatic. They leave Zion, the church, and they go into the world because it begins to look good to them again. Then there are the good ground folks who force feed themselves on the word, and they put it back into their soul. They are not overcome by adversities. They use the stones for their own advantage, and they choke the thorns. They fast and pray. They hold onto the things that are good in their life and let go of what is harmful and hurtful. They accept the tears that come throughout the years. They attend all church services. They may even fall, but they get back up, brush it off, and keep on pressing on.

I began to feel uncomfortable at Meg's church at one point, so I chose to leave to find another church. Because for the months I was attending with my children I felt I wasn't wanted in that church. The people would walk right by us when I greeted them and act as if we weren't even there. When they did look at us, it was always with a stern stare which made me feel uneasy. Thank God the children didn't notice, and if they did, they never said anything to me. My daughter was sixteen, and my youngest son was four at the time. I felt outright discriminated against, especially by the Preacher's Kids and those who were close to them. I found that in most of the churches I attended the preacher's children young and old have a predisposition of thinking they are above everyone and everything in the congregation. They are stiff-neck and callous with the membership. They tend to be the first to form cliques and arbitrary exclude others from their circle. I still do not understand where that behavior comes from and where in the Bible it reads such behaviors exists. I was a newcomer to the church life, but I notice that something was amiss in the manner by which my children and I were being treated. Even a newcomer can tell that it wasn't godly.

The members were so obvious and intentional when they pass by us, not look at me or say hello. For the most part, people in church would greet each other with usual church greeting "God bless you" but not us. It was rare if one of the older women would say something to my children or me. The only few people I expected a greeting from every time I arrived at church was from my friend, her husband, and the pastor and one other sister who made me feel welcome. Church people have to be aware that new converts who come to church carry with them baggage. Some of that baggage can be Domestic Violence, sexual abuse, addictions and the church can really cause serious harm to those people by re-traumatizing them with their hurtful behavior.

My friend Meg made me feel welcome, so I didn't want to leave her church or tell her what I had endured from her church family. She was so kind and gentle. If it hadn't been for my dear friend whom I had known, I probably would never have gone to that church. But you see it was God's will that I did go, and I thank God for my dear friend Meg for inviting me. I love her dearly. I thought that the negative treatment was due in part to my ethnicity. I never thought that the saints would actually discriminate against anyone, I was very naïve. I left my friend's church, and I venture to several of the Spanish-speaking churches, not really committing myself to any at the time.

Let the Adventure Begin

I had heard about this Pastor from an acquaintance of a friend of mine, and I decided to go to his church. This particular church was a corner storefront, and it reminded me like the one I went to with my mom back in Manhattan. It was small inside. The entrance led me right into the sanctuary that was overcrowded with white folding chairs. The pulpit was two feet high, and the band was on the right corner of the platform, and two red velvet upholster royal chairs in the center.

I attended about two to three Sunday morning services, and maybe three Wednesday evening Bible study classes. The first time that I attended I just walked in and sat down. There was no one at the entrance of the church to welcome the visitors, so I went unnoticed except to those whom I sat down next to. I greeted them as I sat and they responded with a very modest greeting of "God bless you." The members appeared to be more genuinely friendly. I could see their genuine desire for spiritual guidance. That church was a traditional Pentecostal church where the women wore their long skirts and long-sleeve blouses. They used no makeup or jewelry and kept their long hair in a bun. The men wore mostly suits or a shirt and tie.

However, the leadership of the church was different, and I wasn't convinced that the pastor was prepared to fill the spiritual needs of their members. (My estimation.) After coming from Meg's church and listening to her pastor preached it was obviously different in that not only in the language spoken but in other ways.

I definitely didn't receive what I was looking for in this church.

I was hungry for the word of God and wanted to learn more about Jesus and how to live right, but that was not the place. I wasn't convinced that it was a spirit led church. The Pastor would not preach but talk to the congregation about some gossip he had heard or other subjects that had nothing to do with the Bible or Christianity.

I continue to attend to give the pastor the benefit of the doubt about his leadership as a man of God. But the more I attended the church, the more I observed that he had no real vested interest in the things of God.

I had the opportunity to speak to him on two separate occasions. The first time was at the church when I approached him after the service to introduce myself and let him know that I was looking for a church home and he seemed aloft. The pastor appeared to be someone of very little words because he barely said anything substantial in his church sermon. Another time was when I saw him in some neighborhood store years after I had attended his church. He smiled and walked out. The person I was with at the store made a derogatory comment about him, something about his reputation but I ignored it.

But during my few visits I managed to connect to one of the female members. She was demonstratively friendly and showed everyone much affection. I particularly admired the way she worshipped during the praise and worship. She was thin, average height with an olive complexion with long dark brown hair that she kept loose. I had noticed her during praise and worship service on one Sunday morning, and she was praising God in such a manner, (it was a firsthand experience seeing someone worship like that). She was spinning around, and her long hair was flying in the air, and there were sisters holding hands in a circle surrounding her. I assumed that it was so that she wouldn't hurt herself or others. I wanted to experience that for myself, and so I approached her after the service was over and introduced myself. It felt really good knowing someone like her as a new Christian. I saw the genuineness in her praise and love for God. She always carried the Bible in her arms as if cradling a baby. I believed that those words in that book meant a lot to her. I saw myself having that same hunger for God's word.

I saw her again in 2013, and she told me that she was pastoring her own church, (her husband died, and she was left to take the position). I was very excited for her accomplishments and pleased that she was leading her own church.

I continued to attend her church several more times and on one particular evening during a Bible study service, after the praise and worship were over, the wife of the Pastor got up and was yelling and ranting like a mad woman talking nonsense. I could not understand what she was saying and the members were bewildered, I could see it in their faces. They all looked stunned, and silence fell upon the church as we all looked in disbelief. I remember the musicians began to play hymns to silence her (my estimation) and eventually she sat down. The pastor stood up and said some nonsensical something that I can't recall. The rest of the service became a big blur to me.

There was something not right in that church. A week before I had noticed a father punch his toddler in his groin because the child would not sit still. I witnessed on more than one occasion, children running around the church and talking out loud. The adult members having full-blown conversations while the Pastor was speaking, maybe that is why I could never make out what he was saying half the time. I thought how inappropriate those behaviors were in a church setting which is why I felt that this was more like a man-made church then a Spirit-led church. Even a new Christian like me at that time can discern that the Spirit of God could not have been in the midst of all that mess. By my observation, there were genuine Christians in that church in search of salvation and a fresh word from God, but they were definitely not going to find it there. Although my newfound friend worshipped God in her spirit, I did not feel the presence of God in that church, and I stop attending.

Void of Love

I ventured into another Spanish-speaking church, and this time it was independent of any religious organization. According to my friend who had been a member there from birth told me the church had been a member of the 'Assemblies of God' at one time. I was invited by another friend, I had met her back in 1974 when we worked together in a children's department store in downtown Eastport (it closed many years ago.) She was a sweet person and very smart. I admired her very much. We lived in a four-family house. She lived on the first floor on the left side of the house, and I lived on the second floor of the right side of the house. After a year of living in that apartment, I left it to my older sister and went to Puerto Rico to live with another sister and her husband.

Many years later, I saw her coming out of a store that I was going into, and she was bent forward (looking to the ground), and I asked her, what was the matter? She said that it was a back surgery she had done several years ago that left her suffering from more back problems and every now and then her back would go out on her which made it difficult to stand up straight. She told me that she had gotten married to a member of her church. She invited me to the church, and I told that "I would visit," and she walked away. I felt so sad for her because she was in her early thirties and she looked like she had aged forty years hunched over like that.

On my first visit to her church, I sat in the back pews. I saw her come into the sanctuary near to where I had been sitting, and I stood up to greet her, and she greeted me back with a nod of her head, but she kept right on walking to the front of the church. I felt embarrassed that I had just been ignored that it crushed my spirit. My friend didn't stop to greet a sister in Christ with the usual blessing, a hug, or a kiss. But she met a few members that were sitting in the front pews already and greeted them with a smile and a kiss. I felt so hurt.

Church people cannot just be attendees and tithers or pick and choose whom they will love and not love in the church. The God who made the heavens and the earth breathes life into all people, and there is no prejudice in Him. We must stop hurting each other and encourage one another. We must understand that people who attend church are not all saved. They are not all saints. People who profess to serve God must live a Christ-like life. Church people must stop pretending to love one another. Christians can't be bitter and holy at the same time. Whatever is hindering us from being true to the Lord must be terminated.

When God calls us, it's because we are a chosen vessel. It's no coincidence that I was a chosen vessel like Paul of Tarsus, (Acts 9:15, NIV). Christians must be more determined to follow the Lord and his command, "to love one another" as He loves us.

The Church is not for Dead People

It's a shame to admit it, but I have found thus far that there is quite a large percentage in the community of Believers aka Christians, who are void of love. My friend's church reminded me of a mausoleum. Please don't misunderstand me I wasn't looking for a perfect church just one that would feed and nurture my spiritual life by teaching me the word and its meaning, to comfort me during my struggles, sickness, trials, and to show me that there is love one for another, "For God so loved the world that he gave his one and only Son, that whoever believes in him shall not perish but have eternal life." (John 3:16, NIV.)

The scriptures clearly state that Christ Jesus commands the church to love one another. So why do Christians find it so difficult to love one another? This will be the only way to identify with Jesus when we love one another. To be discipline is to be a disciple of love and keep on loving those who have hurt us.

The concern here isn't the problem of love but of the attitude. The church family is treating each other with indifference and are being callous with one another. The Lord will cast us off because of our behavior and attitude. He knows that we are hypocrites. I continue to seek God while I was having these different church experiences because I was determined to be obedient. Remember that life will bring us through the wilderness at times but we must take heed to stay in the journey.

The pastor of that church preached above my head by using words that I needed a dictionary to define what he was teaching. So, I didn't hear God's word taught to me. This particular church was well known in the community for the aloofness of its members and the arrogance of the pastor. The church reminded me of a Catholic Church with rolls of pews on both sides and the high ceilings, and the huge altar in the front; and the coldness of the marble floors. There were always a few members each time visited that I could feel the coldness in the church. The members would sit far from each other, sort of scattered throughout the sanctuary. I dare say that only two of the members ever said anything to me the few times I attended. I did not feel welcome. I got the impression that it was mostly family and close acquaintances who attended this church (my estimation).

My experience at that church was short live. I notice how the people who walked into the church would sit away from each other and say hello from a distance. But there were small groups who would sit together and appeared to be more amicable to each other. I knew that I wasn't going to find that human connection and warmth I so desired from my believing brother and sister. I thought of this church as a mausoleum, and I was very much alive to be in such a place void of warmth and loving expressions. I just felt totally out of place. So, I decided to stop visiting the mausoleum. I am not lying when I say that it felt very cold in that church and it had nothing to do with the cooling or heating systems. It was a dead coldness operating in that church.

Believers must stay out of the graveyard if we are going to be the disciples in the Lord's service. We have been raised from the dead, and we have the resurrection power, through Christ Jesus. We must learn to get away from dead people, places, and things. We need to stop operating on things that don't possess power and get away from things that are trying to take our power source, life. "I have come that they may have life and have it to the full" (John 10:10, NIV.)

My young friend told me (she was a teenager and had been traumatized by what happened at that church) that when the incident occurred, she and her family left the church shortly after. The scandal involved an extra-marital affair apparently a child was born out of this affair. I was told this after I left the church by my young friend who was hurt to the core because she loved the pastor. That church had been her life (she grew up in that church.) There was a breaking away of many of the older former members. That is why the church appeared empty every time I attended service most of the members had left the church. The scandals in the church can do serious harm to the youth in the church.

"These are the words of him who holds the seven spirits of God and the seven stars. I know your deeds; you have a reputation of being alive, but you are dead. Wake up! Strengthen what remains and is about to die, for I have found your deeds unfinished in the sight of my God. Remember, therefore, what you have received and heard; hold it fast, and repent. But if you do not wake up, I will come like a thief, and you will not know at what time I will come to you," (Revelations 3:1-3, NIV.)

The church members need to break with traditionalism and move on to what God wants from the members. The members should be living in God's presence daily not just on Sundays and mid-week. The church has the water – the well of living water to help others get it. The people who come to the churches are thirsty and need to get the living water but instead, are drinking stagnant water supplied by its stagnant leadership. The church needs to clean house and get rid of everything that pollutes it. Read in, Matthew 21:12-13, (NIV)

"Jesus entered the temple courts and drove out all who were buying and selling there. He overturned the tables of the money changers and the benches of those selling doves. "It is written," he said to them, "'My house will be called a house of prayer,'"

Jesus was upset to see what was going on in His temple. The same may be said of the modern church today that entertains unclean and ungodly behaviors. God has a purpose for us, and we should be holy without blemish.

I was still an infant in the faith. Imagine if I had walked away from the church then. It scares me to think how many people have gone through what I experienced and have decided not to pursue God because of what they see with their own eyes and hear from church members. It was getting a little discouraging, but I kept pressing on because I had already committed myself to God. I kept on searching for God's church. The church must at all times seek Christ-likeness.

Don't let Satan shake your faith. Call God when we are going through some things and keep on hoping. Hope is the expectation of good things to come. We must never lose our focus on God nor allow the enemy irritate us for our help comes from God, not man. There will be many distractions but whatever you do don't lose your focus. The scriptures instruct us to "seek first the kingdom of God" that we may keep our feet planted on solid ground. The enemy will attempt to remove you from the word, the church, and from congregating with the saints. But stay the course don't forfeit your future…wait patiently on the Lord.

CHAPTER THREE

THE POTTER'S HAND

Religion is born out of a church that doesn't allow the Potter, Jehovah, to mold them. They're disfigured clay and continue in that way because they refuse to be Christ-centered, Christ followers, and Christ-like. Church members must constantly be in the Potter's hands.

> "This is the word that came to Jeremiah from the LORD, "Go down to the potter's house, and there I will give you my message." So I went down to the potter's house, and I saw him working at the wheel. ⁴But the pot he was shaping from the clay was marred in his hands; so the potter formed it into another pot, shaping it as seemed best to him..." (Jeremiah 18:1-4, NIV.)

Mold Me Lord

The church needs to be committed to serving the spiritual needs of those who seek God. We should not take our focus from God and put it on ourselves nor the world. The church should look to God and the things of God. When the church focuses on who they want to minister to and ignore the other lost souls they have constricted the spirit of God. Anyone can minister to his or her own family and friends, but God calls us, His servants to serve others outside that realm. People who love God preach the gospel to everyone who is willing to hear. It doesn't matter what the color of their skin is who or what ethnic group they belong to. People who are unkind to other believers are friends of the world, and their behavior is opposite of the Christ Jesus. The church becomes sad and can't experience joy when there is sin among the members. So that when the church wants to praise and worship, they can't because the spirit is constricted. The church can very easily become contaminated by unholy and unclean saints. Eventually, the church will not want to congregate with each other, with others outside their church; and there will be no fellowship and no compassion for the non-believer. The church would have lost its way and turned its back on God.

But there is hope because of the Potter! God is the Potter, and we are the clay. We must listen to what God wants us to hear. His sheep will know His voice and know that He is their Shepherd. The church must live in such a way that it allows God to break them and mold them in the process of making them more like Him.

I grew up in Spanish Harlem also known as "El Barrio" in upper Manhattan, New York City. I was a toddler when my parents moved to New York City from Puerto Rico. I lived in poverty for most of my childhood and teenage years. My parents were alcoholics and, I witness domestic violence in my home. When my father drank, he would get so angry at my mom that he would beat her and break thing in the apartments. Many times, my mom and my sibling would have to run into the street in the middle of winter leaving our coats behind. As a young child, I heard all sorts of profanity and saw the ungodly things adults did. I should never have experienced those things. I hated their lifestyle but I was a product of their environment, and I soon learn to live the life I hated so much. Many times, I wished that I had not been born into my family. I suffered brokenness due to childhood sexual abuse, parental neglect, and abandonment. Unbeknownst to those who know me, those experiences had caused emotional and mental instability in me for a long time.

Those childhood memories were a constant torment. The fear of being abandoned, abused and neglected had been a constant companion for me. I learned that early childhood relationships, in certain instances, affect how we relate to others in later years.

I hated living alone, and so I was always seeking attention, affection, and love from everyone and always ended up with having my heart broken because I asked far too much of people.

I had several failed relationships with men because I demanded more loving affection, security, and protection from the relationship than they could give. I hungered for something that my parents never gave me.

In my mid-twenties I started to work the second shift at a local entertainment bar. I would get home in the early morning hours. While working as a bartender, I dated my future husband.

I say all this about me because like me there are people who come to church broken and are looking for help. I needed God so desperately in my life during my beginning steps as a Christian.

There are things in the life of a Christian that it is best to leave alone but the memories, however horrible, always manage to surface in our thoughts to remind us of what a terrible life we lived prior to our conversion.

When we give our lives to Christ and begin to attend church and seek God for ourselves, there has to be an overall transformation in our thinking, in our behavior, and in our attitude. We should never try to justify our sin or disobedience to the law of God since we were made new by the blood of Jesus. That is why I am so glad that God took a wretch like me, He broke me, made me, and mold me into the person I am today. We should all be desiring God to do the same with each and every one of us, who is reading this book right now.

There is no doubt in my mind that the Lord is King and He desires to rule over us not like a tyrant but like a loving father. But first, we must establish a relationship with Him. He will have mercy and grace in abundance for those who believe in Him. Second, we must do His will (be obedient) in our lives to be able to enter the Kingdom of heaven and reign with Him forever. Third, the church here on earth is only to guide us into the kingdom of the Lord not to deter us by man-made laws.

The goal of the true Christian believer is to have a close intimate relationship with our Father Abba and to be mature witnesses for the kingdom. The Lord is looking for mature Christians.

The Bible challenges us to take up the mind of Christ and follow God wherever he leads.

During Joshua's time it was the mind of God that he followed. Joshua feared the Lord, he loved God, and he looked to God for direction. Joshua's name means "To endure and strength.' Joshua was a slave and a soldier in the army of the Lord. He was also known as a Statesman, a servant, and a spy. He became Moses successor and a man who made up his mind to serve God. Joshua had a mind made up. For the believer, a mind made up is to serve God without conditions and go where He wants us to go and do what He wants us to do.

It Matters To God What Happens To Us

"But anyone who hates a brother or sister is in the darkness and walks around in the darkness. They do not know where they are going, because the darkness has blinded them" (1 John 2:11, NIV.)

I wanted so much to change my pagan lifestyle because it had been destroying my family and me.

If my friend Meg had not found me when she did and invited me to her church, I would have died in my sins. I made up my mind to attend the church regardless of the member's behaviors. I ignored them and kept coming back. I didn't want to go back to that lifestyle. I wanted God to make it all better. I hate to think what would have happened to my children and me if I had not sought the Lord when I did. Or should I say if the Lord had not caught up with me when He did.

It was mid-Spring, and I was leaving the church with my daughter and my son. I was driving down Nigel Street in Eastport when I was about to turn right just as the light had turn green but a voice told me to wait. If I didn't listen to that voice, I would not be writing this book and my children, and I would not be alive today because a car going eighty miles (my estimation) ran the red light, and the impact would have killed us instantly.

Another time during the summer of the same year my children and I are driving down Edge Street in Eastport, and I hear the sound of a semiautomatic (weapon of choice for gang members in the late 80's.) I look to see which direction the sound was coming from when I saw a youth out my driver side window running toward my car and another youth chasing him. I didn't panic because I felt the presence of God in the midst of all this. I knew that the youth near my car needed the protection of my car to shield him from the bullets of the other youth and so I told my children to get down on the floor of the car while I help this youth gain distance from the other youth. I tell you as I am recounting this story that my heart beats heavily and I rejoice over what God did for those two youths, as well as, my family and me on that day. It was God who kept my children and me alive that day because it was my car that kept those two youths from killing each other. All I knew is that they were some mother's child. I thank God for His omnipresence that He sent His angels to encamp around my car that day. I had just left the church, and God's angels were with me.

So, I ask myself if we who are made in God's image how can we (meaning the church) be so mean to one another. We can never be God's people until we love. Those who are planted in the house of God should possess God's love. When Christ Jesus gave His life for us, His blood represented the love of God, and if we don't love, we are nothing. The faithful believer must put on love and love his fellow believer. A love that will help us love even the people who are so negative. We must have the patience for people the way God has it for us. Through the Scriptures, we learn that love is accommodating not rude or obnoxious. Thank God that he is a specialist in our situation and will prune what isn't fruitful and cut out everything that is hindering us in our life, such as the sin of selfishness and vainglory which are the spirit of disobedience.

"For out of the heart come evil thoughts—murder, adultery,

sexual immorality, theft, false testimony, slander. These are what defile a person" (Matthew 15:19, NIV.) To have a love of God in us, we must have a circumcision of the heart because out of the heart come evil intents.

It matters to God what troubles us. God felt my pain and saw how disappointed I was at my Christian brothers and sisters for their ungodly behavior. God cares for all His children. To be Christian, we have to be willing to be Christ-like. I had to keep up my part of being a new Christian and not let their behavior interfere with what God was doing in me. God detest proudness. I rejoice now that I did not let myself be pushed out of the will of God during those uncomfortable moments in church.

God is our Shepherd

God says, take the negative and make it a positive. Drive out the negativity. Possess what God has said already belongs to us. Don't call a problem a problem anymore but call it a challenge. Change the negative into a positive with the power we have in Christ Jesus, our Lord and Savior. We can defeat the challenge and receive the blessings. Embrace the fact that God has given us the power to excel and take the authority to defeat the challenge.

God knows how to deal with negative people, and I did not have to say or do anything. God says, come down from your pedestals. Christian people should be an example and walk through life as if God is holding their hand. I did just that and would not allow my emotions from distracting me from what God was doing for me at that time in my early walk with Him. He blesses the humble at heart. God cares and preserves us until we get to our future, which is in heaven. God's desire is to save us from what is trying to destroy us. God takes our situation in His hand to secure our future through the power of Jesus Christ. God will send His angels to encamp around those who need Him.

When God is in charge no weapon formed against us shall

prosper. Every tongue that rises up against our family and us shall be condemned for judgment is condemned by God. Righteousness is of God, and He covers us with His righteousness. God is in charge, and He promised to keep us strong and secure.

My intent was to seek unity with the church family because I needed to belong. But there can't be unity unless the Spirit is present. The Bible clearly states it that unity in the spirit is being fed from the word and being in the presence of the Lord all day long, staying in prayer; and in being in praise and worship all day long. We must always make time for God.

God had plans for me, and only He knew where I was to start my ministry. I realize now that my friend's church was just a stepping stone to where God really wanted to me to go. Most of the members were cruel and unrelenting, but I held the course until God decided that I had enough. I was not part of their ethnic group, and they made it perfectly clear that I wasn't wanted there. I stayed because I was having such a good time in the Lord.

Where is the Compassion?

"Therefore, as God's chosen people, holy and dearly loved, clothe yourselves with compassion, kindness, humility, gentleness and patience" (Colossians 3:12, NIV.)

We must have love one for another. The love of Christ is not in us when we can't love others. Compassion is nothing if it doesn't move us to action. In the Bible story of the traveler who was beaten and left for dead and the attitude of the three strangers who took the same road. What was their response or action? The stranger who stopped to care for him was called the Samaritan. Something in his heart made him see the beaten man. He made a conscious decision to help the stranger.

When we have compassion, we see things others don't see. When we have compassion, it moves us to do something about it. Godly conscience moves us to compassion. The man had compassion.

The compassion sees the need in the person, the community, and society. God expects us to be compassionate about people's plight. We must look at others as our prodigal other. The Samaritan made contact with the injured man. He took action and got involved to do something. Jesus made it a point to touch other's lives. We must be available for the hurting people around us, begin with those who come to our churches seeking salvation.

The church should be reaching out to people such as the addicts, the mentally and emotionally disturbed, those in a domestic violence situation; the abused and oppressed. The church is to take care of the person, the community, and society at large. We need to help bandage them and care for their wounds and not inflict them. The church needs to invest in the lives of the hurting people in our church first.

Then the church can go out into the community and meet the needs of the single parent, the lost youth involved in drugs and gangs. The church should take a stance on social justice and change the abortion laws and other laws that are un-Biblical in our society. We can offer help with our time, and money. But first and foremost, let us invest in the lives of the lost souls. Go and be merciful, just and compassionate with all those who are in need that God puts in our way. Jesus loves us. He saved us. He cared for them and for us as well.

The church is a hospital full of sick people. More are seeking to be healed of all kinds of wounds inflicted to them by the world. Wounds that were caused in the battlefield of life and they come to God's hospital looking for healing. The church members should huddle around them and know what ailments have hindered them and what infirmities must they be delivered from. Instead they are ignored and left to bleed on a gurney in an empty and cold corridor all alone.

It is a shame how the church members and the leaders have lost their zeal to minister to those who need a brotherly and sisterly hand and embrace. Instead, they are encountered with indifference and rejection because they do not belong to their clique. And, their attitude is if you can't take the rejection then move to another church. The blame is placed totally on the new converts who need God's healing, guidance, and protection. The church may as well close their doors if they are not going to fulfill what they have been called to do. They have forgotten that they there for the lost and the destitute seeking salvation.

God desires that we pursue peace with all people and live holy. The word Holy means pure and blameless. It's having a right and clean heart. Holiness has transformed minds that reflects the Father's love. The church isn't to be entangled with the yoke of hate, anger, gossip, discord, and jealousy. Holiness is being redeemed from all ungodly attitudes and behaviors. Stay in the presence of the Lord and let Him discipline us for our good.

CHAPTER FOUR

OUR FAITH IS NOT IN VAIN

The devil is still looking to discourage God's people. He will try anything to come against us. But we are going to make the journey and stay with God because God is still faithful to us. We should hang in there and not give up because God will reward His faithful people, and give those who believe what He has promised them. We need a faith that others can't believe how we can go through so many challenges and continue to stand. The promises of God are worth fighting for. We must be sure our heart is right. Make sure our attitude is right. Remain in the work of the Lord. Do the will of God. "We want each of you to show this same diligence to the very end so that what you hope for may be fully realized. We don't want you to become lazy, but to imitate those who through faith and patience inherit what has been promised" (Hebrews 6:9-15, NIV.)

My life had been pathetic for so long, but now I had found meaning and purpose. I was so excited to have received Christ Jesus as my Savior and to have joined the army of believers. I thought maybe I had started off in the wrong church, but this kind of behavior from church people continued for the past thirty years. I found more genuine love from my pagan friends, co-workers, a total stranger in the clubs than from the church family. The emotional pains I suffered in the church was and still is utterly unacceptable. No one in the church should have to suffer such humiliation.

I write this story because I am angry that the church didn't take care of me emotionally, spiritually or physically. I know that God loves me and I did experience his mercy and grace during those trials. I also know He didn't take pleasure in seeing me suffer in the hands of those who called themselves Christians. If it were not for

God, I would have walked away from the church a long time ago. But every now and then He would put a saint to give me a glimpse of His love as they smiled and greeted me with "God bless you sister" or get that hug from a church mother that felt as if God himself was hugging me and saying "I love you daughter, hang on just a little longer."

I was satisfied with my life since I met Jesus and allowed Him into my life. I never lead on that I was going through emotional pain every time I had to attend service. Everyone around me thought that I was doing alright. I knew how to pretend to be strong, especially for the sake of my family because I wanted them to come to church with me on Sundays. As a new convert, my faith was steadfast, and all I wanted was to stay connected to God. We should never allow anyone to move us from our faith in God. "Without faith, it is impossible to please God," (Hebrews 11:6, NIV.)

We Must Remain Faithful

We must show our faith through the belief and the existence of God. In faith, we obey and praise God. Because of faith, we have favor with God. By faith, we are helping to build a spiritual life in our children and their children to come.

Imagine if Noah had given up his calling to build the Ark when the people around him were humiliating him and scorned him and were insulting to him. But by faith, Noah believed God and built the Ark, and hence we are here. By faith, we will build our home on the Rock of Ages, Christ Jesus. By faith, you can believe that God will keep His promise if you only wait on Him. Trust Him because He is the "friend that never fails." It's not sufficient to believe that God exists, but through our good works, we show it. Regardless of what I was experiencing I would always come to church with a fresh feeling and expecting something new from the Lord. I wanted to indwell in the fullness of the Holy Spirit and get the blessings God promised.

The old is gone, and the new has come that is what I learn early on in my newfound faith. If I wanted to change things I had to live right, do good and be faithful to God. I had to get rid of the spirit of resentment and anger and let God take care of every situation that came my way.

The scriptures instruct us to do good and remain faithful and work wholeheartedly in the kingdom of God. We must stay away from depraved people who are deliberately doing the things that the scriptures specify as sinful in the sight of God. We must consecrate ourselves and worship God at all times in spirit and in truth. God has kept us from death, and we must praise Him at all times.

> "And he gave the apostles, the prophets, the evangelists, the shepherds and teachers, to equip the saints for the work of ministry, for building up the body of Christ, until we all attain to the unity of the faith and of the knowledge of the Son of God, to mature manhood, to the measure of the stature of the fullness of Christ" (Hebrews 4:11-13, NIV.)

In the first stages of my conversion, all I wanted to do was tell everyone around me about what I experienced in my first encounter with God. I was on fire for the Lord and was not ashamed of showing it. I would talk about how God calls people into the kingdom for service and ministry. I immediately felt a desire to tell people about Him and His love for them. I enjoyed sharing the word of God with people in my immediate circle, my close friends, neighbors across the streets; to my nephews and nieces and cousins. I remember being at a supermarket once and this female shopper tapped me on the shoulder and said, "You have the light of the whole world all around you." I knew deep down in me that I was "on fire for the Lord," and wanted others to know Him. No matter where I was, in a store, on the street, visiting friends and family I would share with everyone about the love of Jesus Christ and His salvation. I wanted them to feel what I felt.

In the early part of my newfound faith, I would volunteer to help in the different ministries. I volunteered to help in the Homeless Outreach ministry. I also served in the usher board. I determined to volunteer to assist wherever the need was. I knew that I wanted to do something big that would draw hundreds of people to God, especially the youth. I always wanted to work with the youth and teach them to go out and minister to other youths. I felt in my heart that the young generation needed and still need a lot of guidance and that the adults should do more for them. I was too afraid to venture on my own, and that fear restricted me from reaching out to the youth. I wanted to do more than just attend church on Sundays. God always knows what is best for us even when we don't have any clue.

Since I was new to the whole Christendom thing, I did not know that there is a waiting period. There is a waiting period to become a member and a waiting period to be chosen for a ministry and/or to serve in one. Even when we have a willing heart to serve, we must wait. While I waited to serve in the church, it was told to me that the pastor is actually observing the newcomers to the church. In the waiting to be called to a ministry, I had to go through the discipleship process.

Discipleship

Discipleship is denying ourselves and picking up the cross to follow Jesus in spite of the circumstance. Discipleship is where God should take priority over all relationships. Discipleship in the church are disciples who go out to the highways and hedges and tell the sinners about Jesus Christ. The new convert must develop the kind of spirit that will live a life for Christ Jesus. Our lives should be like living waters. Our lives should be as living unto Him in our jobs, our homes, and every place we go. Have a mind of humility and never complain but come into His gates with thanksgiving and enter His courts with praise.

I thought that I had found my true ministry when I ushered in one of the churches. I recall one Saturday morning when one of the top leaders in the Baptist Ushers Board visited the church to train us on the model of a church usher. All the ushers had to wear their proper attire of white dress and white shoes or black skirt and white shirt and black shoes. We had to stand in our different stations in the church. I was partial to the right side of the church, and I would stand there. We had to learn the signs for calling another usher to relieve another usher. We learned signs for seating people and amount of space available and the like. I never knew that there was an organization for ushers.

I got started in the usher committee when the church was hosting a huge event, and the church was looking for volunteers for ushers. I jumped on the opportunity to do something for the church. In the beginning, my having volunteered was greatly appreciated, but as time went by, I was back to being the outsider. Whenever it was my Sunday and Wednesday to usher, I would be there and serve with delight. There were several ushers who would greet me with a smile and "God Bless you sister." As for the lead ushers they were always so serious that I didn't know if I should greet them or ignore them. But I couldn't play their game, so I would greet them knowing that I would get a grunt as a reply or no reply at all. I would be afraid to insist that people move to the front pews instead of seating in the back pews (I was told by a head usher to insist). On my days on, the members would ignore me and seat wherever they wanted. I remember being told that I was to encourage people to seat in the front pews and I told the head usher that I would try knowing that the members would ignore me. I could always encourage a new convert to the church because they were always willing to comply but when it came to the longtime members, they gave me a difficult time, and some would refuse to move. I would get a glance from the leader, and she would motion to me to let it be. I didn't have a good experience in the one and only church I ever ushered in. However, it didn't discourage me from ushering because I was doing it unto the Lord. When we do ministry, no matter where we serve, we must do what the Lord expects of us.

Unfortunate, church people can't see what God wants them to see because they are blinded by hate. Ignorance hardens the heart creating blindness. God encourages us to see ourselves blessed and wants us to get away from those who are evil. I would be appalled by the way church members would look at one another, "if looks could kill," most church members would be lying dead all over the church carpet.

But, when God looks at us, He sees neither Jews nor Gentiles. There is no racism in God's Kingdom. Only holy eyes see what God sees. We are supposed to wear God like a garment and be in His presence all day long. We have to get used to being redeemed and walking with the redeemer. We are our brother's keeper so let us treat each other right. While I waited to find my home church where I would start my Christian ministry I entered into a different ministry. I started taking college courses.

Deny Yourself

In the Spring of 1989, I decided to attend Eastport's community college, and take classes in the field of Human Services. I had no idea where that thought came from, but I would find out later. I walked into the school one morning that was located in the eastside of Eastport and went into the Admission Office located on the first floor next to the front entrance to the school. There in the office as soon as I walked in was a female in her middle twenties, sitting at the Admission desk. She was pleasant and all too ready to assist. I asked her what did I have to do to start taking classes? She told me with a smile to go upstairs to the second floor to the Financial Aid Office that someone would assist me in completing the proper forms. I thought that was easy and went up the stairs to the second floor. I found the office, and someone assisted me with the forms, and I was told that I would have to complete a placement exam and that someone will contact me. I took the placement exam and was put in remedial classes which I passed, and I was on my way to taking college courses. I was in my thirties taking my very first semester in college. I was so excited that I was going to college for an Associate degree in Human Services, but still, I wasn't sure why I was attending Human Services courses.

I started my very first internship at the Hopkins Community House working with the youth counselor who was also a Christian. A polite and considerate male around my age that was always smiling which made me feel comfortable being in a strange environment (all this was new to me as I mentioned before.) Only God knows our future, and therefore He equips us for the journey. We just have to take our cues from Him and follow wherever He leads us.

When God calls us to ministry, He will take us to another level. God's deliverance has a purpose, and it's called ministry. When God's hand is upon us, we can't get away because He wants to be all in our business. God will come to us in different forms. He may appear to us as an Admissions person in a college and as a Financial Aid Officer and grant you the finances you need to attend school. "For whoever wants to save their life will lose it, but whoever loses their life for me will save it" (Luke 9:24, NIV.)

If we want to follow Christ, we must deny oneself, carry the Cross, and follow Jesus. To deny oneself is like saying to the self you are not first. The Lord will put us through a proof test. The trial is to see where our interest is. For some us church members it appears that our interest is more important than God's interest. God puts us through a test to see if we will deny oneself and follow Him. Jesus uses the parable of the rich man to illustrate this point of view.

> "Teacher, what good thing must I do to get eternal life?" "Why do you ask me about what is good?" Jesus replied. "There is only One who is good. If you want to enter life, keep the commandments." "Which ones?" he inquired. Jesus replied, "'You shall not murder, you

shall not commit adultery, you shall not steal, you shall not give false testimony, [19] honor your father and mother,' and 'love your neighbor as yourself.'" "All these I have kept," the young man said. "What do I still lack?" Jesus answered, "If you want to be perfect, go, sell your possessions and give to the poor, and you will have treasure in heaven. Then come, follow me." When the young man heard this, he went away sad, because he had great wealth" (Matthew 19:16-22, NIV.)

We will never be perfect here on earth because there are some things, we are not going to deny ourselves, but that's all right. In denying ourselves, we must do what God instructs us to do. If God tells us to love our enemies and pray for them, then we do it. Do good to those who hate us and forgive them seventy times seven. By all means, don't stop coming to church but be encouraged and encouraged others. We must be servants first. Do good and no harm. Don't do evil for evil. We must carry our Cross daily and give up our pride and our personal gain. We need to adjust our life to what God wants from us.

God's goal for us is to accomplish God's plan. Submit our dreams and aspirations and goals to God and see them come to fruition. Jesus submitted His will to God at the Garden of Gethsemane. "Not my will but God's will be done." We must understand the love of God. The love of God will take what Satan wants for evil and turn it into something good. The love of God transforms us into a new creation. To receive the love of God, we must have our harden hearts and everything that is sinful taken out. The word of God tells us,

"For God so loved the world that he gave his one and only Son, that whoever believes in him shall not perish but have eternal life. For God did not send his Son into the world to condemn the world, but to save the world through him" (John 3:16-17, NIV.)

The Pilgrim's Journey

In the book "The Pilgrim's Progress" (I highly recommend you read this book), written by John Bunyan, a 17th-century Puritan preacher, tells a story about a man named Christian. The book is more of a parable about the Christians and their frailties. You will read about Christians struggles to stay the course of a true believer and follow Christ Jesus into heaven. Christian is being tempted by Mr. Worldly Wise (the legalism in the church and the cultural morals of the time) while he is looking for the "Celestial City," (following Christ to heaven.) Mr. Bunyan uses the character Christian to illustrate the epitome of the Christian life and how easy it's for Christians to fall prey to the deception of others when we are not following the narrow road that leads to heaven. Mr. Bunyan pens these words while he is in prison for preaching without the support of the Catholic church,

> "When Christians unto carnal men give ear,
> out of their way did go, and pay for't dear;
> For Master Worldly Wiseman can
> but show a saint the way to bondage and to woe." [11]

The Bible gives witness to what happens to Christians who continue to sin against God, the Son, and the Holy Spirit. When we try to please the world, we give our backs to God. We cannot serve two masters. God doesn't share His glory with no one. God is a jealous God. God loves us but the word is plain if we willfully commit sins knowingly and don't confess them then enough is enough. We must fear God and stop playing church. We must take heed to the witnesses in the Bible. People who have gone before us were punished for their disobedience. God gave us His Son that whosoever believes Him will have life and that more abundantly. We are responsible for living right before God and to confess our sins. If we continue to sin and don't repent and we ignore it as sin, then we are fooling ourselves. But keep in mind that God is not mock. Punishment will come. God forgives us of every sin under the heavens when we acknowledge that we sin. But if we keep doing it over and over again and come to church and pretend everything is all right it is a lie. The scriptures remind us that Satan is the father of all lies and that is whom the sinner is serving.

The word of God reminds us in Romans 12:2, (NIV), "And be not conformed to this world: but be ye transformed by the renewing of your mind, that ye may prove what is good, and acceptable, and perfect, will of God."

We must start by presenting, "Our bodies as living sacrifices pleasing unto Him" (Romans 12:1, NIV). Allow God to transform our minds and renew our heart to be more like His Son. Let us come to the throne of grace and let God change us.

Change begins when we turn to the Lord, and He lifts the veil that covers our heart and mind, and we take authority for our life. The actions start when we meditate on the Book of the Law, day and night that we may be successful in our Christian walk.

> "This book of the law shall not depart out of thy mouth; but thou shalt meditate therein day and night, that thou mayest observe to do according to all that is written therein: for then thou shalt make thy way prosperous, and then thou shalt have good success," (Joshua 1:8, NIV.)

The actions should be effective, efficient, and eliminate the hindrance. Change won't allow us to let our family, friends or enemies fall through the cracks. We are changed to want to save everyone. We must not fail to tell our family the truth. The wise builders listen and obey. They build on a solid foundation. The foolish builders listen but didn't obey because they build on sandy foundations that wash away. Jesus Christ is the solid foundation. If we build upon the rock of salvation, Jesus, then no matter what kind of trial and tribulations may come our way they will not sway us. Do not quit.

The followers of Jesus Christ, should ask God daily to deliver us from the evil one. We should challenge church members what God is doing for them and encourage them to continue to believe. Let them know that they might go through some hardship to enter the kingdom, but God will see them through it. Having these attitudes symbolizes the attitude of Christ Jesus. This is the style of life we should seek after and God will give us hope. God will give us our basic and fundamental needs. God is going to prepare us and give us what we need to do His purpose. The church must believe that God really does exist and have confidence in Him.

Our friends and family have strong influences and can easily distract our focus it's in our innate nature. Don't follow the directions of the church member who knows they are sinning and don't care.

The word of God is the way to grow and prosper, and so whatever you do, meditate on the word always. We must take the word and understand it and use it when we need it. We must stay planted in the word. There will be doubt in the life of the unbeliever until they enter into the sanctuary of God, then they will know the truth.

When we are rejected for bringing the message of God, it will be their responsibility if they are condemned. Those who reject us will face judgment. We must not worry about being rejected just as long as we shared the message of the Lord.

Bring the word of God to the people where they will want to repent or should repent. The truth of God will cause them to change. The outcome of bringing the word of God to the sinners is that they repent and are saved. We have the authority and the power to rebuke demons by anointing the sinners with oil. It's time to see God for who He truly is and what we can accomplish with Him on our side.

CHAPTER FIVE

KEEP IT HOLY

To deal with holiness is to deal with our own weaknesses. I like to watch American Movie Classics in black and white screens. I would spend hours in front of my television (I don't subscribe to Cablevision any longer.) Watching movies took away time from reading my Bible and praying.

Holiness living starts with our mind – it is being disciplined twenty-four hours a day and seven days a week. Doing the work instructed to us in the word of God and being a witness for the Lord at all times is holy living. Holiness is repentance, confessing our sins, and professing Christ Jesus as our Lord and Savior. You are God's chosen people. You are holy and dearly loved. So, put on tender mercy and kindness as if they were your clothes. Don't be proud. Be gentle and patient (Colossians 3:12.)

Two years after my conversion I experienced some remarkable things in my life. The first was when I started taking college courses and was doing an internship. The second was when I got married to the man I had been living with for the past ten years. We had been living together in sin, (I didn't know that.) Suddenly, he asked me to marry him and I, of course, was very excited because I wanted so much to be his wife. I had to wait until he suggested marriage. Because when we met, I had told him there would be no strings attached in our relationship. God was not in the equation back then. I strongly believe that God put it in his heart to marry me that I would not live in sin any longer. He, of course, used the reasoning that our son, who was five years old, was starting kindergarten. We were going to have a Justice of the Peace perform the wedding and have a private dinner with just a few couples. But his father told us that we should get married in the church and have a reception.

During that year we were in a financial slump. I was working at a fast food restaurant part-time, and he worked for his brothers at their grocery store for a small weekly salary. My father-in-law decided that he would pay for the reception hall. My friends and I cooked the food. His father also encouraged us to get married at his church and told us that he had already spoken with the Parish Priest.

What a blessing it was to have a church wedding. My older brother walked me down the aisle. He was honored I asked him to walk me down, (it was not planned.) I had on a cream color suit and wore a cream color wide brim hat with a lace bow in the back, and my husband wore a black tuxedo and a black bowtie. We both looked so handsome together, and so did our children. My daughter was the bridesmaid, and our son was the ring bearer. All the wonderful changes that were taking place in my life were nothing short of miracles. God made an honest woman of me that day, and I praise Him every day for what he was doing in my life and for what he continues to do till this day.

God had reconciled me to Himself through the righteousness of Christ when I received Him as my Savior. I repented, and all the sins had been removed from my heart and I was no longer fornicating but a married woman to enjoy sex with my husband the way God had intended. I had said to myself that I will abide in Christ Jesus and will stop my sinning.

> "Do not conform to the pattern of this world but be transformed by the renewing of your mind. Then you will be able to test and approve what God's will is—his good, pleasing and perfect will" (Romans 12:2, NIV.)

I grew up in a very dysfunctional home (as I mentioned earlier) and all I ever wanted was to have stability in my life. In my journey for spiritual growth and healing for my brokenness, I believed that the church would be such a place. The church is a hospital where the sick go for spiritual renewal and healing. To be encouraged for their emotional issues and prayed for their physical healing. I know that the church building is just an edifice but what is inside is the real church, the members who should welcome with open arms the hurting and down-trodden and offer comfort and reassurance. I was chasing for the impossible, but God is faithful. God has been with the church since its conception.

People who attend church are not all saved. They are not all saints. Church people can't just be tithers and monetary givers and then hate each other, nor can they fight the purpose of God for their lives. Church people must stop pretending to love one another but ask the Lord, "what will thou have me to do? The time to stop 'half-stepping and wavering in our belief is now. Whatever is hindering us from being true to the Lord must be terminated.

Today we must go after God like never before and grab hold of Him. We must stop hurting each other and encourage one another to grab hold of God and not let go.

Get What We Need At Church Depot

"Restore us to yourself, LORD, that we may return; renew our days as of old" (Lamentations 5:21, NIV.)

There is an association with a human who is broken and needs fixing to a family who depends on heat to stay warm in the middle of winter but the heater is broken. We must understand that when someone goes to church seeking God is because he or she needs to fix his or her life including his or her family. When we go to church, it is like going to a supply store. We go looking for salvation and healing, for God's mercy and grace, and for the love of the One that borne our sins, Christ Jesus and His peace. These are the tools we need for our lives. We don't come to church for form or fashion. We don't come to church to be entertained or just to warm up the pews. We come to church to seek God, be transformed, grow spiritually and to fellowship with each other. We come to church to glorify Him for His goodness and love. Let us understand that the spirit of pride is the opposite of humility and creates conflict with the Holy Spirit. Christ humbled himself to be an instrument to bridge the world to God. And, we are to go out into the world and offer that same bridge to the unsaved. To see God's glory, we need love. Agape love is the unconditional love of God that He demonstrates toward the Human Race on a daily basis. We can love those who don't love us because God first loves us.

I had continued my search for the church that would show me the love of Christ and teach me sound doctrine. I was desperately seeking because I had concerns that the old lifestyle would pull me back. I had left that life behind and needed to have a place of safety, and I thought that being with other believers would keep me from going back to that life again. "Hasten, O God, to save me; come quickly, Lord, to help me" (Psalm 70:1, NIV).

Do Not Lose Focus

I knew that the Lord was with me and that He would help. I could feel His presence and hear His voice bring scripture to me, "be strong and courageous." Make God's word our authoritative guide to all things. We must study and meditate on the word daily.

Don't lose faith when God doesn't move fast enough. To lose faith is to lose hope. Hope is the expectations of good. Try not to lose focus, or allow the enemy to irritate you. Pray and call on the Lord when you are going through difficult times. Don't stop calling on Him but call Him more. Keep your eyes to the hills from where help comes from – it comes from the Lord. Don't lose your footage but keep your feet on the word of the Lord. The enemy will attempt to remove you from the word and the church. Stay rooted on His word and don't forfeit your future but wait patiently on the Lord.

My life had started to change for the better, and I knew that I owed it all to God. I met a female student who told me about a Spanish Pentecost church located on Webber Street, and the services started late afternoon. I was so on fire for God that I wanted to know more about Him. Sometimes we question what God wants us to do, and we struggle with it. The enemy blinds us and lies to us about how God has forgotten us in our struggle, but that is not true. No matter what rules have been set for us the safest place in the whole wide world is in God's will. When we accept God's will for our life, He is able to make it easier. "Therefore, everyone who hears these words of mine and puts them into practice is like a wise man who built his house on the rock" (Matthew 7:24, NIV).

I decided to visit the church the following Sunday. As I ascended the stairs to the church, I was somewhat wary as to what to expect. It was the third in my search for a church. I entered through double doors into the sanctuary. The lighting was dim, and it was extremely quiet. The service had not yet started, and members were still greeting each other, and several of them came to greet me. The service started with the usual praise and worship team singing their songs. The music was quiet void of excitement. Before the pastor preached, I was acknowledged by him who knew that I wasn't a regular member. After he asked my name, a few members came over to greet and shake my hand. I told them that my classmate had told me about their church.

I Was a Babe in the Faith

I was an infant in the faith and was in desperate need of sound scriptural doctrine to keep me from straying back into my old lifestyle. It is easy to pick up on people's routines, and that is what I observed. Some people go to church because it is the thing to do, but their heart isn't in it. It's void of the presence of God. Some pastors spent most of the service sharing their life story and how they got started in the ministry and others share personal things about their family life that should not be made privy to the congregation.

The times I attended I didn't understand most of the pastor's preaching due in part to my inability to fully understand Spanish. At times, the message would come through as fragmented. I couldn't understand it nor make sense of it. What did I know? I was a babe in the faith. I visited the church several times and decided to leave because I was not getting my spiritual needs met. I had developed a hunger for the word and the spirit of wanting to live a life for Christ Jesus. Our lives should be as living unto Him in our jobs, our homes, and every place we go. God will be with the believer as long as there is a relationship with Him. Everything we do in life should be made through the will of God. God should be consulted about every move a Christians wants to make in life. We must reverence the Lord. The Bible reminds us that it is a team effort, a partnership, if you will, with God.

Give God praise in spite of our circumstances. Praise Turns God to us, and He turns things around for us. Praise begins with being grateful and giving thanks. We must sing to the Lord songs of praise and lift up the name of God. How important is praise? When the praises go up the enemy is consumed. For God will defeat the enemy on our behalf and give us the blessings. Keep in mind that as people of God we are always under attack. Don't get out of character in your waiting. No matter what we're going through, we should still praise God.

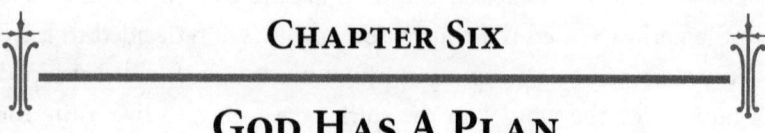

Chapter Six

God Has A Plan

Hopkins Community House is an agency that houses several social programs, and it was there that I met Tonya. She worked with the Day Care program. I would run into her in the mornings. One day she stopped me to invited me to her church. At that time, I was transitioning from one church to another and was unsatisfied with the ones I had visited thus far, so I took her invitation.

Make the Connection

It was a Pentecostal church on the other side of the railroad in Eastport. The sanctuary was small compared to the last two churches, and the altar was much smaller. When I started attending the church services, I always sat by the aisle closest to the window to the right, and three to four pews in front of the altar. It was easier for me to go to the restrooms or leave out the side door.

I was determined to attend a Pentecostal church because it was what I felt in my heart to do. On my first visit to that church, I sat quietly in the seat where I felt the most comfortable. I smiled at everyone that would give me eye contact and greet them with "God bless you," and most times the members would return the greeting.

As I continue to attend services, I felt drawn to a few of the older females in the church because I felt safe around them. They happen to be the members who smiled at me and blessed me every time I came to church. So, I liked sitting close to them because they helped me to stay grounded and somehow connect me to the rest of the congregation. They made me feel welcomed and a part of the church. I soon became acquainted with them as I introduced myself and they may a difference in my staying in this church. I met the person in charge of Saturday outreach program. She served the community's destitute Saturday after Saturday, and I never heard her complain. The other sisters I remember for their heavenly hugs and precious smiles which made a good impression to the new converts looking for affirmation. I will never forget one sister Eliza whom I became much more attached to because of her genuine love for God and people. She wore Christ all over her, and this is not just me saying it. She was the saint everyone wanted around for solace and comfort, and she was as close to an angel than anyone I have ever met.

Being a Christian is an everyday practice. Those who have been saved by the Father in earlier years should encourage the new converts. They need to minister to the least of the people, the poor in spirit. Because the only thing that can raise the poor in spirit is the gospel of the 'Living God,' and older members, for the most part, make the best mentors, (my estimation). The new converts will not be complete until the more seasoned Christians minister to them from their hearts. The scriptures clearly state that new converts are just like the sheep who have to be led. God is the one that saves, delivers and makes whole those who will receive Him, and having a spiritual church member to mentor the new converts makes the transition all the better.

I was still a new convert to the faith, but I could see the spirit of the Lord over the shepherd of the house. When I heard the Pastor of my friend Tonya preach, I knew I had to come back to hear more of his preaching. The Pastor of the church was an anointed man. I didn't say that he was perfect, but there was definitely a spiritual anointing that I had not seen before. Every word he spoke was scriptural, and it was most times directed toward my situation. I guess all new converts think that way.

I believed in my heart that it was my season and my appointed time to be in his church. I pray in faith, waited, and God answers me in His set time. The Holy Spirit knew where I was in my faith after all I had experience. I was prepared. We must stay encouraged and wait on the Lord and what God has for us because He will make it come to pass.

"We who are strong must be considerate of those who are sensitive... We must not just please ourselves. We should help others do what is right and build them up in the Lord. For even Christ didn't live to please himself. As the Scriptures say, "The insults of those who insult you, O God, have fallen on me." Such things were written in the Scriptures long ago to teach us. And the Scriptures give us hope and encouragement as we wait patiently for God's promises to be fulfilled. May God, who gives this patience and encouragement, help you live in complete harmony with each other, as is fitting for followers of Christ Jesus. Then all of you can join together with one voice, giving praise and glory to God, the Father of our Lord Jesus Christ. Therefore, accept each other just as Christ has accepted you so that God will be given glory" (Romans 15:1-7, NIV.)

I felt that I would receive my spiritual mentoring with the Shepherd of the house, as he was called by everyone in the church. Obeying God and submitting to godly leaders is our godly duty and I had no problem doing both. People who claim to believe in God must follow the leadership that God puts them under. We must submit to their leadership and obey what they preach to us. As we imitate our spiritual leaders, we will succeed. In the farmlands, the sheep must first know their shepherd's voice so that they will not get lost. It is the same with church members in that we must first examine ourselves to admit that we need help. We must stay the course by listening to wise counsel from our anointed leaders and be willing to be mentored and taught.

Godly men and women must not allow themselves to be influenced by people who rebel against spiritual leaders. But allow being guided and instructed in the way of the Lord. Believers should take heed to make the contract to serve the Lord. We must take a stand and make the decision for righteousness and holiness. We must purpose in our hearts to stand for the Lord and put all of our faith and hope, as well as our life in His hands. I had found what I was looking for in Shepherd and had decided to stay in that church but not knowing for how long. All I knew is that I had made a decision to live for the Messiah and this church preached nothing but Christ Jesus.

At first, I didn't know whether this stirring inside of me was a normal thing and didn't want to embarrass myself or appear out of place since I was a new convert. But every time he preached, I felt like I wanted to run, jump, scream out and praise God. I was very careful not to overstep my bounds because I was new to the church and needed to get acclimated first. I felt that I needed to respect the house because I was a guest. It took me some time to give the spirit the freedom to run around the church in total praise.

God's love is relentless in His search for us, the sinner. God will take us to where He wants us to go and eventually, we will do what He has planned for us. We need to be connected to God for He has a plan for our life. "No eye has seen, no ear has heard, and no mind has imagined what God has prepared for those who love him" (1 Corinthians 2:9, NIV.)

There are things that God called us to do that we have no idea until we are actually doing it. When we are connected to Him, we are brought to life, and we allow God to do His will in us. We may start off as infants in the church, but God will guide us toward maturity.

Do Not Look Back

"Not that I have already obtained all this, or have already arrived at my goal, but I press on to take hold of that for which Christ Jesus took hold of me" (Philippians 3:12.)

I knew that my old life had to die for God to do a new thing with me. To say yes to the Living Water is to have life and that more abundantly. At the time I didn't have a hold on what God wanted me to do. I was saved and delivered but didn't know what the next step was?

Several things began to happened to me all in the same year

that appeared to have me on the right track. I guess what I needed was to stay spiritually focused. I was to live holy and do the things that would please God. It was going to be a challenge to be where God wanted me to be, but I was willing to be obedient. It appeared to me that it was Tonya's church where God wanted me to be and so I was all too happy to oblige. I knew I was to pray, read my Bible and go to church.

In the road ahead of where God was going to take me, He had to break me to transform me. God wanted to break my old patterns of behavior the enemy was using against me. God wanted to break my negative view of things. All this spiritual stuff was new to me, and I had to be strengthened and encouraged to move forward. God knew me and knew that I was self-sufficient but He had to break my auto-sufficiency. He told me what was for my own good. It was no coincidence that God brought me through those churches if only to teach me a lesson. God taught me that things didn't have to go my way. I had to leave the world behind me and take the world's lifestyle out of my system. I had to stop the love affair I had with the world. I realized that God had to break me to bless me.

How can putting someone through difficult times and hardship bless them? The road to the kingdom is a difficult one with much suffering, but only Jesus can save us from such hardships. For the most part, in our spiritual journey, our pride, and our ignorance of the scriptures, and God in specific is a hindrance that doesn't allow God from breaking us. We should cooperate with God. Ask God what is the pattern of behavior I need to have broken? Things that don't allow God's plan to come to fruition. We limit God's blessing on our children and family when we don't allow Him to break us of our worldly lifestyle patterns.

What is God trying to break in you? Allow God to break you. Don't be resistant to His breaking. God will let you keep what He wants in you and get rid of what is not pleasing to Him. God will make you and mold you. If we profess to be Christ followers, then we must be willing to give in and stop resisting God's breaking those sinful patterns of behavior? Surrender to God this moment and don't look back. The gatekeeper opens the gate for him, and the sheep listen to his voice. He calls his own sheep by name and leads them out (John 10:3.)

CHAPTER SEVEN

WHEN GOD CALLS

When God calls us, He draws us. We come to church because we know there is something we need that we didn't have. Before God called me, I was nothing, and there was nothing good in me. Where I was, there was no structure; there was no light, no joy, and no happiness. There was nothing. "Before I formed you in the womb I knew you before you were born I set you apart; I appointed you as a prophet to the nations" (Jeremiah 1:5, NIV.)

I enjoyed learning about God, about Jesus Christ and loved all the Bible stories the Shepherd shared with the church. I was not looking for foolishness. I was very serious about learning about God and why I was chosen. I knew that I should have died in my sins. I was pleased with what I was receiving from God and ignore all the other nonsense.

God Called Me

We must be aware of the Pharisees and understand they are those church folks who will keep the rest of the members down and distracted from doing the will of God. We must ignore the Pharisees. The Pharisees in the church are the members with negative attitudes. When they saw me, they did not see a sister in Christ but an outsider who didn't belong in their church. But I was determined to learn more about God and refused to take Satan's bait. The preacher was really preaching to me what God wanted me to hear. It was always something new that I was learning about Christ Jesus and holy living. I wanted the holy living part because it was what was going to keep me from my sinful lifestyle. The preaching helped to keep me grounded.

I was enjoying the uplifting gospel music and praising God. The hymns were so inviting that I just could not sit still. I literally loved the dancing and singing and seeing the church come alive in praise and worship. I invited my husband and my daughter and her family (she had recently married and had a baby girl), but my husband and her husband didn't want to attend the Pentecostal church. My oldest son was not interested in attending church, but I prayed for them all.

God saves us for His namesake and not because of anything we have done but because He is good and His mercy is forever. God is our wonderful counselor and comforter. The characteristics of God's mercy are expressed through His love, righteousness, and justice. We must never discourage anyone who comes to the church. God doesn't show favoritism but accepts everyone.

I was at that church for almost two years, and I made it my mission to stay no matter how the member treated me. The elder female's kindness made the transition much more bearable, and I was intentional to receive the positive and ignore the negative. I was beginning to get to know the members as they were acclimating to me as well. I had not become a member of the church at that point simply because I was ignorant of the process. Come to think about it I was never asked in any of the churches to join their church. I would think that church membership would be a priority to make sure that the convert becomes part of the church where they will assist them along the way to leading a godly lifestyle.

I was being transitioned one more time to attend another church and this time not by my own volition. I told Tonya since she was the person who had invited me to her church and I needed her to know the truth about why I was leaving. Like myself, she was also born elsewhere and moved to Connecticut on a whim. She told me the following story of how she came to live in Connecticut.

She was at a conference for musicians and choirs when she heard a group of male choir members singing, and she was so impressed with their voices that it led her to where they were. She sat and listened tentatively to them until the preacher got up to preach. She said, "he was full of the anointing, and I felt the presence that was upon him, and I wanted to hear him again." She was invited to come to Eastport by a female member from his church, and she accepted the invitation. She moved to Eastport, and her first job was at Hopkins Community Daycare, where we met. She was absolutely right about the preacher because when I heard him, there would be no one quite like him.

I felt a spiritual connection to her. I invited her to family events. I really did not know her that well but she liked Spanish food and she attended my parties. She gave me a Bible on December 29, 1991. She wrote these beautiful inspirational words. I can quote them because I still have the bible.

12-29-91
Zamora,

God is Great and
Greatly to be Praised. Run
with this word – pursue it
day & night – for it is this
the word that will change lives –
I love the Lord and I
love you – Muchas amor (lots of love)
Siempre! (always)
Pray for me continuously –

Tonya

God Will Work It Out

I was on my way to a Catholic church environment that I knew would be different in many ways than the Pentecost church, for sure!

It was the Fall of 1992 when my husband told me that he had decided to attend his parent's church. I thought, just when I felt comfortable and had decided to stay in my church.

I had just come from work, and I saw my husband sitting in the loveseat watching television. I walked over to him and kissed him which was the norm for me. But there was something different, and I noticed his solemn look, and I asked him, what is the matter? He immediately responded, "I want to start going to church." I was elated but did not want to seem so excited that he would change his mind. Our youngest son had been going with me to church on Sundays but would stay home with him on Wednesday evenings while I was at Bible study. I had been attending the Pentecostal church for the past several years, and he never seemed interested in going with me to any of the churches I had visited, and I never forced him to go nor argued with him about it. So, I immediately said, I'll go with you because a wife should attend church with her husband. With his serious macho tone and the cute smile, he said, "okay."

His parents were longtime parishioners at that particular Catholic church located in Eastport, a predominately Hispanic neighborhood.

God had answered one of my many prayers. We soon began to attend the church as a family. Even, my daughter and her husband began to attend the same church as well. I could not be happier than to see everyone in my family visiting the house of the Lord. My husband was to me the man of my dreams, and by agreeing to attend church, he had made my world complete.

I met my husband in the summer of 1978 at his home which he shared with two of his younger brothers. I had been invited by his brothers to cook lunch for them and their friends while they painted the exterior of the house. The house was located in a quiet residential neighborhood in the suburbs. It was a hot and humid day. I was inside the house where it was air-conditioned cooking their lunch. I remember standing in front of the kitchen sink rinsing off the lettuce and tomatoes when I suddenly felt a presence behind me like someone watching me and when I turned around, I caught him looking at me with this cute smile on his face. I have to admit that I instantly found this 5'9" man very attractive. He wore a nicely trimmed black mustache and sideburns. He had high cheekbones (some freckles around the nose), and a cute slim nose. I was immediately drawn to him like a magnet is drawn to metal. It was as if we had this invisible connection that pulled on us to connect. It was unexplainable. It was getting late, and I had to get home with my two kids, and he immediately volunteered to drive me home, and I was all too happy to have him take us. It was obvious to the both of us that we wanted to spend a little more time with each other that day. When we got to my home, he walked me to the door, and we kissed.

I married him (the man of my dreams) ten years after that first encounter. He was smart, a good father to my two children and our son, a good provider, and a great companion. I would tell the kids, "You kids have nothing to worry about because dad and I will never ever get a divorce." I will always treasure and love this man.

God knows what he is doing even before we can fathom or imagine it. God had us in mind from before our existence. God had already reconciled us to Himself while we were still in our sins. I could just imagine the conversation God was having with Jesus Christ about my husband and me. Jesus told God, "I will save her first, and she will sanctify her husband, and then we will reconcile him to us." God told Jesus, "that sounds like what we had discussed back eons ago, and it worked."

Reconciliation has to do with repentance, confession, and convictions. Reconciliation has to do with what God and Adam and Eve had before they both sinned. But something went wrong. However, God calls us to repent of our sins and confess them to Him. God loves us so much that he gave us His Son so that we can see just how much, arms stretched wide. We had lived a sinful life for many years, and at last, we were both saved and served the Lord. "And we know that in all things God works for the good of those who love him, who have been called according to his purpose" (Romans 8:28, NIV.)

When my husband and I decided to change our sinful lifestyle some of our friends were respectful of the decision we had made. But there were other friends who were disappointed that we didn't want to indulge in the use of drugs and alcohol anymore. We would still attend their parties, but we didn't enjoy them as we did back years earlier. Slowly the friends began to dissipate, and we were all right with that. We thought if they value our friendship they would stick around and appreciate what we were doing. But it doesn't work that way because they were now living in darkness and our light shined too bright. The spirits that were operating in them could not tolerate that we were walking in the light. We must shake ourselves from the sins of this world when we are in the will of God. When we are working for the kingdom of God, there is nothing we can't do in His name.

I remember being invited to my friend's house for a party after my conversion. Her husband and my husband were longtime friends even before I came into the picture. We had partied together for many years, and we enjoyed each other's company. I adored her and considered her more like a sister than my bestfriend. The house was full of all our friends, and I was the only one not indulging in drinking and drugging. I didn't mind being there because they were my friends but I noticed that every time they wanted to do drugs, they all went to the downstairs room of the house (it was a raised ranch) and they'd let me know that it was out of respect for me. I felt the presence of the enemy encouraging me to indulge, but at the same time, I knew that the presence of my spirit was too strong. They could not enjoy what they were doing if I was in their presence. She came up to me and said, "I'm sorry we are leaving you alone up here, but we will come back after we do…but I know you don't… anymore." We hugged, and she left and after a few minutes came back upstairs, and we laughed and had a good time that evening. I thank God that he kept me. I wanted to be a beacon in a dark place.

I don't see them anymore, but I still pray for their salvation after all these years.

The Bible tells us to flee from ungodly passion such as fornication, the love of money, lusting after ungodly men and women, adultery, thinking self-righteous thought, desires to do drugs and drink alcohol, covertness, and jealousy.

When people are jealous of us Christians, we just have to let them go and not feed into their negative behavior. We should continue to follow God and do His work. We must flee from temptation. We must understand that God can be trusted no matter what we go through He can still comfort us. We must trust God even when our children leave home, and when a loved one dies. We must know that God is Sovereign and there is nothing He will not do for us if we walk right before Him. "It's not the healthy people who need a doctor, but the sick ones. "For I have not come to call the righteous, but sinners" (Matthew 9:12-13, NIV.)

God Wants Our Family

God wants our unsaved families. We are to reach out to the unsaved husband and wife, our children and grandchildren. Saving our house is a ministry ordained by God. Wives are to be helpers to husbands- as Jesus is to us. Wives first ministry is to their husband, then children and then the church. The spouses are to love one another and their children as God loves the church. We must obey God by doing what is in the scriptures. God will bless our families and us through our obedience to Him. Let us always pray in the morning and before doing anything so that God can send His angels to keep our families and us in the way of the Lord. The enemy will try to fight against our families and us, but God will fight the enemy for us. Pray to Christ Jesus who washed us in His precious blood. We are cleansed from sin through Jesus Blood. He who knew no sin became sin for us that our families and we may be saved, set free and delivered.

My husband and I were both in love with the Savior. He was such an affectionate husband, father, and grandfather. God knew what he was doing when he gave him to me for a husband. He and I had such a remarkable relationship with the children and their families.

My sons received Jesus Christ as their Lord and Savior when they were younger but aren't fully committed as I am to serving God. I am still claiming their deliverance from the snares of this world, and they are in my prayers daily. I do witness to them every opportunity I get without frustrating them. I let them know that I will always make myself available to them and they know that I will always love them until God calls me home.

The saints shall always pray and not faint. We shall pray and wait. Never get frustrated with God if we don't see the results immediately. It's all in God's timing. All we need to do is have faith. I am talking about faith in God. Faith comes from hearing the word of the Lord for our lives. Which is why we should always seek God in the sanctuary where the preacher, who hears from God will give us the word to live by. God has our destiny in His hands. He conquered kingdoms, and He fights our battles, and He never loses a fight. He is the Righteous King who delivers promises. We need someone we can trust, and Christ Jesus is it.

Chapter Eight

For the Sake of the Father

The parish Priest was no stranger to us because he had performed our wedding back in 1989. But I knew it was God orchestrating everything that was happening to us both after my conversion. It was the Patriarch of the family who had suggested we get married in his church. My daughter also got married in that church; the associated priest performed her ceremony.

We attended the English service although most of the parishioners were Puerto Rican. It was a beautiful church that had recently been built. The round shaped sanctuary was enormous with solid oakwood pews semi-circle from right to left with four aisles. The altar stretched from right to left connecting with the sides of the church. Behind the altar from ceiling to floor was a mosaic tile wall with the figure of Jesus Christ in His white robe holding a scepter with a banner. Painted on the banner was a red cross.

God will plant new growth in the life of the believer through establishing new friends, attaining new things, having renewed health and new blessings. If we can't make sacrifices, then don't look for new growth. Self-sacrifice is what should be our goal to empty out self-efforts. For the sake of others and our own salvation, we must throw out the imperfections in our life such as our pride, our negative attitudes, and habits that are a hindrance to our spiritual life. We will have new growth when we can be perfect in love, in faith, in the way we speak, and in our obedience to God. New growth is allowing God to help us stay in our spiritual walk with Him.

I had been saved for several years and basically had stayed away from my old lifestyle. I had been trying very hard to keep God's laws. I did not want to fall prey to worldly behaviors and its bad habits.

But I would quickly find out that being a member of the Catholic church would be a challenge.

Sacrificial Years

Coming to the Roman Catholic Church was a challenge for me for several reasons. I didn't agree with the reverence they held for the mother of Jesus, Mary. I couldn't understand the reason for praying to Saint Mary (with all due respect to the Catholics.) I didn't see the point of repeating the same prayer with the rosary beads. I couldn't understand the liturgy of the Priest, most times it sounded muffled. I could never understand the correlation between the scripture and the message. I didn't have the freedom to express my praise outwardly hence constricting the spirit. I decided to sacrifice myself the freedom to outwardly praise and worship the Lord. I went along with a different doctrine for the sake of my husband's salvation. I knew that God had it all under control and all I had to do was to be obedient. This new adventure was either going to break me or make me into the person God wanted me to be.

Not long after I had become a member, the church secretary (who I had been buying a brand name cosmetic product from for several years) announced that she and the parish Priest and a couple of other members were going to see a live comedy show and if my husband and I would be interested in attending. I am by nature a very sociable person, and I quickly jumped to the occasion to fellowship with some of the church members. My husband and I went with them to the comedy show. We sat at a table with the secretary and the priest and a few others. The waitress came by, and everyone ordered their drinks, and to my surprise, I was the only one drinking soda. I was shocked to see that the parish Priest was drinking shots of Tequila and the other members drinking alcoholic beverages as well. I didn't know what to think about what I was witnessing. Being an immature Christian, I thought since I was among church people and the parish Priest then it was all right to drink alcohol and attend comedy shows with adult themes. Because after all, he is a man of God and the church leader. Keep in mind that I was new to the body of believers and was not equipped to understand such matters.

I had heard from Catholics and seen on television that the Roman Catholic Priest do drink wine and I didn't see the harm in it. I also heard that wine is offered in the communion. I am not their judge. "Que sera, sera." But as for me I was in a delicate situation and very vulnerable at that time. I saw some things with the church members that I was beginning to find disturbing.

The Roman Catholic church celebrates most of the secular holidays that other churches of different denominations celebrate and there is nothing strange about that. But in my first Christmas dinner with the church, I witness the same parish Priest sitting alone at the head of a table and on the table was a bottle of the highly expensive Cuevas tequila. There were members drinking all sorts of alcoholic drinks and dancing to the secular music. I was confused about all that. I didn't know what to think about the Roman Catholic Church at that point. My experience with the Pentecostal church was very different. I was encouraged to live in the presence of the Lord and seek guidance through the Holy Spirit. I suppose there is a great distinction between the Catholic and Pentecostal beliefs. I just didn't realize the great chasm between them.

It was my second summer after being a member when I decided to volunteer to help in the annual summer carnival. I noticed a carnival prize spinning wheel and the people were putting money on a number to win a prize. I thought to myself, that is gambling because I had seen those machines in the casinos. But I didn't share it with anyone for fear of getting a negative backlash from the members. I didn't approve of the Bingo games either because of the exchange of money. It appeared innocent, but I thought it was a form of gambling (my estimation).

For the entire five years that I attended Sunday service at that church, I had a routine going. I would greet everyone in my path and head straight to my seat located left side of the church and sit three pews from the altar of the church kneel on the kneelers and praise God in silence until the priest start giving his liturgy. I needed to enter into the presence of God to forget where I was for a moment. I wanted God to transport me somewhere else but there. For the benefit of my family, I had to pretend I was alright attending the church. I was there for them.

I decided that I would volunteer in the hospitality committee and engage more with the members and maybe it would make things better. In some way, it did make me feel better because I was doing it unto the Lord. I wasn't being fed spiritually in the church the way I was at my former church, but I would carry on and read my Bible at home. I continued to say my prayers and praise and worship God with Christian music. I listen to Christian on my car radio. In my office, I had a radio, and I would turn on the Christian station WFIF, 1500 AM, and listen to pastors preach to keep me fed with the word of God. Those spiritual exercises kept me grounded for a while. My experience in the Catholic church was odd, to say the least. I never understood the message because it was more like mumble jumble even though it was spoken in English. Several people would read the scriptures, and then the priest would chime in and talk about something totally unrelated which confused me. I wanted and demanded solid doctrine and was not getting it. I didn't go for rhetoric I wanted something more substantial. I am speaking from having experienced five years in the Catholic church and can honestly tell you that I didn't learn absolutely anything from their way of preaching.

Back in Egypt

After 4.5 years (of my conversion) of struggling to avoid going back to my old lifestyle, I began to slip away from God's laws. I had just returned to Egypt without realizing it.

Throughout the years as a Christian, I have learned from reading the Old Testament and the preacher's interpretations that Egypt and Babylon although real places are symbolic for everything that is against God. In the book of Exodus, God calls it, "the wilderness of sin" (Exodus 17:1, NIV.) Wilderness is symbolic for not knowing which direction to take in the church and in our spiritual life. People turn away from God when they turn to worship graven images, idols basically.

We must never put our confidence in man because man will cause us to change routes and get lost. I was very naïve to look at the parish priest and think it was all right for me to start drinking again. I am not insinuating that because he did that, I had to follow his cue. The word of God is here to teach us and guide us in the ways that we must go. God knows our heart, and He will help us come out of the wilderness. I had to continue to attend the church for my family, and I never stopped giving God praise. I thanked Him in the midst of the trials.

Praise God no matter the situation because praise is an attitude and through it, God turns things around. God is greater than anything we are going through. We must continuously sing to the Lord songs of praise and lift up His name. Praises begin with thank you. Thank God in spite of what we are going through we can tell Him we love Him more than what we are going through.

In the situation I found myself in I knew that I had to keep believing and trusting God. Regardless of how much I had backslid, I did not allow my faith to be moved. I felt in my heart that I wanted so much to live holy. But holiness starts with our minds first. Holiness is a discipline of twenty-four hours and seven days a week. Holiness gives no place to the devil. Holiness is dealing and working right in the sight of God for His Kingdom. Holiness is when we get the spirit of the Lord Christ Jesus and become a witness for Him.

Slowly I began to take subtle steps backward until I was hanging out again doing drugs and drinking. However, something was different in that I didn't enjoy doing these things anymore as I did before my conversion. And, I would feel so guilty that I wanted to hide from God and everyone from the Pentecostal church as if they knew what I was doing. I ran into my former pastor (it was after 2 AM in the morning) as he was leaving the diner and I was walking in after leaving the dance club. I tried to rush past him, but he grabbed my arm and asked me, "how are you doing?" If I could have become invisible at the moment, I would have done it, I quickly responded, "I'm okay" and walked away so fast that I knew I had been rude to him. I couldn't erase that moment from my mind. It bothered me for a long time because he didn't deserve such treatment. I assumed that he knew I had backslid.

On another occasion, I was up-all-night doing drugs that I felt so guilty I called my friend Meg, (I always called her every time I felt guilty about what I was doing) and she told me to go to another church for prayer. It was Sunday morning. I went to see the pastor from the Spanish church and told him what I had done, and he called the women of the church to pray for me in the back room. After the prayer, I was invited into the sanctuary. I was standing in the front pew when all of a sudden, I fell back into the pew and laid there, not sure how long, the service was over when someone woke me. I obviously needed the sleep, and I was sober when I woke up. I felt so embarrassed and guilty because former church members knew I had backslid. I definitely felt separated from God. There is no doubt that sin makes us weak and vulnerable.

The scriptures clearly state that we are born with proneness to sins. Sin will not allow for God's word to live in our heart. Every time I sinned, I wanted to hide from God because I didn't feel worthy of Him. I continue to attend the Catholic church but also accommodated my sin nature. I prayed to God to forgive me because I knew that I was sinning. But before my conversion, I didn't even know what sin was or how it would make me feel. When God took and cleaned me up again, I had to learn to live in this world but not be of this world and to sanctify my life and live godly.

Things Are Looking Up

I decided, after four and a half years in the Catholic church, to go back to my former church for the Wednesday Bible study while still attending Sunday service with my family at their church. I never wanted the Catholic church to be my church. I was so relieved to be back to the Pentecostal church even if it was one day a week. It kept me grounded. I walked away from the alcohol and drugs and stayed away from clubs and the people from the Catholic church and their worldly influences. I had developed the kind of spirit that wanted to live a life for Christ Jesus. Therefore, it was no longer I but Christ who lived in me. I wanted to live the righteous life for Christ Jesus. I had to have a mindset for God and pray unceasingly. I knew I had to live by faith and not by my own ability and that every day I had to practice living in Christ. I went back to giving God genuine praise and thanksgiving for saving a wretch like me one more time.

Besides serving in the hospitality committee, I also volunteer for wherever the church needed an extra hand. One day I was cleaning the sanctuary with a female member and as we were leaving the church, (it was a Wednesday), she asked me what I was doing that evening? I told her that I was going to my former church for Bible study. She looked at me quite strange, and I found it odd when she told me,

"you shouldn't be going to that church." I told her that I had attended that church before I started attending her church and I liked their Bible study sessions. Several weeks later the priest asked to meet with me. I went to his office and sat down, and he began to lecture me about attending my former church. He told me that he had heard I was going to the Pentecostal church. He said, "the Bible those people read is full of lies, and they are evil." I said, "with all due respect, the same scripture that was read here on last Sunday was the same scripture the pastor read on Wednesday, and there was no difference." So, he jumped to a different subject and asked me, "I had not seen you in confession when was the last time you went to confession?" I said, "with all due respect the Bible tells me to go directly to God and confess my sins to Him. It is between God and me." At that point, he appeared to have been frustrated with me and told me that if I insisted on going to that church that I should not be serving in any of his committees. I looked at him and said, "I have decided to go back to the church, and I will no longer be a member here." There was nothing else to discuss, and with that, he dismissed me by saying, "I have another appointment have a good day." I told him, "have a good day as well."

A year before this meeting took place, I had met with an interim priest to ask him a few pressing questions about praise and worship. I desire so much to praise God outwardly in the church but felt ashamed of doing it because it was not the norm there. The most the parishioners were allowed to say before the taking of the communion was, "Lord, I am not worthy to receive you but just say the word, and I shall be healed," Matthew 8:8, NIV) or the Lord's Prayer (Matthew 6:9-13) at the instruction of the priest toward the end of the service. I asked the priest, "what would happen if I stood up and said hallelujah and just express praise outwardly?" The priest told me the following, "the intellects will say that you should learn to be more compose and the less educated will say that you are crazy." That wasn't the answer I wanted to hear. In other words, outwardly expressions are not the norm in the Catholic Church. I had to learn to follow their norms as a member.

I knew that I would not find what I needed attending this church and that I had to find God for myself. I felt sad for the people of this church but didn't want to offend anyone, especially my husband, so I kept silent about how I truly felt.

In the parable in Matthew 25:3-13 Jesus illustrates the different mindset of the church. I am reminded that the wise church is the church with the true believers that are spirit filled and that the foolish church is the church with its non-believers. The lamp is symbolic of our prayer life, and our praise and worship life. We must take heed to the scriptures, live sanctified and please God not man.

We must have our mind made up to live right as it's mandated in the Bible, not by man-made doctrines.

I finally felt it in my spirit that it was time to tell my husband that I was returning to Tonya's church. I was on the right track and had given up on all that old man stuff, and it was time to put on the new man and get serious about my walk with God. I was very cautious in my approach to him because I didn't want him to stop attending church if I wasn't going to attend church with him. But I should have known better because God had it all under His control. When I asked my husband if I had his permission to go back to my former church, he told me yes. I was so happy not only because he gave me his blessings but because he was going to continue to attend his church. My daughter also continued to attend with her husband for several more years and then she left the church. She reconciled with the Lord years later and decided to attend a Christian church, non-denomination.

Remember, we will all stand before the judgment seat of God. For the Scriptures say,

> "As surely as I live,' says the LORD, 'every knee will bend to me, and every tongue will declare allegiance to God." Yes, each of us will give a personal account to God. So, let's stop condemning each other. Decide instead to live in such a way that you will not cause another believer to stumble and fall" (Romans 14:10-13, NIV.)

CHAPTER NINE

RECONCILIATION

Rather than doing the ungodly things I did, I should have led by example. I should never have taken my eyes off God and where He was taking me. I should have expected the adversary to attack me, especially being a new convert. "Dear friends, don't be surprised at the fiery trials you are going through, as if something strange were happening to you," (1 Peter 4:12, NIV.) Our meaning in life should be to serve God not a man and live a holy life according to the scriptures.

Starting Over

When we sin, we are giving our weakness strength. Sin must be completely removed from our heart. To continue in sin after we have been saved is to flagrantly ignore having known Jesus Christ and His reason for coming to earth. We must never get to the point where we arbitrarily forget that Jesus came to take away our sins and His desire for us to abide in Him, (1 John 3:4-6.) We will never be righteous or live righteous on our own except through Him. We will not be able to do ministry until we die to the self effectively.

I resumed my journey at my formal church that would take me into nine more years of learning more about God and my reason for being. I would hear messages after messages from my Shepherd about God's instructions on living for Him and doing kingdom work.

However, those nine years would not be uneventful. I finally became a member of the church a year after my five-year hiatus, and I was proud to call it my home church not only because of the great teaching and preaching but for the stability it brought to me. I was warmly welcomed when I came back by the older sisters. I met one of the sweetest younger sisters in the church, and we got close, but it was short lived because she left the church under unusual circumstances. I could still sense that the majority of the members were not ready for me to attend their church and they were not going to be openly accepting of me. I had resigned myself to that, so I thought. I even noticed my friend Tonya was quite different and I could not figure out why.

I came to the realization that I was in that church because God wanted me there and no matter what they said or how they felt about me I was going to ignore it. I thought maybe in a few years they will change. The following year I joined the usher board. The church needed volunteers to usher, and I obliged because I thought that it would get me more connected to the female members. The head usher was pleased, and at least two of the other ushers made me feel accepted. I knew the head usher from her job where I used to have lunch sometimes. As I mentioned my being an usher did not make me inclusive at all, especially to the veteran ushers.

Like I said I had just spent five years in a church I felt I didn't belong. I saw it as a sacrifice so that my husband would begin his journey toward heaven bound.

In my experience after visiting the different churches, I can say with certainty that this occurs in all denominations. Where church members fragrantly ignore you and walk right by you and not say a word or they try to dodge one another so as not to say hello.

This would be my experience with most of the church members throughout my years of attending God's choice of church for me. It was that church God had called me to be mentored by the shepherd of the house, and thus it became my home church.

It had been two years after I left the Catholic church and returned to my home church. I would leave the Wednesday Bible study service knowing more scripture and Bible history and its relation to us in this modern age but at the same time regretting being there.

Ungodly Among the Godly

That Wednesday night I was feeling more distraught than ever that I rambled in my car on the way home about how fed up I was regarding the member's treatment toward me that I was telling God, as if He didn't know what was going on, "They don't want me there. They don't love me. They hurt me." When I hear a faint voice that comes from within my head, that is pounding at the temple due to so much crying, say to me "because this is where I want you." At that moment I couldn't say another word. There were times that were worse than others. I couldn't stand it anymore. Week after week and month after month, and for years I left crying my eyes out and feeling the pain in my heart caused by their indifference toward me. I could not stand their mean-spirited behavior toward me and intentional cruelty, but God would not allow me to leave. I could hear the voice tell me over and over again, this is where you are going to start your ministry. I stopped complaining to God about it because He had placed me in that church to learn from the shepherd of the house. From there on I had to love them or ignore them. I will be very honest I choose the latter. It took me some years to love them because it did not just end there. Never would I have imagined that this could happen to me in this modern age and in this place of all places… Church.

God gave us the truth, the way, and the light to separate us from the bondage of hate, anger, jealousy, envy, strife, and all carnal lust. The church must learn to let go of their love affair with the darkness. God gives us the power and the authority over any and all unclean spirits to rebuke and dispel the darkness. This power and authority came when we changed from our pagan life to a life in the Lord. Don't let the unclean spirit steal your blessings and victory because of your behavior toward one another.

Sometimes we may need to rededicate ourselves through baptism and ask God to put us back on track and shape us and make us new again. Let us take heed and know whom we are taking counsel from, turn and refocus.

People who have a negative influence on our lives will eventually leave because their job is done, to turn us from God. Look around and get rid of people like that because if they are not talking God's love to the brethren and to the loss, they should be gone from our lives.

If our own family, long-time friends, relatives don't believe or respect us for our belief and are bent on turning us from God then let them go and just pray and ask God to help them. That is why our prayer life is so important.

Most times those toxic relationships we refuse to give up bring more disorder to our lives anyway, and that is why Satan sends them. We need order in our homes, in our family, and in our life. Only in our relation with Abba Father can that be accomplished. There is no two-way about it. It is either Father God or Satan. The Lord is the King, and we need to allow Him to bring order and rule over us. It is crucial that we establish a relationship with God and enter into His will and obey His command that everything may go well with us. As Christ followers, there is no question how we are to live. It is incumbent that the church shepherd guides the members to have a true relationship with the Lord.

Godly Leadership

Pay careful attention to yourselves and to all the flock, in which the Holy Spirit has made you overseers, to care for the church of God, which he obtained with his own blood (Acts 20:28.)

Is the church lacking in integrity and in godly leadership? What does it mean to be a godly leader? The leader of a church should lead by God's command and be careful to obey all the laws. Leaders must be the catalyst for change in the body of Christ, which is the church. Leadership in the church should exact all the good quality as required by God's word. It should not be business as usual. I believe that if a person doesn't have the calling from God to be a preacher, then him/her should not appoint themselves. Leadership is about influencing the right things in the life of a believer and bring light to their dark areas. God needs spiritual leaders who will allow Him to lead them in the pulpit. Spiritual leadership is a doorway to kingdom principles. When Moses died, Joshua was handed the leadership role because it was God ordained.

- Leaders are God's agent of change to be able to move people from where they are to where they should be.
- They must influence and impact the congregation in a positive way.
- They must be able to discern what God wants them to do for the church and the members.
- They must depend on the guidance of the Holy Spirit and bring about spiritual growth in the body of Christ.
- They must seek God genuinely daily.
- True leadership will be filled with compassion for the lost souls and care greatly for their salvation.
- True leaders should not be puffed up men and women nor attempt to manipulate the members in any way form or shape.

It will cost them greatly and will require a strong commitment to serving God and their members. Godly leadership goes hand in hand with integrity, and we can't have one without the other. Integrity means maturity and honesty, and it will get the church leader in place to hear from God. It's important that God sees the leadership's integrity in order for God to move on their behalf. If a leader knows that he knows that he is not under God's anointing, He needs to step down because the church family will definitely suffer the consequences of that leader's disobedience. God wants to see leadership standing under His anointing and with it comes stability, longevity, destiny, and purpose. I appreciated my shepherd, and I saw him as a no-nonsense kind of preacher when he was on the pulpit and off the pulpit. He was serious but also friendly and funny when he wanted to be and was highly respected by many people in his hometown, and throughout the different states, he visited to preach.

In 2000 he encouraged me to attend a ministry workshop where I receive a certificate from the church's school of discipleship – Preparing God's People for Ministry. I got the certificate, but I still didn't see myself doing ministry. I continued to serve in the church as an usher. I also volunteered on occasions in the Homeless outreach program on Saturdays by helping with the cooking and serving of the luncheons and organizing the community closet. I guess what I called ministry was going out into the community to evangelize in the street corners of the railroad side of Eastport. But I had not been given permission by the church leader to do so. I realize that there are protocols and I had to follow them and wait patiently to me be instructed by the church leader.

I didn't know what God was doing and why He had placed me in that particular church where I would experience certain unpleasant situations, but I had to trust him. I allow people to make me doubt what God had given me to birth. I stayed regardless of how I was made to feel because I believed that it was really God's will that I stay and learn from the pastor. I decided to stand firm and believe that God had a plan for me. God leads us and guides us if we allow Him to do so. As members of the body of Christ, we must seek Christ-likeness, and He will keep us strong and secure. We must live a sanctified life which is our Christian duty. God instructs us to respect your fellow saints and the church leadership. Hold on to the good and avoid all that is evil.

But while I waited to find out what my true ministry would be, I continue to share the gospel of Jesus Christ no matter the wounds that were being inflicted upon me by the saints.

"What counts is that you put up with it for God's sake when you're treated badly for no good reason. There's no particular virtue in accepting the punishment that you well deserve. But if you're treated badly for good behavior and continue in spite of it to be a good servant, that is what counts with God" (1 Peter 2:19-20, MSG.)

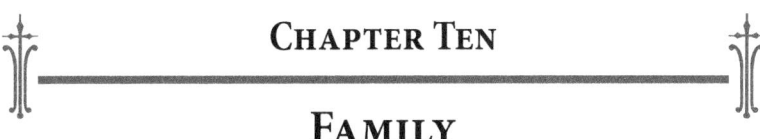

CHAPTER TEN

FAMILY

My home was a place of peace, love, and joy and laughter was greatly encouraged. Most weekends my home would be filled with my children lounging around the house and the grandchildren running around in the yard or jumping on the trampoline. I loved having them come over and cook their favorite foods. There was so much love in my home than I have ever experienced. For sixteen years after my conversion to Christianity, my home had become a sanctuary where only the love of Christ was professed. My husband and I were both in love with the Savior and served in the church. Life was good. I had a good job, and we were both financially stable. We had a remarkable relationship.

Beloved Son…A Marine

In June my son enlisted in the United States Marine Corps, (during peacetime) to pursue a career in communications. He planned for the military to pay for his education, taking the burden of paying for it off of his father and me. I was disappointed that he didn't want to go straight to college after graduation, even when we told him we would help pay for his education. His father and I couldn't dissuade him from entering the military. He was scheduled to go for training in February the following year at Parris Island in South Carolina. In the meantime, his girlfriend was pregnant with his child and was due that same year. I became the grandmother to my first grandson, (I had four granddaughters by then). He left for Boot-camp in February and three months later my husband, and I, along with my daughter and her family, as well as the girlfriend with a baby in hand traveled to Parris Island for his graduation. When he got home from graduation my son, and his girlfriend got married. The pastor of my church was asked to perform the wedding ceremony, and he agreed to marry them in such short notice because my son had to go back to base soon. They had met in high school and hung out together for several years, but he never told me she was his girlfriend because I always encouraged him to get his college degree before getting serious with any girl in high school. The day of the wedding my daughter-in-law looked very pretty in a white all satin empire fitted bodice wedding dress with her long blonde hair made into pipe curls. My son looked slim (he had lost much weight in Boot camp) and handsome in his black tuxedo. His sister was the maid of honor, and her husband was the best man. The married couple had a private dinner at the bride parent's home with a few friends and family members.

The 9/11 Twin Tower attack by terrorist forced the United States into war with Iraq, and my son's division was the first to be deployed to Iraq. The day it happened I was in my office sitting at my desk writing progress notes when a co-worker knocks at my doors and steps in to tell me that a plane intentionally flew into the one of the Twin Tower's building, "let's go to the eighth floor and watch it on the television." When we got off the elevator workers from that floor already had on the news, and they were commenting on what had happened in New York City. As I enter the community room and stare into the television, the second plane flew into the second Twin Tower building, and it exploded right before my eyes. I was shocked at what I saw. It was so surreal.

I never thought that I would be the mother of a soldier fighting in a war. I was devastated, to say the least. I would pray all day long even when I was at work, driving in my car and even in the middle of the night. I even took a frame with a photo of him to church and placed it on the altar reminding God to keep him alive. I didn't remove it until he came home.

I would have been lost but for my prayers and thank God for a few good spirited women in the church. My experience of having a son in the military during wartime told me that I had no choice but to trust in the Lord for my help.

People think that they can do it on their own and that they don't need help from God. I don't know what I would have done if it hadn't been for God in my life. We need God's help whether we want to admit it or not. Our God cares enough for His sons and daughters to concern Himself with where we are getting our help. Mankind's help is in vain, and this is why we need spiritual leaders and church family we can call on to assist in times when it is most needed.

I can't stress this enough in that the church family need the indwelling of the Holy Spirit in them to change their ungodly attitude. They must possess godly attributes to be empowered to help themselves as well as others. The people of God must know where their help comes from because the systems of this world are evil and have no place in the lives of the church members.

G.K. Chesterton was a journalist in the latter part of the seventeen Century. I can agree with him on a few remarks and observations that he had made about religion and people during his time that aren't so far-fetched from our time. I assure you I don't agree with every one of his opinions due to the many controversies, but for the subject at hand, I will share just this one remark with you to 'drive the point home' of just how far the church family has strayed from God. He writes,

"The human race, according to religion, fell once, and in falling gained the knowledge of good and evil. Now we have fallen a second time, and only the knowledge of evil remains to us." [12]

Keep in mind that man does not have the answer, the Bible does. And I am not saying that the entire human race has gone astray, but there still remains a remnant that is following Christ who has not been swayed to the dark side.

Beloved Husband...

I was truly at peace with myself. My home had also become my sanctuary a place where only the love of Christ was professed. I had been with my husband for twenty-four-year. I only had God to thank for the joy and happiness of being with the only man I had ever truly loved. I felt such admiration for him. I celebrated his fiftieth birthday with friends and family to show him my appreciation for everything he had done for the family and me. To see him happy made me happy. I asked my Pastor's oldest daughter to minister a worship dance at his birthday party. I chose the song by Hezekiah Walker, "I Need You To Survive." I stood next to him on stage holding his hand and told him, I love you and I can't survive without you. Little did I know that it would be his last birthday celebration. Our last vacation together was a few months before he died. He lost his battle with cancer.

When he died, I was so destroyed and hurt that I wanted to die. Yes, honestly speaking, I wanted just to drop dead. I was torn apart and felt alone in my grief. I cried every day and night for one entire year. Although, after many years have gone by my heart still aches when I think of him.

During the time that he was in the hospital, my dear sister in Christ Eliza (she died sometime later) would come after work and sit with me in the hospital room praying for my husband. I will never forget her, she was the sweetest human being I had ever known in the church and I know that she has won her crown in heaven. My pastor also visited one late afternoon and prayed while my husband's four brothers were visiting (he was asleep already under the influence of the morphine, but I was unaware.) I didn't really expect anyone from the church to come to visit.

No matter how much I wanted to feel God's peace and comfort, the pain was much more than I could bear. I pretended that I was doing alright for the sake of my family. I realized that knowing God intimately, attending church, serving the church, and living a godly life didn't exclude me from suffering the loss of a loved one. I had to learn to depend on God and know that He will be with me throughout my trials and tribulations.

This had been my first time being a widow, and I didn't know what to expect from those around me. But definitely didn't expect the treatment I received not only from my family but from the church family. I went back to church, and it was business as usual. The church knew I had lost my husband. I remember the pastor telling the church on my first Sunday back, "she just lost her husband and look at the way she continues to praise God." And, he asked the church members, help her praise Him.

I was hurting bad but and pretended that everything was alright. I wasn't going to get sympathy from the church members. After my husband's death I felt so alone in my pain and so grief-stricken. I thought how things may get worse for me at the church since now I was a widow.

However, I had to think about why I was there, and that even the death of my husband wasn't going to distract me from God's purpose. Although I was emotionally a mess, I was financially stable. But not every woman who widows may be as fortunate, and the church should step up to the plate.

The Scripture describes God as the Father to the fatherless and the defender of widows and that He places the lonely in families, (Psalm 68:5-6.) "Pure and genuine religion in the sight of God the Father means caring for orphans and widows in their distress…" (James 1:27, NIV.)

The church must understand and accept the realization that widows go through rejection, suffering, sorrows, and poverty.

Fortunately, this rejection can bring those who have widowed to have a greater relationship with God, and their faith will grow more as they trust God unequivocally. For the widows in the church, this is for you. Don't allow yourself to be sidetracked by the rejection of others just turn to God.

Remember, that rejection is external, and it can do you harm if you internalize the emotions of sorrow, pain, hurt anger, bitterness, and hate. People are innately evil, and if the spirit of God doesn't live in them, they are incapable of being sensitive to people who are hurting. When the church is Spirit-filled and living godly there will always be someone to lend a hand. The church's widows should never be made to feel that they are a burden to the church nor be financially and spiritually impoverished.

I had been a member of this church for six years, and I honestly didn't want to be there, so I pretended and went through the motion because God was preparing me for ministry. I received the word and wrote journals after journals of the sermons and bought the cassette tapes Sunday after Sunday. I attended the Wednesday Bible study but was still not feeling connected. I felt very much alone.

Widow...

When I widowed, I didn't have someone in the church I could seek out for guidance or connect with.

My dear sister Eliza who had been kind to me became fragile due to her own illness (I never knew how seriously sick she was) and I hardly saw her in church.

After my husband died, I didn't seek advice from godly people during my struggles as a widow.

Instead, I went at it alone and made some really serious mistakes.

When man fails, God takes over. But God should always be the first consultation. Everything we do in life should be made through the will of God. God should be consulted about every move a Christians wants to make in life. There are perfect examples in the Bible to guide us through a better understanding of how to live a life totally reliant on God. Christians must give God total surrender of their will and let Him have His way. God gave mankind free will because he wants us to love Him and make sacrifices to Him because we want to – not because He forced us to do it.

I made plans to reinvent myself since I was a single woman. It occurred to me that things only would get worse in church since I was a single woman. I did observe that a bigger chasm had been created between some members and me. The men were very cautious when it came to greeting me, and most of the women ignore me. Not that it didn't happen before it just got worst after I widowed. But it was their issue, not mine and I had no time for foolishness. I was there because God wanted me there no matter what they thought or how bad they behaved toward me.

However, in my own personal life, I was moving forward and moving too fast. In my decision to move forward with my life I met a man, (a relation to a former co-worker) whom I hired to fix the roof leak at my soon to be hair salon business. I had no previous business experience and had no idea about owning a business, but I had the money and owned the property.

We dated for several months, and he proposed marriage a few months later. We had our wedding ceremony three months later. Several of the church members came including the pastor and his wife. A few members of the dance praise team came to the wedding and ministered in dance. God didn't ordain my marriage, so it was doomed to fail from the very beginning. God knew that it would be a disaster, and He did make several attempts to help me avoid what was coming, but I didn't want to listen and didn't take heed to His warnings. I completely ignore my purpose and vision.

My disobedience caused me one devastation after another. I would loathe myself for what I had done and whom I had become. A great division was created between my children and me. I went from being the happiest woman in the world to the most miserable. I became insecure about my future and frightened to the point of almost losing my mind. In my desperation to end the grieving process after the death of my husband, I rushed into a marriage.

I would walk around in a fog unable to see what was right or wrong. I had become religious and a poor excuse for a Christian. I didn't walk away from the church but had created, in my mind, a distance between God and me. I was ashamed of myself and hated whom I had become. I lived in a fake marriage that had been influenced by demonic forces that I was unaware of at the time. Even when I tried to run away, as far as I could from my tormentor, the devil, he followed me wherever I went.

We must seek the scriptures for ourselves to see if we are doing the right thing in the sight of God. We must not be a slave to sin. When God delivers us from sin, and we continue to live in it, then we have made a choice not to live right. We are enjoying the sin nature, and we aren't confessing because we like what we are doing. "If we claim we have no sin, we are only fooling ourselves and not living in the truth." (1 John 1:8, NIV.)

When we make plans without consulting with God, we are asking for trouble of the worse kind. I had opened the door for Satan to make himself at home in my life. "For he has rescued us from the kingdom of darkness and transferred us into the Kingdom of his dear Son, who purchased our freedom and forgave our sins "(Colossians 1:13-14, NIV.)

I realize the importance of knowing the voice of God and taking heed to it. I should never have taken God for granted. When God tells us to flee, he means it, RUN! Rejecting God is an awful offense, especially for a Christian because nothing good can come out of it.

I can thank God for having kept me even when I rebelled against Him. "It would be better if they had never known the way to righteousness than to know it and then reject the command they were given to live a holy life" (2 Peter 2:21, NIV.)

Chapter Eleven

Servant's Heart

As I mentioned in the earlier chapters that I had started my usher ministry and felt much more connected to the church. The female members were the worse when asked to move because they would roll their eyes and push right by me almost knocking me down and others would just tell me I'm not moving. I only speak from what I experience. The other ushers also get treated the same even when asking them in a kindly manner. Even when it comes from the pastor, he would have to repeat himself and be stern about it to get a reaction from them.

The Pleasure is Mine

I had acclimated myself to the church environment and culture and had been in the usher ministry for three years and was attending church three times a week, twice on Sundays. I was obedient to God because He had a purpose for me. One afternoon one of the veteran ushers asked me if I wanted to be in the First Lady's Committee and I jumped to the occasion to serve the First Lady of the house and that way I would get to know her more and her me. I thought this would be my break to feel more like a member and not a stranger if I befriended the pastor's wife. My responsibility was (when it was my turn to serve) to meet her in the front of the church and walk her down to her seat and sit behind to assist. I was told to make sure I had a bag filled with mints, tissues, a writing pad, and a pen. In whatever ministry I found myself in I did it all unto the Lord because He appreciated it. I hardly entered into conversation with the pastor's wife because there were not many occasions that

I would be in such close proximity to her. Since I started attending the church, I was never given the opportunity to talk to her because she never opened that door to me. Many times, I would greet her on the way in or out of the church, and she would walk right by me. Maybe on one or two occasions she smiled and whispered a greeting. When I tried to make conversation with her, they were few and far between, she rushed by me. "For who is greater, the one who is at the table or the one who serves? Is it not the one who is at the table? But I am among you as one who serves" (Luke 22:27, NIV).

I bought two tickets to attend the shepherd of the house 60th birthday party and was very excited about going. I was in the foyer on my way into the banquet hall when I noticed with my peripheral vision both the First lady and pastor sitting at a table by themselves. I told myself to go and say hello because it will be the only opportunity you will have all night to talk to them. I walked over to them, and I wished him a happy birthday and gave them a sisterly kiss and asked if I could have a photo taken with them both. The photo still sits on a table in my living room.

God saves souls to serve in the kingdom. Be encouraged in your hearts when doing the work of God and know that God is in charge. If we have been called by God, don't be afraid to show the world your stuff but speak the truth in love. Stay close to God and in a rich relationship. We must never become spiritless where people feel that we are unapproachable and haughty.

I remember getting an invitation from the pastor's wife to her daughter's baby shower; I was amazed to have been invited. I arrived early and walked into the house the door was open and wondered from foyer to living room to kitchen and saw groups of women talking and greeted them but wasn't acknowledge and I kept on wandering around the house. After a while of being ignored, I put the gift with the other gifts and left. I was appreciative to had been invited, but I felt like an intruder, and I could not get anyone to sit and talk to me. I thought it worth mentioning to give the reader a picture of how I experienced rejection to such extreme that I couldn't wait until God would give me permission to leave the church.

When God gives us a vision, we should not allow people to take our vision away nor distract us from it. The enemy is never happy when God gives us a vision. But we must take ownership of that vision and go with it by faith. We must be in constant prayer on our knees about what really matters to God. The enemy will use even our brothers and sisters in the church to distract us. We must never forget that the enemy is mad and wants to destroy us. The enemy will attempt to come between our victory and success. Let us follow the vision and ignore the foolishness of the ungodly.

In the book of Mark, he demonstrates that he is a realist and he and doesn't mince words. In other words, we don't have much time to fool around and play church, (having one foot in the church and one in the world.) We know that people will fall away from the church for whatever reasons, and only they know why. But when we are determined to take Christ Jesus serious, then He will take us seriously. When we are being confronted with issues that deal with the church, we must take it seriously and address it immediately. God will make things right. God knows every sacrifice we make because He knows everything.

At Your Service

God's plan for me was to learn from the church's designated mentor. Through that pastor, I would receive the assistance I needed to go out into the neighborhoods of Eastport and ministry the gospel of Jesus Christ to the youth hanging out in those streets. I had no time to waste. But because of the lack of church connection, it was easy for me to flow away from my vision. I insisted on making the connection through volunteering in the different church ministries. I would join them in the fellowship hall to connect only to be left sitting alone.

I never received instructions from the evangelistic ministry as to what to do. I didn't dare take the initiative because it wasn't my place. I felt like I was wasting my time because no one would tell me anything. The only time I was given the lead to do something with the church was for an 'international luncheon.'

I was the co-chairperson of the Cultural Diversity Affirmative Action Committee at my job, and I had organized an 'international luncheon' for the employees. The staff brought their traditional cultural plates, and the kitchen supplied the drinks and other foods. I had mentioned it to the sister in charge of the feeding program, and she mentioned it to the pastor, and they both thought it was a good idea to celebrate Hispanic Heritage month at the church and I would be the lead. I was finally doing something that involved the other church members. I was so excited that I was going to fellowship with the church in something we all had in common, food.

I went to see a seamstress and asked her to make me the typical traditional Puerto Rican costume dress. This type of dress was traditionally worn by the women of the mountain region during festival season called, (Fiestas Patronales) Patron Saints Festivals.

> These festivals are yearly celebrations held in countries influenced by Spanish culture. Most festivals feature live entertainment by famous international or local singers, amusement parks, and street vendors, among other things, during the celebration. [13]

Every member who participated had to set the table with artifacts from their original ancestry (Jamaica, Poland, Africa, Early American, and Puerto Rico), and wear their own culture's traditional attire. It was a good turn-out. This was not the only time I had a fellowship with the church members, but it was the first time I was involved in leading it and I felt connected.

Follow God's Lead

Everything God does is for our good. Although we are followers of God, we are also leaders of men. God is still making way for those that receive Him and believe in Him. As leaders for God's kingdom, we are to lead others to Him. We shouldn'tt allow the negative attitudes in the church to stop us from taking the lead. When we take the lead, it is God's vision and wisdom guiding us, and we do what He asks of us. God will send us to help those who need help and equip us with the energy to stay the course without excuses. Remember, that when we were without a vision, God sent us leaders to guide us. So, we must do the same for others that they may continue to do the work of the Lord.

God has a mission for every one of us. There is a purpose for the church, the members, and the leaders. In the latter days, God is going to establish the church. God is going to exalt the church. God wants us to be the church of the New Testament. Christ Jesus wasted no time and began to preach, teach, and save souls. And, God is asking for laborers to go out into the fields because the harvest is ready.

The sons and daughters of man are waiting for the true followers of Christ Jesus. God's people must stop playing church and stop creating division among the church family. God wants to send His army of believers with power and authority if they submit to His will. Yes, God will give us the Spirit of wisdom and revelation when we are walking in the truth and loving one another. God will open our eyes to see things yet unseen, and we will be empowered to get the job done.

But we must not just have a relationship with God but be in fellowship with Him to receive His might and glory. God desires that we change the circle of negative influence and get loose from those people who don't want to move forward with the church of Christ Jesus. We need to be around people God sends our way and recognize that God sent them with such anointing. The Lord will open our eyes to new opportunities and to evangelism, and to things, He wants from us.

I was obedient to God as I continued to attend church and was living a godly life, praying, reading the Bible, and on occasion, I would fellowship with the church. I participated in attending church events and activities to remain a part of the body of Christ.

CHAPTER TWELVE

UNHOLY ALLIANCE

After nine years of attending my home church, I left against my better judgment. At the insistence of my newly-wed husband, I started attending the Baptist Church. He said to me, a wife should go where her husband goes. It was a Spanish speaking church in Eastport. The church membership was predominately Puerto Rican and a few from other Spanish-speaking countries.

Where is the Holy Spirit?

When I first entered the church, I was met by the hospitality member Laura who had a smile from ear to ear. For the most part, those who served in the hospitality committee in that church always welcome people with a smile and a loving embrace. The sisters enjoyed hugging one another more than the men did. The men appeared to be more reserved. I had learned to hug males and females alike at my home church. I soon found out at this church that hugging males, especially married men were awkward and it was not encouraged. I then realized that I had been physically inappropriately hugged by the male members at my former church. I was a newcomer to church, and I didn't know what the hugging protocol entailed. The single men took advantage and hugged me so tight I had difficulty catching my breath. And, all this time I thought that was a normal brotherly hug. New converts, please be aware.

They welcomed the visitors with a big smile and handed them a gift bag (first timers.) I felt like a fish out of water in that church because it was a different denomination than I had gotten accustomed to. Prior to learning their way of worship, I outwardly praise and worship and danced in the Spirit as I was led. But as the months went by, I saw that it was not the norm there, and I started to feel awkward about it. I began to constrict the Holy Spirit after something the pastor said to the church regarding order.

After several months of being at the church, I noticed this young female, mother of two young children, began to dance during the Sunday service. But her dance movements were more provocative than the usual praise done under the Holy Spirit. One of the older male members called her attention to it, and she got upset. Maybe this is why on one Sunday the Pastor told the congregation, this is a house of order, and people should learn to constrain themselves. I felt like he was talking to me directly on my manner of praising God. Maybe I had started a new trend of praising God they were not accustomed to it in his church. I began to feel uncomforted and was thinking about leaving and going back to my home church. But I quickly made friends with most of the congregation and decided to stay. The young female approached me one Sunday and told me, "I want to praise God the way you do." I explained to her that "it is through the Holy Spirit that I praise God." She said, "I want to feel the Holy Spirit." She needed the indwelling of the holy spirit at all times.

When the holy spirit is invited into our lives, we go from feeding the flesh to feeding the spirit. There are church members who should be walking by the Spirit and not by the flesh. Every negative thing that operated in us before should be canceled. But for that to happen there has to be a relationship with God for us to be filled with the holy spirit.

It was apparent to me that she hadn't been attending church for very long. She had a pretty face and a curvy body with blonde/brown highlighted long hair and men found her very attractive, and she did wear very provocative clothing to church. It was obvious to me that she needed a veteran Christian female perspective on decorum and learn more on the leading of the Holy Spirit.

The older male member and his wife had issues with that sister dancing during praise and worship which made them both feel uncomfortable. I thought that maybe they should not have been so focus on her during the service. But I realized that everyone has issues and demons they have to confront and be delivered from. My husband and I became very good friends with both the young sister (she kind of adopted us) and the older couple became our friends as well.

Apparently, the dress decorum hadn't been addressed in that church because some of the female members wore very provocative clothing. I remember after church service approaching one of the youth praise team dancers and calling attention (indiscreetly of course) to her about wearing a low-cut t-shirt during her dance ministry. She was dress inappropriately for the dance ministry because every time she bent forward, she exposed her breast to everyone in the church. Well, after that she and her mother stopped talking me.

In my opinion, the pastor and the church's more season women should have had a discussion with the young sisters to address what they can and can't wear to church and the importance of being filled with the Holy Spirit first before going on instinct to display what they think is praise and worship. "God is a spirit, and his worshipers must worship in the Spirit and in truth" (John 4:24, NIV.)

Therefore, we can't allow our walk with God to be less important than the interaction with the world. The provocative clothing has to be thrown into the fire and burn along with the old self. God must be given top priority and complete access to our lives. The word of God tells us that our spirit is willing, but the flesh is weak.

The Flesh Needs the Holy Spirit

The flesh is weak and dirty. Our flesh will resist God and temptation will entice us to lust after the things of the world, and we will sin. The flesh has an appetite that can't be satisfied unless we have the holy spirit. Even when we are believers of the word, we continue to have a war within us -- the mind and the flesh. We need to be delivered from our sinful nature, but the flesh refuses to be put to death. We will never be judged guilty if we walk in the spirit of the living God.

I later will discover that the church had its cliques as well, but they were not as isolated as my former church. For the most part, the members were cordial to one another. But there were a few members who had taken ownership of the different ministries. In particular, the drama and arts ministry, the choir and the psalmist ministry. They would take offense if anyone wanted to bring in a new perspective.

For example, if I wanted to join the worship team, I had to wait to be invited. So, even if I showed an interest and had a good singing voice if the leader didn't want me on her team, then I didn't get to sing. I had volunteered for the talent show, and when I sang I received good reviews from most of the members, but the leader and the worship team didn't acknowledge me at all. I was never invited to be part of the worship team in the six years I was a member.

The arts and drama ministry were even tighter to get into than Fort Knox. There was one person who had been there for years, (she grew up in the church) and she didn't ask anyone for help because it was her ministry and she did most of the work for all events.

After several years in the church, I dare to volunteer to do the Christmas pageant. I asked for volunteers, but it was like pulling teeth to get any of the members to help me put it together. I finally got a team together and to get them to come to rehearsal was a major hassle. The pageant was done but I told myself never again will I plan another pageant. However, other members decided to do their own pageant, and everyone wanted to volunteer. Please don't misunderstand what I am saying here although it may sound like I am whining or complaining. What I am conveying is my experience in a church that is so knit tightly together that only the old members can run the ministries. I was a newcomer with great ideas, but they were already set in their ways.

Another example had to do with the annual health fair that the church did on the church location. God had given me the vision to bring the health fair to the neighborhood park, down from the church, to give it more exposure in order to minister to more people. The park was known as a place where alcoholics, drug dealers, and prostitutes frequented.

I wasn't happy about doing this because I knew their attitude about someone "putting their two cents in where it wasn't asked for." But on God's persistence, I finally gave in and moved forward.

So one night, after the Wednesday Bible study, I approached the pastor, and I told him about it. The pastor had not been their long and was aware of the antics of the old members, and so he asked me to see sister Laura (she grew up in the church) on the matter. He abruptly ushered me to speak with the person in charge who was known to do this every year by herself. She had the connections and sent out the emails and made all the arrangements. When I approach her with the vision, she was hesitant and looked at me as if I had 'two heads.' I had to insist that it was God's idea and not mine. I had to present my case to her and ask her if she would put it in prayer and get back to me. Several weeks passed by and I approached her again, and she gave me the task of going to the Park and Recreation Committee meetings and request the date and time of the event. I was to do all the footwork on my own and get back to her. I went to the meeting and requested the park permit for the event. I went to the Police Department and to the Fire Department and to all the departments I had to get signatures in order to move the event from the street venue to the park. I did the work with much joy. The event was a success, and the church accomplished to ministry to more people who frequent the park. I got a stage (church paid) for the musicians to do their praise and worship and for the guest speakers to preach. I did that for three years in a roll, and when I left the church, they went back to the street venue. I was given the challenge and didn't quit or get discouraged even when I received no help. She always received the accolades for her work, and no one else was ever mentioned for helping her get the health fair up and running.

But even with all the challenges in the church and the struggles I was having in my private life I continued to serve God. I become connected to most of the members in this church and I could not see myself leaving at that time. For the most part, they were lovely people who shared their love for one another even if they were set in their old way. They were not perfect, but they got along with one another even if superficially. Every so often I would get a glimpse of their own shortcomings. Once in a while, a member would approach me with the latest gossip in the church, and I would kindly excuse myself and not entertain it.

Most times, I had an activity at my home, and the majority of the church family would attend, and have a great time together.

When I graduated with my Master's degree, they celebrated with me. I could always count with them to come for Christmas dinners. We celebrated the Christmas holidays with 'caroling' every Friday in a church member's home who would volunteer to open his/her home. Every member who came brought food and drinks and stayed until midnight sometimes.

The Church Needs the Holy Spirit

My issue with that particular church was not so much the member's attitude but with being put in an awkward position about praising God. I felt I was going against the norm in their church being the outsider. Most of them did join in singing the worship songs but there was no outward expression of praise except by the praise dancers once a month. I had been in the church for three years when one Sunday morning I felt the need to outwardly worship God, and I got up from the pew and ran down to the lady's restroom and started praising the Lord aloud and dancing in the women's stall. When I was done, I said to myself aloud, "I am leaving this church and going back to my home church." As I was leaving the restroom the Assistant Pastor was standing outside the restroom, and she asked me, "what is the matter?" I told her, "I am leaving this church because I can't praise God the way I want and I am going to where I can!" I was so angry that I wanted to leave right there and then. But she put her hands on my shoulders, looked me straight in the eyes and told me, "you go right ahead and praise God however you want and don't worry about it." Even though I continue to praise God in the sanctuary, I still felt awkward.

Following that incident on one Sunday morning, a young couple came to church. They came from a Pentecostal church. She would get up and stomp on the floor yelling out hallelujah! I believe she was an answered to my prayers. Sometime later, her sister began to attend the church, and she also praised outwardly. More members began praising God in the spirit, and I was no longer alone in my praise.

There was a young adult female who began praising God through laughter. Her mother became my confidant in the church, and I really admired that sister for her wisdom and honesty. She told me that it had been years since her daughter praised God that way (she started praising God as a child.) She was pleased that I was a praising woman who made it possible for her daughter to start praising God again. I couldn't stop praising God because others refuse to do so.

I stayed in the church because God was going to use me to bring about a change. I volunteered for the usher and hospitality ministry (the church can always use more ushers), and I enjoyed serving the church. I volunteered in the kitchen when cooks or servers were needed for special events. I even volunteer to do Sunday school and assisted in the nursery during the Sunday service. I was finally being used in the church and felt part of the Kingdom.

I believe I had been at that church for four years when the pastor called to lead the Evangelistic Ministry. I was to report to him on the church media's issues and concerns and make sure we had enough supplies in that department and the handouts used for the outreach events. On my first attempt to connect with the members in charge (mainly young males) of the media department, I was met with resistance. I asked several of the youth who were working in that department if there was something I can assist with and I was completely ignored. There was so much chaos in that area, with supplies thrown everywhere. No one was interested in straightening out the mess. After several attempts to be of assistance and no one care to acknowledge me, I decided to leave it alone and not bother. I didn't attend that church to get frustrated with mundane things.

I made myself available in wherever there was a need, but I enjoyed being a greeter.

The leader of the usher board had been out for several months because she was working overtime on Sundays. She had asked me if I would assist in that area while she was out and I was more than happy to assist her. I soon realized that there was no weekly list for the ushers and the supplies of pamphlets to give out to the visitors and other materials had been ordered. So, I decided to step in and take charge after all she had been gone for months. One Sunday the person who was to be the greeter was also singing with the worship team that morning. I asked her to please do one or the other, and she ignored me. The following the Sunday the leader of the ushers came back to church and asked me, "who left you in charge? I am still the leader." I told her "you asked me to help you when we spoke on the phone. I told her about the incident with the sister. She told me what right did I have to tell that person to do one or the other because she is one of the Psalmists. I told her that she couldn't volunteer to do both on the same day. I needed someone at the front entrance greeting, but she was in the front singing. At that moment I told her, "I'm no longer in the usher board" (this was my fifth year at the church.) After several months I noticed that the church needed greeters and ushers and decided to ask for my position back. I went back to her, and she told me that the Pastor had sat me down. At that point, I decided to start transitioning myself out of the church and go back to my home church since I was no longer useful there.

I was having personal problems at home and was contemplating divorce and moving out my home. I spoke with the pastor about leaving the church, and he wasn't in the least surprised with my decision. He knew what I had been going through in my marriage and about getting a divorce in the near future.

I Need the Holy Spirit

During those years at the church, my marriage was causing me much stress and sleepless nights. I had lost the properties my late husband had left me, and I was in credit debt. The first property that I inherited I had to sell to my late husband's family. The second property that I inherited I brought from them only to lose it. That house was involved in a fire caused by the next-door neighbor's house (a make-shift heater in the basement blew-up that killed three lives). The business (hair salon) was damaged in the fire. The money I received from the home insurance money was used up to pay the mortgage and the constructors (who took off with the money after several months.) The bank took the house.

I was pretending that everything was alright because I was ashamed of myself and what I had done to lose everything. I continue to have faith in God, but my flesh wasn't right. I had been faking having a happy married life. The only person I spoke to about my home life and what was really happening to me was powerless to help me. As long as I was laughing and happy outwardly, I was alright.

I thought that some people don't know how to deal with other people's tragedy or drama very well. It seemed that everyone was doing good in church and if they were not, they hid it really good. So, I learn to hide the fact that I wanted out the marriage until I couldn't take any more of the emotional abuse. I made an appointment for a counseling session with the Assistant Pastor.

When my husband and I met with the assistant pastor and her husband they had no words and just stared at my husband and me which confirmed that they really didn't know what to do. They more or less said indirectly figure it out (my estimation.)

When the church is unable to assist us in our mess, God is always available. I prayed in ignorance. I had been out of the will of God for some time. I should have had that conversation with God beforehand.

Many of us lack having that conversation with God, and we start talking to Satan instead, and that is where our prayer connection or relationship with God is broken. Many times, we come to God with phony prayers that have nothing to do with being in the will of God nor His purpose. Even Christ Jesus went to God in prayer with a purpose. We must know in our heart that when we go to God in prayer with a purpose, He will help us through it all. Our prayers must always line-up with the covenant of God, and He will grant us the desires of our hearts. What do you pray for and is it in communion with God?

I kept going to church week after week. I attended Sunday service and Wednesday Bible study. I had no one in the church to guide me through this. But the only way I survived this was through having hope and faith. There are some things we must go through to know that it's not about us but the Lord. He can make the way. We must look at the reality of what we are going through and realize that we can't do it by our self – but God. Know that whatever mess we have in our lives God will fix it. We must know that there will be moments in our lives where we will be alone – void of people around us. God will isolate us so that we can run to Him. We need to deal with that situation that separates us from God – deal openly with what disconnected us from God. Look at what God has done for us in the past and that He will take care of what we are going through in the present. I knew that I couldn't do it by myself and that if God didn't do it, then it couldn't be done. But I never gave up in my expectations of God's blessings because He has the final say in my life. I kept the faith and kept on praying for a relieve and way out. Remember that you and I are a work in progress.

People believe in God according to the measure of their faith. I thought that I was there. But there are certain thorns in our flesh that we blame for walking after the flesh. The Holy Spirit of God puts us in charge of our temple, and it is up to us to clean up our lives because God will not dwell in an unclean temple. The carnal mind is an enemy to God, and that is why we must worship Him in spirit and in truth.

I eventually reconcile myself to God after I went through some very serious spiritual attacks and major losses. I prayed to God to release me from the marriage (I know what you are thinking but this is between God and me.) I moved out of the house into my own apartment. I started a new year concentrating on my spiritual life and on pleasing God. But, for the grace of God, I would eventually be made whole again. God showed me how I had allowed Satan to enter my life and my home. I had to cut somethings out from my life that didn't help promote my purpose. I had gotten too comfortable at my husband's church, and I had lost my vision and God's purpose. I should have known that when we are anointed for God's purpose, we can't hang around everybody. Sometimes things that appear good are not always good for us. As much as I wanted to stay in a relationship with the church family, I had to make the decision to move from the people who were binding me and go a different direction.

Therefore, we must ask God to help us with our spiritual eyes and depend on Him only. God is a way maker. Don't give up and know that whatever problem you are facing he will make it work out for your good.

CHAPTER THIRTEEN

THE CHURCH

The only way we can have a true relationship with the Father in heaven is through the Holy Spirit that helps us. We will no longer be indebted to the flesh, and there should be no excuse to sin.

After much prayer and supplication, I felt in my spirit to move to another state. In 2012 I moved to the southwest.. I was going to start a new life, and meet new people. I rented a spacious apartment with cathedral ceilings, two bedrooms, two full baths, with community swimming pool and fitness center. I knew the church I was going to attend. I had attended the church a year before when I visited my ex-husband's cousin. The church is a non-denomination charismatic contemporary mega-church with Twenty Thousand members, a sanctuary that seats Fifty-four Hundred that comprises an equal proportion of Anglos and Latinos and a few African-American.

Although the church was huge in membership, it offered those who wanted to attend a weekly Bible study group. There were cell groups around the city by zip code so that no one was amiss. Sunday school was opened for everyone who wanted to attend. But it was mainly for the cell group leaders to get their weekly lesson. In 2014 I became a cell group leader and had a Single Women Bible Study group. I belonged to the Simeon Tribe. I like the way this church was organized. I was looking for order in my life and needed a change from the chaos I had come from.

A Church is a Church is a Church…

I know that no road is without bumps and that all churches come short of the glory of God but I would take this church over all the other churches I have attended in the past thirty years. In this church, I saw things differently in many ways.

Because of the church membership size, the Pastor wasn't always available for all twenty thousand people, but he did provide services to suit every need in the congregation. The Pastor established a cell group in every zip code surrounding his church to take care of his flock. The Pastor wanted to make sure that no member went unnoticed and left without some sort of support. I experienced firsthand one of the many ministries the church offers. While I was there, I went to visit the special programs ministry to discuss my divorce, and I found the counseling purposeful.

The church offered the following ministries: the ministry of reconciliation for backsliders, the ministry to provide help to the church family through encouragement, educate, and community resources, and funerals, adult ministry and special programs that included but not limited to issues of marriage, grief, divorce, and parenting.

My first year I had the privilege to attend the Pastor's birthday party (he does it annually) at a huge campground that he owns. For five dollars (that is donated to charity) I had a delicious meal (beef brisket) bottle water in every station throughout the area, all the cake you can eat, free mid-way rides and real horse rides. There is even a lake if anyone wants to go swimming or take a boat ride. Families are welcome to have their own mini picnic. I admired that pastor for sharing with the church what God had blessed him with.

God has equipped each one of us with the material resources around to build what God has in store for us. God will send us and will also supply all we need to build and succeed so that He can get the glory. People will be indignant and get upset when God begins to use us to show His greatness. I was satisfied and confident because I knew that it was God moving in my life. I found the church's Sunday morning services to be more on teaching the word through explicit visual and art. The Sunday evening services had more of a Pentecostal flavor. I enjoyed both services and tried never to miss a service. I was getting all my spiritual needs met and felt I was growing in faith and in the wisdom through the word of God. I equally enjoyed the praise and worship music.

I had the privilege to see the following Christian music artists, such as, the Gaiters, Natalie Grant, Ricardo Sanchez, Canton Junction, and countless others perform on the church's pulpit.

I also enjoyed the dinners after the evening Sunday service. If it was a warm night the members would sit outside otherwise, we would go into the fellowship hall.

Again, I say that no church is perfect because they all have issues and dramas. I would be lying if I said, "that my church is the God is coming back for."

The Bible informs me that Jesus is coming back for His church, and it also echoes that he wants a church with neither spot nor blemish. "…Christ loved the church and gave himself up for her to make her holy, cleansing her by the washing with water through the word, and to present her to himself as a radiant church, without stain or wrinkle or any other blemish, but holy and blameless" (Ephesians 5:25-27, NIV.)

Strangers In Church

That church was definitely different then the churches I attended in the northeast but far from perfect. I had several disconcerting episodes with different members on different occasions during my three years at that church that shocked me but didn't surprise me.

I usually sat in the same area (center of the church on the second set of pews) most of the time. Depending on the time I arrived at the church I could get my usual seat. I had been attending the church for maybe a year and a half when I noticed a new face sitting next to me. I approach her with a friendly greeting, "God bless you." She looked at me as if I had two heads (no smile) but responded with, "same to you." I told her my name and asked for her name. I knew that there was not going to be any small talk with her. Two Sundays later, I came early and noticed that she had sat in the pew in front of me. I approached her again and greeted her by her name. I greet everyone that I meet at church, especially when we sit next to each other. She was not smiling, and I found it odd because she would smile with those around her. After several months I noticed that she had become part of the greeter's ministry. She didn't sit around my area anymore. I saw again some months later at the monthly midnight vigil, and I smile at her.

There was a young female member who sat in the back pew from me, and we had begun to talk to each other before the start of the service. She also had attempted to talk with that female member, but she would discourage small talk with her as well. One Sunday that female, whose name is Gina (very sweet and kind) came to church with two plastic grocery bags filled with soft-cover books, several flash drives and copies of literature (Perry Stone materials) and offered them to me. She said, "Take one and give the other one to Josey." When I approach her to give her the bag, I said, "Gina asked me to give you this bag, she also gave me one. She is so kind to do this, so I took it." She took the bag and sat down. After that episode, I decided I was not going to force her to acknowledge me. Later on, I would see her and just smile at her.

I am a very friendly person who says hello to everyone who is at close proximity to me and doing it in the church is no exception. As a matter-of-fact, it's to be expected. I greeted every one of my brothers and sisters in church whether they liked it or not. We are a family in the church, so I thought.

I can't help it if I happen to be very observant of people and their behaviors. I was trained to be observant because of my clinical background. I received my Master degree in Social Work and worked with the mentally-ill for twenty years, and observation is primal in this field. For months I had been observing all the people that sat in the vicinity of where the Pastor's family sat. So obviously I spotted several female members sitting there. One sat with her husband and the other female I noticed was never accompanied by anyone. She would sit one pew in front of the Pastor's wife and his family. There were many times I would see her in the church corridor or outside and I would greet her.

There was an episode that occurred with her and me about two years at the church. We were no strangers to one another at least as far as recognizing each other as members of the same church. That particular day I went to the back of the church during service to ask their 'Lost & found' if they had found an earring (14k gold with diamonds) I had lost. I saw her standing by the counter having a cup of coffee, and I approached her. I told her my name and stepped in to give her a sisterly hug (I did that with all the other sisters), and she stood there with a serious look in her face that made me feel terrible. I smiled at her and left. I had seen her greet others with a wide smile on her face as they hug each another. Why was my hug less important?

During the summer I volunteered for the Vacation Bible School camp. On my break, I went to the lady's restroom, and I saw her standing by the entrance. I was in a hurry to use it, and I looked at her, and she turned her eyes down, and I didn't know whether to greet her or not, so I rush right by her. For the most part, those I sat around were kind and friendly, and we would exchange names even phone numbers. But like many other churches, I had visited in the past this one was no different in expressing common courtesy.

There are those who come to church sit and listen, and as soon as the service is over, they are out the door leaving without a word to those around them. They don't greet coming in and don't care to greet you going out. Every Sunday it would be the same, and I knew not to be bothered by it. Church people would walk right past each other and not say a word even when greeted. I was taught as a child to greet my elders because it was the proper thing to do. It is common courtesy is what it is. Common courtesy as defined by the Merriam-Webster Dictionary as, "politeness that people can usually be expected to show."

The church has lost its moral compass and something as simple as saying "hello" and "goodbye" or even saying "please" and "thank you." has been lost. The adults in this generation are teaching the children and the youth that common courtesy isn't important.

Church Worship

That is why in some sense I appreciated the cell groups because it made me feel connected to a body of believers. In the cell groups, we would have Thanksgiving dinners together and celebrate birthdays and attend church events together. I might have been estranged from my biological family, but I had another family that I felt some kind of connection to. Sometimes I thought that I was too spiritual for them. There was a female member (she did not believe in the indwelling of the Holy Spirit) in the group, and she had a tendency of interrupting me when I would be sharing a spiritual thought or experience. She would talk about herself and some deed she did. There were times when I would be talking, and the group leader would say something like, "due to time constraints we must move on," but this sister would be allowed to continue her lengthy story.

I understood that I was the newcomer (from the Northeast), but it would hurt my feelings that I was cut short of something I felt the spirit wanted me to share with them. Most of them didn't believe in the indwelling of the Holy Spirit. Their way of thinking was that it didn't take all when it came to the worship of God. They sang their song and on to business as usual. So, if I lingered on a little too long in praising God, (during cell group Bible study nights), I would hear it by the group leader about the time constraints and that everything had to be done in order.

However, I truly enjoyed when we took time to pray for one another. I witness miracles for healing and restoration in that cell group because they prayed in faith believing.

In the church, I observed that very few of the members openly verbalized any other forms of expression in worship besides singing the songs. There was no dancing, no running around, and very few members lifted their hands. There was a small remnant of exalters who would stand up to accentuate the preachers preaching and raise some hallelujahs and Amen outwardly. I recollect a time that the pastor mentioned that he grew up in a Pentecostal background. When he preached, it was evidence of his Pentecostal upbringing.

When I make a judgment call, I am making an observation for the interest of why I am writing this book. I mainly want to share my insight into the church members reactions and responses in the church venue.

I remember many pastors call out their members about the lack of worship in their church. The comparison the pastor always using is between a sports game and the church. The Pastor would say to the congregation that they cheered the loudest for their favorite team in sporting events and don't care who is seated next to them. But in the church when it comes to praise and worship some members don't even let out a whisper.

During the time I was attending the church I was amazed at how much politics was introduced into the sermon to 'drive a point home' about the conduct of society and the church. I found the pastor to be well versed in everything from politics, religion, the Bible, and life in general. I found him and his son to be very concern for America and the salvation of the lost souls. They not only preached the word of God but they sang it as well. Overall, the pastors of that church openly demonstrated a love for God that anyone with a pure heart and willing spirit would be contaminated by them.

I realized that in every church there will be members who wish to remain silent and those who are more demonstrative in their reverence to God and both responses are to be respected.

I thought that when people go to church is to reverence the God of the universe, the Creator and to rejoice and bathed in His presence. That they shout, jump, dance, and run around. I was wrong.

"I once was blind, but now I see…" When I am in church, I can't help but get excited and worship Jesus. I am there if for nothing else but to give Him all the glory. When I am in church, I feel that it is required of me as a believer to hear and feel Jesus. Jesus anointed me anew by dying on the cross for me, and he washed me with His blood. I could never pay Him except to praise and worship Him in the sanctuary. For when I was blind to Jesus He helped me and showed me His mercy that endures forever. We must glorify Him, worship Him, and give Him all our praise. Through our praises, we will hear the voice of Jesus and feel His hand.

A Little Heaven in Church

The church needs to know what it takes for us to get to heaven and to be blessed. We need to go to church to hear the truth because holiness is a lifestyle and only through the word of God can the church get it right. The church needs to know that heaven is for those who are redeemed. Heaven is for those who have allowed God to do His will in them.

I was determined to rid myself of all the junk that I had experienced in the church in Eastport and from my old self. I had decided not to allow others to make me feel less than a child of God. I would not hang around people who hurt me but be delivered from them forever. I told Satan that he is a liar and that he had no right in my life. That he had no authority whatsoever in my life at all.

I started with the new church's dance ministry that introduce me to a different world in evangelism. I fell in love with praise dance and the prospect of ministering to lost souls through my own dance ministry in the future. I felt at peace in my church. I liked going to the other churches to minister in dance. My desire was to live holy and blameless and be filled with the spirit at all times.

Believers must never look at the church as an exclusive social club but a community center where everyone is invited to participate. It is what God wants. We should be tired of just having church. Let us move from church to where God wants us to be. Whatever God wants from us we should be saying yes to it. The Kingdom is past, present, and future and remains the same forever. Things would be so much better if we can only stay the course and let God take the reign of our lives. Jesus started that process in Peter, "on this rock I will build my church, and the gates of Hades will not overcome it" (Matthew 16:13-20, NIV.)

The Church is the Place to Be

The first person I met in the church was Irene. My friend, Irene's great-grandfather, has a town in the Midwest named after him. He was the first settler in that town.

Irene invited me to the monthly Women's Brunch on the second Tuesday of every month. I had never seen anything like it. There were women from different church denominations and ethnic backgrounds coming together for four to five hours just enjoying each other's company. This event took place in another church. The church's banquet hall would be exquisitely decorated to reflect the theme of the month. I met women who were from different religious denominations.

Irene had warned me about some of the women strong Catholic belief. She told me, "don't try to convert them." She said that was her job because she had been trying for months. Her thinking was that she would lose them if I appeared to be too spiritual.

She knew how much I loved God and my decision to help others to know Him as I did.

Well, after several months they saw how spiritual I was during the praise and worship service in the sanctuary.

After the brunch, we would go into the sanctuary for a devotional time. I was ministered to and receive a word from God that encouraged me and helped me stay focus. In the group, there was a younger female who wasn't a member of any church, and God used Irene and me to minister to her. She became more interested in the things of God.

On several occasions after the service, we would occasionally go shopping to an early supper at a nearby restaurant. The young female would ride with Irene and I. I attended these brunches for about a year and then stopped because I got busy with my writing and traveling with the dance team. I spoke with Irene several times after and she told me that the young female continued to seek advice from her about God. I began to get more involved in my church's events.

When the church announced the "Mother and Daughter' event (an annual event.) My spiritual mother Ms. Carmen told me that she had attended it last year with another cell group member. I saw how excited she got so I decided to take her. I became her partner for these church events, and she enjoyed them to the fullest, and so did I. I wore a yellow hat, and she wore her red hat. Church members actually thought we were mother and daughter. I adored her tremendously.

I couldn't believe that she was in her eighties when I first met her because she looked younger. She attended the gym three times weekly along with her husband. Ms. Carmen was born in Mexico and move to the Midwest twelve years old, and at nineteen she met James. She was a waitress at a restaurant James frequent often. She and her husband adopted me as their spiritual daughter, (I happen to be their daughter's age). I would pick up Ms. Carmen up on Sunday evenings and take her to the church, and after service, we would sit and have dinner on the grounds. She enjoyed our trips to the mall and to one particular store where she would pick up her coffee for the month.

The church had another event for the ladies, the 'Night to Honor the Ladies' (an annual event). Those are moments that I will cherish forever.

I had so much energy and wanted to remain active in the things of God that when the opportunity to volunteer to be a counselor for VBS (Vacation Bible School) camp I took it. I especially enjoyed attending the Annual Eagles International Training Institute Summits held in Dallas.

The Church in Us

The Eagles International Training Institute founder is Dr. Pamela Hardy. Every year for the past eleven years (2016 was their 10th year anniversary) men and women from different ethnic backgrounds, States in the nation and countries (15 countries as of this writing) would come together for graduation and a week of praise and worship. From morning to night people walk around in their praise garments, (civilian clothes come off and praise garments come on.)

All of the dance graduates had to be in the graduation dance that was presented on the evening of the graduation. I remember one year there were one hundred dance graduates, and the dance finale was a phenomenon.

I graduated from the TEN Network Year One (2014) and Year Two (2015) basic dance school and from Authorship School in October 2016.

Rehearsals for the finale was done in groups from those in year one and year two to those graduating from a different category such as choreography, flags, mime, and arts and drama. Attendance was mandatory to these rehearsals. In these groups, I would meet people from other states and countries, as well as, from Dallas itself. For the most parts, people tended to connect with those they knew from their own church or from previous years who had attended the summit, and it was to be expected. The problem I saw was that most times people did't exchange greetings with anyone else outside their group. If I would run into them outside of rehearsal and greet them, they would walk right by me and not say a word. I observed that it happened not only to me but to others. It would happen by the elevator, sitting at the breakfast café and just in passing. We are all wearing praise garments even though we are strangers to one another but should that matter? We are all in the family of Christ. I would think that common courtesy would compel us to say hello at least.

Is it not our calling to minister to strangers? I would feel so out of sort and say something because the Bible tells me that we are to love one another no matter where we come from. I started to feel awkward to greet them with 'God bless you' which would cause them to respond with the same. Why would Christians treat each other as such? It is beyond me that people professing to be Christ followers would behave unfriendly toward one another.

No matter where I moved to people are people, and so for those three years I had my fill of church disappointments. I also witnessed that no matter the ethnicity, like groups will tend to gravitate to each other. I believe that everywhere I go, I will find there will be church members who have not been delivered or have not fully surrender to the Holy Spirit. That people who hurt other people have themselves been hurt, and they bring that hurtful behavior to church with them. There were some hurtful moments caused by a few of that church's members but the friendships I made and relationships I established outweighed all the negativity I experienced.

CHAPTER FOURTEEN

A NEW HUMANITY

However, I did experience a new humanity in the southwest unlike what I had experienced in the northeast.

When God changed me, He gave me the sight to see who I really was – a child of God. It was nobody but Jesus who healed, blessed, and kept me. And he will do the same for you. I was so grateful at what God was doing in my life that I didn't want anyone or anything to separate me from God again. I began to remove some stuff from my mind like guilt, shame, depression, discouragement, and anger. As children of God, we can't build a new life until we get rid of the old rubbish in our life. We need to put it in order and start over again with a solid foundation. We need to speak words of encouragement to ourselves and do not allow the enemy to speak negative words into our life again. There were many unexpected things that came my way, but in spite of them, I continue to praise God more than ever.

I began to spend more time in prayer and in the word. God was changing my season. I began to write my memoir about my years in the marriage I termed, a 'marriage made in Hades.' I had retired and was living solely on my State Pension. By God's grace, I was provided for, and He supplied everything I needed.

We have a purpose here on earth that has been assigned by God, and we must trust God to sustain us and guide us. We must pray to God to give us the strength to finish the good race. Sometimes we will be discouraged, but we must remember that God is in control. "And I am certain that God, who began the good work within you, will continue his work until it is finally finished on the day when Christ Jesus returns" (Philippians 1:6, NIV.) I humbled myself before the Lord and praised Him for all my blessings, accomplishments and everything I received.

Kingdom Living

Moving to the Midwest was a dream come true, and I had other reasons. I was listening to the news on the radio when I heard that the governor was about to pray on the steps of the State Capitol and that spoke volume to me. I liked that their government believed in Jesus Christ and was not ashamed to share God in public. I saw something in the Midwest church that I didn't see in Eastport churches, the common denominator there was Jesus Christ and kingdom living.

It's all about kingdom living. Let us understand the difference between the kingdom of God and the church. The kingdom is both accessible and livable because of God's gift of Jesus Christ and the abiding of the Holy Spirit. The word of God tells us to seek first the kingdom. It's a sphere where God is, and it belongs to the poor in spirit. We are learning Kingdom living in Church, but some refuse to learn it and live any old way. There is a difference between churching and kingdom. Those who can look beyond their ethnic group and connect with other children of God who look different than they are uniquely different for the kingdom of God. Wherever the King rules there is where the Kingdom is, and He is the only one we are to serve not our Race, our ethnic group or the culture. Jesus had to come to put humanity back on track. Why do you think Christ Jesus preaches on love so much because He knows that we are mean? The believers must be Kingdom minded and be the influence in their church. I believe that when a church is Kingdom minded the members will see many manifestations of God. But those members who do not do the work of God and who murmur and complain will not only see the manifestations in their own life but will not enter the kingdom.

When I made this move, I had no choice but to have faith and believe God. My decision was a bold one, but I knew that God my Father would keep me safe. There was going to be a time of manifestation and expectations, and it was the time to move from the realm of saying to the realm of seeing. I had come to this earth to make an impact. I felt in my heart that as long as I stayed in Connecticut, I was not going to move forward in the kingdom. I truly believed that the church in Connecticut had lost their charisma and character as well as their dignity and honor. I was focused on my destiny in the kingdom. When we make decisions, we must stay focus. It is our decision that decides our destiny.

God as Our Navigator

Whatever situation you find yourself in remember there is a way out, and with God, as your navigator, you will be alright. Just walk in what God has called you to do. Just be concerned with what God has to say about everything you are doing. God is looking for believers. Don't waste time with the pretenders in the church who don't truly believe. The non-believers will begin to plot against your blessing and destroy your dreams; and will make you doubt God. Be tough and don't allow anything to turn you away. God has a way of turning things around for those He has chosen, that is you and me. God is waiting to turn some things around in us so be still and know that he is God. God has chosen us, and He has a way of renewing us that together we can help free others who are lost. There are too many people who still need to be delivered, and we have no time to waste with pretenders in the church.

There are going to be some hard hits from the enemy but there are Christian brothers and sisters still praying for you and me, and they are standing in the gap for us. Let us put our attitude and flesh to death so that it will not hinder our walk with God. The Christian must embrace the word of God because it is plain in explaining how followers of Christ should treat one another.

I spent three years enjoying my cell group members, the new

friends I made in the Women's cell group, and the praise dance team. I don't mean to say anything derogatory toward the people in Connecticut. I am sure you will agree with me when I say that sometimes it takes us experiencing something new and different outside of our comfort zone to help us along the way to reflect on what was missing before. We must be sincere about life. God will prepare us, and He will supply us with the necessities to get where he wants us to get. We must be one with God.

I had no idea of the wonderful things I was going to experience there, but God did. I was determined to trust my Savior Jesus Christ because through Him I have access to the Father.

The church family can't afford to be at odds with God if they are going to walk with Him into eternity. The church needs to have a deeper relationship with God and let Him direct their path. God wants to make one new man and one new woman. The church loses its light when it loses its first love, Christ Jesus. Before anyone of us became a new convert (I am speaking to both the new and seasoned Christian) and was baptized in the water we walked according to the flesh and did as the world did and we satisfied our flesh through pleasure caused by our sinning. We are still sinners. God works with us and reminds us of His grace daily.

God has predestined our path, and He will do more than He promised and not less. God saw that we were without hope and through Christ Jesus, He made a covenant with us.

Kingdom Humanity

God showed me how He is bringing together people from different ethnic groups that are of one mind. It is called the new humanity.

I had to leave the Midwest and travel back home to reconcile myself with my family and resume the ministry God had in store for me. During those three years, I was traveling three to four times a year back and forth, and it had taken a toll on my finances, and it was beginning to affect my mental health and physical body. I received some money unexpectedly, (blessed supernaturally) and was able to move back to Eastport. I was looking forward to doing ministry and felt joyous about being around my children and their family. With much pain in my heart, I said goodbye to my spiritual parents.

However, I knew that I would be returning in the fall of 2016 for my last graduation in Dallas and would visit with them at that time, which I did as I promised.

I went back in November of 2017 to visit Ms. Carmen and Mr. James and spent Thanksgiving with them and a few of the cell group members. Mr. James went home to be with the Lord in March of 2018, and Ms. Carmen went to Arlington to be with her daughter.

I had learned about total surrender and dependence on God while I was there. I witness that there are still good Christians who care and love one another. I realized that I was still useful to be used in the kingdom and I was bringing back a wealth of knowledge to implement in my ministry, whatever it would be. I met some of the most interesting people, and I didn't have to travel out of the country. The dance ministry took me to places I never dreamed of and what great experiences I had. One such experience was dancing at the Tobin Center in San Antonio where Pastor Kim Burrell was the main attraction, and she praised God like never before.

I was also invited to dance for the Annual 'Love Fest with Jesus' event in San Marcos Texas. I have also danced for the Christians United for Israel, 'A Night to Honor Israel.' event and at the 'Seder Dinner Night' event.

I was going to miss all of my sisters in Christ and all of those activities, events and more. I thought I'll bring what I learned and teach it to others. That was my enthusiasm talking.

PART TWO

✝

TRUSTING GOD

A Woman Washes Jesus' Feet

When one of the Pharisees invited Jesus to have dinner with him, he went to the Pharisee's house and reclined at the table. A woman in that town who lived a sinful life learned that Jesus was eating at the Pharisee's house, so she came there with an alabaster jar of perfume. As she stood behind him at his feet weeping, she began to wet his feet with her tears. Then she wiped them with her hair, kissed them and poured perfume on them.

When the Pharisee who had invited him saw this, he said to himself, "If this man were a prophet, he would know who is touching him and what kind of woman she is—that she is a sinner."

Jesus answered him, "Simon, I have something to tell you."

"Tell me, teacher," he said, "Two people owed money to a certain moneylender. One owed him five hundred denarii, and the other fifty. Neither of them had the money to pay him back, so he forgave the debts of both. Now which of them will love him more?"

Simon replied, "I suppose the one who had the bigger debt forgiven."

"You have judged correctly," Jesus said.

Then he turned toward the woman and said to Simon, "Do you see this woman? I came into your house. You did not give me any water for my feet, but she wet my feet with her tears and wiped them with her hair. You did not give me a kiss, but this woman, from the time I entered, has not stopped kissing my feet. You did not put oil on my head, but she has poured perfume on my feet. Therefore, I tell you, her many sins have been forgiven—as her great love has shown. But whoever has been forgiven little loves little."

Then Jesus said to her, "Your sins are forgiven."

The other guests began to say among themselves, "Who is this who even forgives sins? ⁰ *Jesus said to the woman, "Your faith has saved you; go in peace."*

Luke 7:36-50 NIV

CHAPTER FIFTEEN

A CHURCH IN DARKNESS

Where I was there was no light, no joy, and no happiness.

When God called me over three decades ago, I had no structure, and I was living through the see nothing days. I came when He called me because I knew there was more then what I had. In the world that I was in, there was nothing good for me but death and hell. But God drew me to Himself and made me what I am today.

There are Pharisees Everywhere

In the process of God making and molding us, He will show us to be aware of the Pharisees, those who will keep you and me down and abstract us from the will of God. God will give us the wisdom to ignore them. The Pharisees hated Jesus because of who He was, and they will hate us because of who we are in Christ Jesus.

I learned to live through painful and hurting days and learned to praise God during those times because my heart wants God's will. What God has for me and you will be awesome. When we have questions of God, we have to give Him more praise. God is too big for us to understand but He is not ignorant, and He knows where we are emotionally, mentally, and physically. We must learn to forgive those who hurt us and those who even hate us because it is God's will.

God has created us to worship and praise Him and to go out and make saints out of the lost souls. God is looking for warriors to do kingdom work. God is looking for people who are desperate to do kingdom work here on earth. But first we must be desperate for the presence of the Lord, and when we get to the presence, we will be changed and have the mindset of Jesus. We are to bring to God the problem we want Him to fix for us or save us from. He is waiting for us to ask Him. God just wants us to ask Him for whatever it is we need help with no matter how difficult it is so that we will realize that only God can do it. In the church, in our social life and work, we have to move some people out of our way to get to Jesus.

I just want to get to Jesus, and I will not allow anyone to distract me from what God wants from me. I want to do the will of God and what he wants me to do.

In January 2016 I returned to Eastport and found an apartment exactly how I had prayed to God for. I went back to my home church, but the founder had gone home to be with the Lord. There was another pastor. I had been away from (my original home church) for about eight years. I noticed some changes in the church that sadden me.

Before I returned to Eastport, I had spoken to the pastor about returning and that I wanted to be part of the evangelistic ministry. I spoke with the pastor regarding the leadership classes that I took in the Midwest and about my interest in the Evangelistic Ministry and he told to see the elder in charge of that ministry.

I met with the minister of the evangelistic ministry, Elder Emery, and he was more than happy to take me into the ministry. I was excited to get started and kept after him about going out into the streets to save souls. In the first year we went out twice, and the following year we went out once around the neighborhood.

Then one Wednesday (beginning of my first year back) before the start of Bible study the pastor informs the church that several of his ministers are forming a group of only males to go into the north side of the city to evangelize young men. So, when I asked the elder about our ministry, he told me, "I am not sure what to think, and I have to talk to the pastor." I was shocked to see how unorganized things were and I could only equate it to that my former pastor was not around who in my eyes was a more organized pastor. The pastor would talk about the order in the house of God and how God was a

God of order. I started to see how things had been unraveling since I came back to the church. I went back to volunteer for the Saturday outreach program, and the same sister was still in charge of it. It was good to see her again. I met a few new members that I had not seen when I was serving in that program years before. One of the new members was not friendly toward me at all, and no matter how much I tried to connect with her it wasn't easy. She would look for ways not to greet me or have any kind of conversation with me. If I'm making such a strong statement against my sister is because I witness it with my own eyes.

One Saturday morning the person in charge of the feeding program did come that day because she was not feeling well. I happened to have shown up early, and no one was there to let me in, so I called Elder Emery who came and opened the door to the church. I started to search in the refrigerator and the cabinets for something to cook, but there was nothing. I didn't know what to do. Elder Emery had to leave because he had somewhere else to be and I was left alone. Shortly after sister Janet walked in and I greeted her, "God bless you, sister Janet," she responded, "hi." I asked her what we are going to cook? She didn't respond but walked out of the kitchen. While we're cleaning the kitchen in preparation for what was to serve those who come to the program her and I spent a good amount of time in close proximity in utter silence. The silence was broken when the other volunteers walked in. She started the conversation with them about what they thought should to serve to those attending the feeding program. Finally, they all decided on serving them tuna fish. Sister Janet told the rest that she would purchase what the church needed and that she would be reimbursed later and left to the grocery store with another sister. I was left with a few of the members I had known from before. I stay in the kitchen cleaning up until the sisters came back with the groceries and I helped them prepare the lunch. The other members spoke to me, but she didn't exchange another word with me.

I used that time in the feeding program to talk to the people we served. I also place Pocket Testament League tracks, that contained the gospel of John, on the tables.

I came back to the church where God wanted me to attend since my conversion. I was obedient.

I had suffered far too much for my rebellious behavior.

I wasn't going to allow church people's petty behaviors discourage me from God's plans and purpose for my life. I decided to let God deal with their ungodly behaviors.

But my story does not end there I will continue to share more of what I witness that left me in shock in the house of God. It is a shame that I can't even call them my church family that is how much they hurt me.

After several months of attending church, the preaching had gotten so repulsive that I would get sick to my stomach and want to walk out of the building. There were times that I would leave midway into the service. The things I heard from the pulpit and what I was observing from the members made me nauseous. The enemy came with ridicule and discouragement, but I was not going to be defeated by his words anymore. To God be the glory.

But for God I was to be obedient, stay focus but be aware of the enemy who would use sisters and brothers in the church to confuse me. I had to be careful of what people said to me when God had something already for me. I believed God for restoration and recovery of what He planned for me. I had to surround myself with the Holy Spirit to save myself from this corrupt generation. We must be disciplined and follow the laws put before us by God because we have been ordained by Him. This generation of Christians is corrupt because of the wrong teachings or lack of good teaching. But we who follow Christ and want to live right before God need to save ourselves from such a corrupt generation. The church members need to be prepared and disciplined. "So that no one can criticize you. Live clean, innocent lives as children of God, shining like bright lights in a world full of crooked and perverse people" (Philippians 2:15, NIV.)

Can They Be Anymore Callous?

The church leaders are encouraged to be mature Christians. The church needs godly men and women in leadership that have the wisdom ordained from God. They need to put on the clothes of Christ Jesus and live a Christian life. We should clothe ourselves in the scriptures.

My first year back in my church during one Sunday Mother's Day service was an experience I will never forget. I am in the altar praying when all of a sudden out of nowhere a strong thick hand is placed on my forehead, and male voice is saying something to me, but I don't understand what he is saying, and then I was pushed. As I am falling, I think to myself someone will grab me so as not to hit the floor, but I was wrong. I go straight back onto the hardwood floor landing on my shoulders first (the pain was excruciating) then my head hits the floor. I immediately heard an inner voice say to me; they don't love you here they let you fall. "Am I dead?" I thought as I laid there. I am in total darkness, and I can't move my body. I am waiting to open my eyes in heaven, and I am excited about it. I thought "if I'm not dead will I be paralyzed for the rest of my life," "I don't feel my body," "it has gone limp completely." "I don't want to be paralyzed. I want to be in heaven." Then, I hear two female voices talking to each other. The one is asking the other, "is she alive?" They try to lift my arms, but they go limp and fall back on the floor. I recognize the voice of one of the females, she is a midwife nurse, and she tells the other female she is alive, I feel her pulse. It seemed like a long time before I could open my eyes and they are asking me, "are you all right?" "Can you get up?"

When I was falling, I really thought someone would hold me but when I felt the sharp pain in my shoulder blades which hit the floor first and then and my head. It was always the norm to have someone standing behind a person when the pastor or anyone else is praying for that person because most times that person would fall back. When I finally opened my eyes, I was so angry that no one cared enough to protect me from falling. The first words out of my mouth were, "who was that demon who pushed me?" They didn't respond even when I repeated myself. They helped me up and walked me over to my seat. I was feeling light-headed; my vision was blurred as well as feeling nauseous and weak. I sat there to listen to the message and when the pastor called all the mothers to come to the altar for a photo. I made myself get up and move slowly there but still feeling somewhat light-headed. My eyesight was still blurry.

After the service, I went home changed and took myself to the hospital for an examination because I wanted to make sure I did not break any bones or injured myself internally. I had x-rays taken of my head and shoulders. Good thing that I was not seriously injured.

The following months after that incident I would not go to the altar for prayer or to dance. It took about a year before I got the confidence to go to the altar. I had told God "I'm going to dance and praise you from my seat." When I did dance the spirit would lead to one of most spirit-filled sisters to watch me, and she would graciously stand with me. I did not trust the church members to have my back, and I'm still a little resistant. I had experienced many awkward moments in that church because of the member's attitude, but I kept attending Sunday after Sunday even when members would sit a distance from me. If a member had to sit next to me they, for the most part, ignore me for most of the service except when I would greet them.

In the summer of that same year, I went south with the church, and I took the coach bus with other members. I didn't know what to expect at first, but it was traumatic, to say the least. The announcement was made on a Sunday of the church's Annual Holy Event. I place emphasis on holy because what I experienced there was short of holy.

Before I made the decision to go to the event with the church, I wanted to make sure that someone I was comfortable with would room with me and share the room expenses. The other reason was that I didn't want to be alone but expected to have someone to sit and talk. In the past, the Annual Holy Event was mainly celebrated in Eastport, and it was convenient, and I would always find someone to talk and sit with who was not a member but a visitor.

I had the money, and I really wanted to go since I had missed so much of those events. I really wanted to reconnect with my old church members. I went to one of the older members, but she was not going, and she suggested that I ask my friend Tonya. I went to Tonya, and she agreed to room with me. She told the room was reserved and I should meet her there because she was driving her car the day before. I paid the church secretary the bus money. When I got to the hotel I called her cell phone, but she didn't pick up, and I felt that something wasn't right and it was very disconcerting. Because I was there in the hotel and may not have a room nor have anyone to talk to was my biggest fear.

I had been at the church for over half a year and hadn't been received very well by some of the remaining old members. But for a few of the more mature older sisters who were still there and I could always count on them to treat me with the utmost respect. But I felt something different in the church's atmosphere since I returned and most of the member's attitude was much more negative than when I was there over eight years ago. That was why I wasn't very sure about going with the church unless we were going to room together and she had told me that we would.

I kept calling her phone, and when she did pick up, she sounded angry and told me, "I have things to do." She told me that I would not fit in the room because it was crowded with her friend and her son. When I finally caught up with her, she was abrupt and asked Rita to help me get situated. I was devastated and crushed. I was so hurt and so disappointed at her. I felt discarded like a piece of rag. All these years of knowing her I meant nothing to her at that moment. That event was the worse experience I have ever had in what is supposed to be a Christian event. I got a room with a double bed (no single beds were available) at full price because the discounted rooms were all sold prior to the event. But God and His sense of humor and love for me put me right in front of her room.

"Our Righteousness Is Like Filthy Rugs"

Before going up to my room I went to register and pick up the bag with goodies and the t-shirt with the event logo, it comes with the price of the conference. I met with people at the registration table who looked at me as if I was her worst enemy. Everyone behind the table looked so serious, and none of them greeted me. That event is to be a joyous event, not a funeral. Not once did any of them smiled at me. I received that same treatment for the whole two days I was there, with the exception of the hotel personnel who were kind and polite.

I was looking for a smile from the church people and couldn't find one that would greet me with "God bless you, my sister." Not a one. I grabbed my things and went to my room to change for dinner. I thought that if I finished before Tonya, then she would not leave me behind. I would knock on her door, and she and Rita would have to take me along. Rita appeared concern, and I appreciated her for that. She offered to save me a seat in the conference hall when we spoke on the phone later on that day.

The event served a special brunch in honor of one of the First lady of the church, and I was able to sit with both Rita and Tonya and a few new members. I had a good time at the brunch talking to everyone. The food was exquisite and very delicious. But I had too much of the chocolate mousse cake that I started to hyperventilate, (allergic to caffeine) and had to go to my room to relax. I took a nap sitting on the chair so as not to ruin my makeup or wrinkle the dress I was wearing because I still had to attend the evening service and wasn't going to change clothes. When I woke up (I had fallen asleep for an hour), I tried to reach Tonya and Rita, and none of them answered the phone.

I went back to the conference room where we had the brunch,

and everyone except the First lady, Pastor's wife and, few other ladies were standing around taking photos of each other with their cellphones. I went over to them to see if I could take a photo with the first lady but I was being ignored. When I tried to edge in to excuse myself and greet them, they would continue to talk as if I wasn't there and they continue to take photos of each other. Just when I thought that the Pastor's wife wasn't going to acknowledge me, she turned to me and said "hello." I quickly greeted her and asked if I could take a photo of her and her mother-in-law. I really was looking forward to taking a photo of the First lady and me, but I had to settle for taking a quick photo before they changed their mind. Mind you that I knew these two women from our home church for eleven years. I wasn't a stranger to either one of them. There were very few times when either of them would talk to me anyway at the home church. I would always go out of the way to greet them, and they always appeared to be in a rush whether to their seat or going somewhere quick.

So, after that awkward moment of trying to get their attention, I went out to find someone to share some time with until the service started. I could not find Tonya nor Rita.

I remember the group of Latino members who had taken the bus with me that morning (they slept the whole trip in the back of the bus.) One of them was my team leader. I called her cellphone and told her how I was feeling lonely and needed company, so she invited me to join her and her family who were at the hotel snack café. I felt awkward having called her because we didn't have a relationship or connection outside of the church. So, whenever I approached her, I was always afraid she would snap at me. But I was alone and desperate, and at that point, I just didn't care if she bit my head off because I just wanted some company. I explained to her why I was left all alone and how awful the whole thing was making me feel.

I went up, and she offered me some hors-d'oeuvre, and we talked for a while and then she told me she needed to get dressed for the event. It was still early, and I decided to go outside of the hotel and venture around but it was too hot, and I went back into the air-conditioned hotel. I saw Tonya by herself, and she asked me, "where have you been?" I told her, the whole story of what had happened to me since I last saw her. I went back outside with her, (the sun had gone down some) and it was much cooler. We sat at an open café in the shade and had small talk about my family and her son. We went back into the hotel and ran into Rita, and we all headed to the main conference room for the evening service. I met most of my church members waiting for the doors to open. I greeted them, and some were glad to see me and others were nonchalant, and others did not care to say anything to me at all. I suggested that we take a few photos with my cell phone and they both agreed and we moved away from the crowd toward some huge windows and open space by the conference hall. We did not want to venture too far and end up with no seats.

I realize that everything in our flesh desires to do wrong and Christians are not immune. In our flesh dwells no good thing and its agenda is for our destruction. The key to dealing with our flesh is discipline by putting the flesh under submission to the will of God. We can start by facing the fact that we are sinners and weak to the flesh. If we can be honest with our weakness, we will be delivered when we go to God and ask Him for help.

The biggest problem in the church is that they can't deal with others because they are self-centric. Many Christians whether new in the faith or a veteran saint are lacking insensitivity to others needs. The saints must stop giving in to their weaknesses. Jesus rebuked His disciples when He was in the garden of Gethsemane, "Then he returned to his disciples and found them sleeping. "Couldn't you men keep watch with me for one hour?" he asked Peter. "Watch and pray so that you will not fall into temptation. The spirit is willing, but the flesh is weak" (Matthew 26:40, NIV.) The church must be more Christ-centric and think of why Jesus Christ died on the Cross for us.

No matter how unkind the members in the church were to me, I was not about to stop seeking the Lord and all His righteousness. The Bible tells me that our righteousness is nothing but filthy rags and it is only through the righteousness of Jesus Christ that you and I are made right in God. If we keep God's righteousness, it will bring other areas in our lives into right standing with Him. If righteousness is not operating in us, it can only mean that the spirit of God is not operating in us.

How can church people say that they are the children of God when they aren't living by His standard? Jesus died for us and bore our sins that through Him we can live. But to live filled with the Holy Spirit and only then can we be managed by the righteousness of God. There has to be a total surrender of our will and letting God who is the righteous one who can help us make all the right decisions for us. I know for sure that there will be fewer hurting people in the church if we all walked in the righteousness of God.

We all sat together in the service. I worship, danced and listen to the preacher. The service came to close. I was headed to my room when I saw a familiar face from (long-time member who also sang in the choir). I went over to her greet and gave her a hug, and made some small talk about the service. She told me, "I am trying to get a glass of milk so I can get to sleep but everything is close." I told her, "I like drinking warm milk myself before going to bed." She turned around and gave me her back which indicated that was the end of our conversation, and I said, "goodnight." She was one of the members who rarely greeted me in church.

React In Love

The next day was an even greater challenge. I woke up got dressed so I will not miss them today and end up alone. This was our departure day, and everything had to be done according to schedule, and there was no time to waste today. I thought I would not see my friend at all that day but I knock at her door, and Rita was doing her hair. I invited them to breakfast, and they both said they would meet me there. I went to eat and waited until I received a call from Rita that she was going to the main hall and find seating and my friend had to have breakfast with the ministers who had been served a breakfast buffet in one of the conference rooms. I ate by myself in the hotel dining. How in the world does one feel so alone in a place filled with wall to wall Christians? I felt alone because those around me were going about their business focusing either on themselves or in their cliques. It was scared to think that my ethnicity had anything to do with the rejection I was experiencing from church people in general. I could not come up with another explanation.

After I ate my breakfast, I went up to the main conference room, and the usher led me to a seat by the aisle on the left pews. I didn't see either of them. I was seated next to a new member from my home church and in front and in back members from other churches. I greeted all those around me, and the only ones who responded were the other members from a different church. The member of my church ignored me. When I noticed that she turned her back to me, it was an indication that she didn't want to speak to me and at that moment I decided it would be alright with me. I wasn't going to let her negative attitude interfere with me receiving my portion that morning. I was going to praise God in spirit and in truth and was going to put her bad attitudes in God's hands. Let Him deal with her. The service was underway, and I was trying to stay focus on the preacher but felt a conviction in my soul. I had to turn to my sister and greet her because that wasn't how the children of God should behave toward one another. I felt so much better and was able to enjoy the rest of the service without feeling convicted. At a point in the service, the preacher asked people to partner up with someone and pray with them. I immediately turned to the sister behind me, and we prayed together. When I began to pray with her, the spirit took over in both her and me, and she began to weep, and I continued to pray as the spirit lead me. After the prayer, we both danced together in victory. She told me afterward that what I was praying for was what she had asked God for and that was confirmation, (we had not met prior to this service.) She told me her name, and I told her mine, and we were to stay in touch, but we didn't because I lost her information. I continued to pray for her after that event. She was the sweetest person I had met in the entire place beside the hotel personnel.

In the situation, I found myself rather than to react to every negative behavior I just needed to respond in love and gentleness. I just had to examine the purpose of my situation and keep my eyes on where God is taking me. As a child of God, I should expect things and adversaries to happen in my life but what is important is to continue to praise God and maintain my relationship with Him intact. I must remember in those difficult moments to speak life over any and all situations that arise. I must learn to stop looking for people to pity me and forgive them so that it will not be a hindrance in my praise.

The church members should be spiritually-minded and expect from God to show us where we are falling short and why is it that we are going through those experiences. I have made up my mind that I would jump for joy no matter what was going on because I trust the Lord and He will help me understand down the road the why of it all.

After the service was over, I found a restroom and changed into some casual clothes for the ride back home. I heard that the bus was already outside and so I picked up my bag that was being held in the hotel temporary storage room. I found a seat in the front of the bus by the window and made myself comfortable. Members began to board the bus a few at a time, and the last to board was the First lady, and there were no more seats left except for the one next to me. She looked around to see if there were any other seats available but that was the only one, and she sat down. I greeted her with, "God bless you. How are you? You look exhausted." She responded, "I just want to go to sleep." I saw how tired she was because she had been there days prior to the event and with all the excitement it appeared to have taken a toll on her (my estimation.) I tried not to make small talk with her realizing that all she wanted was to sleep.

I was hungry and was hoping that someone would suggest stopping someplace to eat and just at that moment the pastor came onto the bus and announced that we were going to eat. I praised God silently and thanked Him for hearing my thoughts. The bus driver was not the usual driver but was convinced by the pastor to take us. He left us at the restaurant and was to for us in an hour. The restaurant let us have the entire upstairs eating area, and we packed it in. I decided to play it safe and put my bag on a chair and hold my spot because there were groups (cliques). I first wanted to see where everyone was going to sit before, I sat. As I had suspected members found their groups and I sat with people who were new to the church. It took longer than usual to bring the food, so I went around taking photos with my cell phone. I would stop and greet them and ask to take their picture most said yes. I passed the time doing that so as not to feel left out. The food finally came, we ate, and it was back to the bus. In the bus, the First lady was so tired that she fell asleep the minute the driver took off and I noticed her head was bobbing back and forth. I reach over to my right and pulled out my traveling neck rest (I use in long-trip airplane travel) and reached over to her and placed it around her neck. She appreciated the gesture and fell back to sleep. She slept all the way back to the church where the bus picked us up the day before. It is sad to say that in a sea of Christians I felt alone. What if I had been a non-believer would any of them care to have evangelized me?

Spiritual Disconnection

There is a spiritual disconnection when people are carnal-minded. There are church members who have no interest in walking with the Holy Spirit. They either don't care anymore, or they have lost their faith. Either way, they have been negatively influenced by the culture of the day. Christians everywhere must fully understand that our spirituality should be very important to us because God is a spirit and the only way to connect with Him is through the spirit. Christians are losing the zeal for God because they are hanging out with the wrong people and visiting the wrong places. They have forgotten their first love, Jesus the Lord.

The church has profaned the covenant it has with God, and they are becoming faithless. They have profaned the sanctuary with their negative behavior toward God and each other. Where is the love? The church has stopped trusting God and no longer love the Lord. The church has become a place of hypocrites. Members are behaving indifferent toward another and are doing what they want to do. They don't believe that God can keep them holy. The church needs deliverance from their ungodly behaviors and attitudes so that the love of God will permeate their very being and they will become more like what Christians should be.

Especially with the 'new millennium' generation in our day and age where submitting to God and the Holy Spirit is not popular. God can't force anyone to do anything they don't want to do because He is a gentleman and it's by choice that people receive Him. Yes, the scripture tells us that He does call us, but if we do not respond to His call, then it is what it is. I know that there are many blessings and miracles to those who search Him and decide to serve Him. I am a recipient of His goodness and love.

Christians have lost sight of their priority and are going after the wrong things which include body piercing, tattoos, and provocative clothing that silhouettes every curve in their body (men and women alike.) And they have taken God out of the Christian equation. But the Bible is very clear when it tells us to seek Him while He may still be found. Christians should be chasing after God not the other way around.

God is calling us out of the darkness and into the light, and we should take heed. There is a spirit of unbelief roaming in every city, town, and country. It is an oppressive spirit that sucks the life and joy out of the believer. But Jesus Christ dealt with those unclean and deceitful spirits, and He will deal with them now if you just asked Him. When the believer is robbed of his hope, there is no question that unbelief will set. But Christ came to free us of all that has us bound.

CHAPTER SIXTEEN

WHERE DID THAT COME FROM?

There is no doubt that there is a war between the flesh and the spirit realm but the goal of the believer is to draw closer to Christ. But that is easier said than done unless the person believes in fasting and prayer to overcome the flesh. Throughout history, there has always been this type of battle in Christians. But in the time that we are living every Christian who is serious about living right must be spiritually prepared. According to the holy scripture and its commandments being holy spirit filled is the way of a Christian.

Even though I was having such awkward feelings about the church members, I didn't have an issue with God's church. I desired to go to church and sing praises and worship God and receive a Rhema word that would take me until the middle of the week when I returned on Wednesday for Bible study. I enjoy hearing the word preached because it was food for my soul. But sometimes I would listen to some preachers and wonder, where did that come from.

Politically Correct vs. Spiritually-filled

It was during the Annual Women's Conference at my church where there were several invited female preachers. There was one preacher in particular that what came out of her mouth made me feel so uncomfortable about being one of the few Hispanics in the church.

I attended all three services and heard a different speaker each time. It was in the Sunday morning service (the other guest speakers had preached on Friday and Saturday) that this particular female minister took to the altar and shared what seems like a good word from the Lord. This was the first time I had heard her preach, and she talked about her family and her own church ministry. She was a strong figure of a woman (very attractive and fashionable) who appear very confident and authoritative in her presentation. I was very impressed with how she had managed the difficulties in her life and with her family. However, she saw it necessary to explain to the church that she was not a Hispanic but Black. I didn't see the need for her to share that with the church except that she too must have been treated differently by church members for looking Hispanic (my estimation.) I thought is there anything wrong with being Hispanic and what was the big deal?

Since my return to the church, I had felt out of sort caused by the negativity in the church's atmosphere and the strange treatment I received, especially from the female population. The males did not seem to care much one way or another who I was they just said hello or hi, and I would respond with "grace and peace" and "God bless you." What had happened to the church in the nine years that I was gone. I come back, and it is more "politically correct" than spirit filled. Hardly anyone is greeting each other with the usual "God bless you" but with "hi, how are you?" I would have to take a step back to make sure I was entering a place of worship and not a government office building.

The culture of the day had entered the church that's what I saw happening. What are the prejudices that keep us from surrendering to God? Can it be our race, culture, gender, intellect, profession, politics, gender and/or our theory about religion? God gives to anyone who wants to receive Him a vision that speaks of His prejudices and biases. Perhaps we need a change of attitude about our prejudices. God wants us to clean that which is keeping us from receiving Him. The church needs a transition from our prejudices and biases to receiving God into our lives.

In an interview done at the Rock Church Point Loma, Jim Caviezel the actor who played Jesus in the movie, "The Passion of the Christ" shared this testimony about what it means to stick to our convictions in the face of opposition:

"Everyone wants resurrection, but nobody wants suffering. ...Much in this way I wanted to do this piece to transcend... But if you look at it day after day that we all are part of handing Christ over when we contribute to sin, especially when we betray Him and we are Christians. The problem I see right now is that many, many Christians have emerged themselves in paganism. They want to be cool to their pagan friends by being a little pagan so they can be cool. There is nothing cool in this. The only thing lacking in you is you don't want to be holy. Well, here is what will happen, we'll all become to task one day and you'll either have a chance to lay it down for Jesus or you get to deny Him. But it will come in our generation in this way. ...You will have to make a choice. ...We need Christians to go look death in the face and understand, ...encourage these people to understand that eternity awaits them. ...God never sends a man into hell people choose this place. ...Can society exclude moral truths and moral reasoning? Set yourself apart from this corrupt generation my brothers and sisters. You weren't made to fit in; you were born to stand out." [14]

The cure to walking holy before God is as simple as not being yoked together with unbelievers. For righteousness and wickedness can't dwell in the same house for they have nothing in common. The Christian who truly lives in the light of Christ has no fellowship with the darkness. For they can't serve two masters. No one can serve two masters. For you will hate one and love the other; you will be devoted to one and despise the other. You can't serve God and be enslaved to money (Matthew 6:24.) There is no way that a believer can have a relationship with an unbeliever less the unbeliever influences the believer and causes him to stumble. The believer must decide in his heart that his contract agreement is with God and not with the idols of the devil.

As the word of God has said:

"I will live in them and walk among them. I will be their
God, and they will be my people. Therefore, come out
from among unbelievers, and separate yourselves from
them, says the LORD. Don't touch their filthy things, and
I will welcome you. And I will be your Father, and you
will be my sons and daughters…"
(2 Corinthians 6:15-18, NIV.)

The scriptures can't emphasize this enough that to enter into
another level of spirituality is to be connected to the Christ and
possess the attitude and mind of the Savior, the Prince of Peace,
our Lord. The more intimate we are with Christ, the more we will
think like him and the more we will seek peace with one another
and reflect His love.

Disconnected Christians

My church was going through some financial problems, and
the local churches who knew the pastor stepped in to help, and they
offered their services by preaching on Sunday evenings to bring up
morale. I couldn't be more disappointed in my church than on this
day. It was during a Sunday evening service when we had the guest
pastor and some of his members visit our church. It was obvious that
the visiting church was culturally diverse by the members that were
in attendance. I noticed that I wasn't the only one sitting alone in a
roll of empty pews, but this Caucasian male was also sitting alone in
a roll of empty pews. I thought does he realize the disconnect in my
church in that no one from my church wanted to sit next to him. I
felt sad for that brother and for my church.

The church members are strangers to the lost, no longer are they
distinguishable from the pagans. Jesus Christ stood out among the
crowd, and He showed them, love. If the church can't love their own
brothers and sisters in church how are they going to love the stranger,
the lost soul? "And the King will say, 'I tell you the truth when you

did it to one of the least of these my brothers and sisters, you were doing it to me!' (Matthew 26:40, NIV.)

There are negative consequences for our behavior that are never favorable, and we should fear those consequences. The church is struggling with an inner conflict that causes the member to decide on doing what is godly and right and doing what their carnal nature wants. This warring or conflict in us that we don't understand is trying to over-power the other. The pleasures of this world have infiltrated the church and have substituted selfishness to holy living. The cell phone is a perfect example with all its apps. I have seen members who have been raised in the church taking selfies of themselves while the pastor is preaching. The Pastor's mother was the guest preacher for the Sunday morning service because the pastor was away preaching at a church in another state. And the first thing she said when she got on the mic was, "I think it is a shame that members are on their phones taking pictures of themselves while the preacher is preaching. I see who you are. You don't disrespect the house of God. If you don't want to be here, then leave."

As I mentioned before when I return to this church after my long hiatus, I noticed a lot of things had changed in the church not only in their behavior but the lack of respect for the preacher and the sanctuary itself. The house of worship was longer revered as being the house of God. I observed on many occasions that not only the youth but the mature saints would sit in the pew most of the service playing "Candy Crush" on their cellphones. Every other pew had one member or another playing on their cellphones. There was such an addiction to that game both the secular and the church. The church had idolized their cellphone. Even during praise and worship they wouldn't stand up but sit in the seat with their game on. Church members must learn to get their spirit in control and pray to God to give them the liberty from the conflict within them.

There are stages that the enemy orders for our destruction. The enemy knows our weakness. The enemy is always trying to find out what our strength lies to destroy us. The enemy would like to put some people in our lives to mess us up. These associations can very easily cause us to make a mess of our relationship with God and the members of the church. The enemy has several strategies he uses to cause us to turn from holiness to the sin. The enemy's approach is through the choices we make in falling in love with the wrong person and through our family.

Sin is in us, and we need to acknowledge this fact. Sin seizes us and gets a hold of us, and its only intent is to kill us. Sin lives in our flesh, and it deceives us, and we don't have the power to control it. We need to know how to deal with this sin because if we don't, we will be a prisoner of it.

If anything, we must remember of when we first got saved and received Jesus Christ as our Savior, and know that He is the same yesterday, today, and tomorrow. Christ came to free us, heal us, and deliver us. He lives to save us and keep us from sinning. Never forget that the purpose of Christ coming from heaven to earth was so that we will know how much God loved us. It's not too late to ask God for His forgiveness.

Rebel With An Evil Cause

I had encountered many conflicts when I rebelled against God and sought to do my own thing. Satan knew my weaknesses and sought to destroy me. I had a hard time forgiving myself even when God had already forgiven me. But God is a patient God, and He waited for me to come to Him to fix the mess I had created. I was most vulnerable when I widowed. God warned me, but I didn't take heed to His warnings. But I learned a valuable lesson in that God is always faithful, just and His mercies never end.

The people in church rebel when they are no longer living holy, and it causes major problems in their spiritual walk. When souls are void of the Holy Spirit, people end up doing what they want to do and not follow the way of the Lord. If we have a Holy Bible and reccive a holy word, then we must live a holy life. As the church continues to move away from a holy spirit filled living the more sin will creep into the church.

There was this young female minister who was very attractive and wore the most beautiful dresses. She was married to a minister in the church, a tall dark, and handsome young man. She didn't greet or speak to me the entire nine years I had attended the church. I would ask myself what in the world did I do to this woman? I thought she is going to Hades because of her behavior and she will get her just reward. I noticed that I was not the only member she didn't greet or speak too. She appeared a bit snobbish. Her attention was always toward the pastor's family or the preacher's kids. There were many like her in the church who clearly didn't care about others in the church except for the first family. That kind of behavior she displayed is a disease, and it can easily infect the church. When I saw how much of the church had been infected, I couldn't be any angrier. I felt a spirit of discrimination in the church against those who were different in shape, status, and looks. Everyone was carrying around a chip on his or her shoulders.

I saw that the Church wasn't aligned with the doctrines of the gospels and that it needed to get in place. I witness that their sinful self was refusing to submit to leadership. I sensed a wicked spirit operating in the church that shouldn't have been there. Mostly everyone was operating in the natural instead of in the holy spirit. Their attitude and mood didn't fit that of the Holy Spirit. Most of them grew up in the church, and you would think that they are growing in faith and walking in the truth not regressing as I witnessed.

The church was now down the wrong path, and it needed to repent and turn from their wicked ways. "Restore us, O LORD, and bring us back to you again! Give us back the joys we once had!" (Lamentations 5:21, NIV.)

People nowadays are finding it harder to have a relationship with God. The church has been infected with evil brought in by the same members that attend it. This evil has infected the church with the demons of divisiveness, disorder, and sexuality. The church is serving the secular world with their bodies, language, attitude, and behaviors. The church members have allowed for the paganism and materialism to fester in their lives. The church has lost respect for the Shepherd and the leadership of the house of God. The church is out of order, and it needs to go back to its First Love, Christ Jesus.

CHAPTER SEVENTEEN

GENERATION SL
(SPIRITUALLY LOST)

I had attended one college class with one of the church's ministers many years ago while he was still a layperson in the church. He was dating a church member at the time. As I was exiting the church one Sunday morning, he was standing at the door with her, and he leaned over to greet me with a brotherly kiss. The look she gave me I would have dropped dead that instant if looks kill. After that episode, I noticed that he would greet me from a distance. They got married and have a beautiful family. He is an excellent Sunday school teacher and preaches from the heart. This kind brother stopped saying anything to me even as we pass each other in the church. I could see that he wasn't raised to disrespect his elders, but I had become someone that he felt he didn't have to acknowledge anymore (my estimation). Which in my observation goes back to the church's worldly attitude.

It wasn't out of the ordinary for members of that church to ignore me or each other even when I walk side by side or came face to face with them. They chose not to greet me. Some of them even went as far as avoiding eye contact with me. I would walk by them and greet them with, "God bless you" but they would not respond. I wasn't the only one I am sure, but I can only speak for myself.

Wikipedia describes 'Generation X' as those who were born between the early and mid-1960s through the early 1980s. During that period there was a shift in the social values due to the lack of parental supervision, both parents working, and an increase in divorce. The people became cynical and dissatisfied with the authority figure. [15]

The church is experiencing its own Generation X only they are the Generation SL, the spiritually lost generation. The attitudes of the Christian have changed, and they don't want spiritual leaders to lead them. Each has turned to his or her own self, and God is far from their hearts. They are living out their lives like the secular world. They know the scripture but ignore its teachings. In this generation, many grew up being fed the word of God, but they have been enticed by Satan and his idols. Many come to church service late and do not participate in praise and worship but sit there until service is over. The church has lost many members to other churches less demanding and more liberal in their doctrines where the message is watered down. There is a self-righteous spirit inhabiting this new generation, and they're doing their own thing.

The Selfish Generation

Then there are the 'Millennials, who were born in the early 1980s and mid-1990s to early 2000. They are the children of the 'Baby boomers,' and they are more interested in communications, social media, and digital technology and have a more liberal approach to societal values. [16]

These are the church members who come to church to take selfies of themselves during praise and worship while the pastor is preaching. They leave the service to answer their calls and sometimes they just text throughout the entire service. It is so frustrating and disturbing to see them in the house of God ignoring God's word just to answer a text. I could see if they were doctors on-call but even then, I am sure that would not occur often. The church is out of order!

I was in church but a few months when I noticed one of the ministers that had been with the church for several decades wearing her dress over her knee showing the back of her thighs.

I was appalled at what I had seen in that minister that I called the church office to talk to the new ordained Bishop of the church. I told him about my observation the Sunday past. I had noticed the women in the church were wearing their dresses and skirts shorter than usual and showing more breast with the lower cut blouses and dress style. I asked him, "when did the standard get lower in church?" I continue to tell him about my observations, and he told me to speak with one of the older sisters because she was in charge of addressing such issues. And with that, we said our goodbyes and hung up.

I was able to approach one of the older sisters one Sunday after service to tell her about my conversation with the bishop and that he suggested that, "I speak to you about my observation." As I am telling her about my conversation the female minister is up in the pulpit and leans over the piano to speak with the male who was playing on the piano, and we both saw her girdle (that was mid-way down her thighs) and the further she leaned in the more she exposed herself. The older sister just shook her head in disbelief and comment, "I'll talk to the pastor." She went to her seat to gather her things, and I left the sanctuary and went home thinking how shameful that a minister should not feel the slightest conviction about the length of her dress and dare to bare so much in the church. It was appalling and unacceptable. I had been gone for eleven years and oh my goodness how things had changed in the Pentecostal church. But then again this should not have surprised me because I saw it coming.

Counsel From the Ungodly

How many times does the Bible have to tell us not to walk in the counsel of the ungodly because they follow after their own plans and purposes and for the most part live unstable lives? These are our own friends and family members who have strong influences on us and can easily distract our focus from the things of God. We learn their bad habits because we already have the propensity to sin, it is an inherent and part of our nature.

Many members know they are sinners but just don't care and could care less what anybody thinks about them. And, they refuse to follow after and delight in the things that are of the Lord because it clashes with their choice of lifestyle. The word of God means nothing to them even when they have heard it growing up in the church.

But the successful believer will always meditate on the word of God, take the word, understand it and use it when these negative influences try to overcome us. Successful believers will stay planted in the word, and the spirit of the Living God will flow through them like rivers of living waters. Let us who are true believers continue to choose to grow in our relationship with God.

When did the church lose its way? It is a question that many can never quite put the finger on it, but I can tell you with certainty how it started at my church.

When church people sin, it's not a deliberate act per se (they don't go around thinking I am going to sin today.) but there are those in the church who do sin to violate the will of God, and they do it without remorse.

I began to see the shift in the fashion from more moderate wear to a more provocative look after this young sister returned from being away at school and brought her style to church with her. There was no stopping her from wearing what she felt like or when she wanted to wear it. This female's manner of dressing had a major impact on the church, and the residual effects are still being seen. The female had a catastrophic influence on the church's lack of decorum. She showed no remorse and rebellion was written all over her face. She was born in a Christian home and grew up in the church. She had returned home from school while I was still in the Catholic church. I saw her for the first time sitting over where the first family sat. She, like most of the others members, never smile at me and for many years later her demeanor was always the same. I never saw her sit with anyone in particular except with her children for all those years I attended the church. I observed that her sister-in-law, who was more on the conservative side didn't approve of her choice of clothing for the church by the way she would stare at her. She would wear spaghetti strap dresses and low-cut that was very revealing for church services. She became pregnant with her second child, and I remember the comment her mother made, "she has to get married this time!" I saw that she wasn't a church role model for the young girls to follow. I'm not saying that she was disruptive or outrageous, but there was for sure a liberal spirit in her. The pastor would say time and time again, "we don't come to church for form or fashion." But she was the only member at the time attending church wearing pants and low-cut, short dresses.

It was during Wednesday Bible study night that I first observed her ungodly attitude. She was about to sit (I was a couple of pews behind her), and I heard her tell one of the sisters, "if you don't like what I wear don't look at me." And this is how the church allows themselves to be contaminated by the world through one person at a time.

We must ask ourselves whether we are believers in Christ or not and do we really know the Lord. If we are believers and have lost the way we must find out why and where did we lose it.

Humility Wins

For me, it was the time that I was the most vulnerable after my husband died. I was harboring unforgiveness and was living a lie. I remember putting on a happy face in church on Sundays but continued to live a lie at home. I had become so bitter and miserable. It wasn't until I humbled myself and asked God to guide my way that I got my true joy back.

We never know what kind of situations cause people who grow up in the church, hearing the word for years, to lose their way. They continue to attend church out of habit but have no real commitment nor have they humbled themselves before the Lord.

I found out what humbling oneself before the Lord can do

for the soul. Humility is the key to our joy. I had to learn to be considerate to the person I was living with and the church family. I had to have a Christ-like attitude and not get caught up in my ego. I had to submit to the will of God.

We must never see ourselves superior to God or pretend to be more righteous than others. We must be obedient to the word of God. Be obedient to those in authority in every aspect of our life. Work responsibly for our salvation and know that God desires we demonstrate humility at all times. Every day we must mortify the flesh and humble ourselves. The results of humility will reduce all kinds of negative attitudes, stop the gossip and discord within the church members.

We must give an account for what we do, say, and think. God knows everything, and He sees everything and nothing surprises Him. God knows every decision that every one of us makes, and He has exclusive rights to peek into our future. God knows our ups and downs, our hurts and pains, our misery and anguish.

Attending church will not give us entry into heaven. Our salvation depends on the life we have through His Son Christ Jesus. We must trust God for He will make our way straight.

As the years' pass, I see that the dresses worn by the women in the church continue to get shorter, and the neckline continues to get lower. There is no longer any shame about showing what should only be privy to a spouse. It has become difficult to distinguish between the female who is living in the secular world and the female who calls herself a Christian.

CHAPTER EIGHTEEN

GOD IS OUR BANNER

I have learned to confide and trust in God because He will fight all my battles, and I will have the victory every time. I will stay connected to my banner who will guide me when I am in my deepest sorrows and fears. He will be my caretaker who will nurture me and give me His peace.

What better than to be loved by the Creator of the Universe who will continue to bless us and rescue us from our oppressors. We must admit that outside of God there is no one who is good and merciful day and night and not just sometimes. There are assurances and security in our God that is beyond compare.

Integrity Goes a Long Way

I say all this to say that people around us will always hurt our feelings and make us feel less than but we can move beyond it and know that someone greater loves us and we matter to Him.

I was at a store buying curtains for my pastor's office, and there were only two pairs left. I asked the frontend checkout person to call another franchise to know if they had a third pair. She told me to see the person at the checkout counter at the back of the store. The young female made a phone call to the other store and as we were waiting for the person on the other extension to come back online her and I talked about church people. She told me that her family goes back three generations of attending the COGIC church and that her grandfather is a pastor. She hasn't been attending church because of a negative experience with the church members. The young lady told me, that she had gotten pregnant out of wedlock, and that some of the members judged her. When she had the baby, the same members approached her and wanted to pray for her, but she was indignant and told them, "you will not lay hands on my son or me." She told me, "I peak into the church every now and then, but I don't like going to church. I rather listen to this one pastor online that I like". This young woman was hurt by her own church members who were supposed to have under-grid her during a difficult time in her life, and all they did was gossip about her. She has been disappointed by the church and doesn't trust them anymore. She prefers to listen to pastors preach their sermons online because it is safe and she does not have to fear being hurt again. I gave her a word of encouragement and asked her to visit my new church whenever she had the desire to fellowship. She responded, yes maybe that will be good.

I could have chosen to do what this young woman did and leave the church, but I would have given in to the enemy. Instead, I chose to seek God and let Him deal with the heathens in the church.

Sometimes Christians do waver in their faith. I went through a period of confusion and doubted my own faith. I get it! Sometimes our human emotions can be so overwhelming and can sidetrack our focus. When I was confronted by the attitudes of those professing to be saved, I just wanted to run and never see them nor the church again. But then I thought about my family and relatives and who was going to pray for their salvation and talk to them about God's unconditional love and mercy. I couldn't allow the church people to turn me from Jehovah God. He first took the initiative to look for you and me because He loves us. The behaviors and attitudes of some Christians should not be an excuse not to continue to seek God. It is not His fault that church members choose to act like heathens. It is their sinful nature operating in them.

My friend Cecilia shared an interesting church experience with me. She went to visit a church for an award ceremony for certain public officials. One of the ushers escorted her to the front pew, and she was seated next to another female (different ethnicity). She noticed that when she sat, the female turned her back to her. During the service, the preacher asked that everyone turn to his or her neighbor to the right and to the left and greet them. My friend turned to the female, but she turned the opposite direction, and Cecilia turn to greet the other person. Then Cecilia turned, and as the female turn with her head down, she extended a hand to shake Cecilia's hand and at that point, my friend says to her, "you can look at me you know." When the Pastor of the church began to present the dignitaries, he announced my friend, "here we have Police Commissioner and called out her name, and Cecilia stood up. Soon after the female turn to my friend and asked her, "did he say you are the Police Commissioner?" Cecilia said to her, "you heard right."

Cecilia was an invited guest to this church, and this female was a member of the church by her estimation. What kind of an impression did this female leave on Cecilia? By the way, Cecilia is a Christian (over 35 years), and it is her church that I now attend. But what if she had been an unsaved soul expecting to receive love instead of attitude? Is there no integrity in the church of God anymore? Integrity is very important to our walk with Christ, and it plays an integral part in evangelism if we are going to influence the world. Integrity is a moral compass as to how we should behave and how we should live. When church people live like the non-Christians, there is a definite moral decay spreading in their lives. The secular world doesn't want to reference God and is doing their own thing in which there is unrepentance, unforgiveness, and lack of integrity. Our culture is living in darkness full of sin and depravity and Christians have no time to play church. We are called to be warriors for the Kingdom of God.

God gave us the values in the Beatitudes for Christians to live by. Attitudes that will make a difference in the way we interact with others in church and outside of the church. The profess Christian needs a transformation and a renewal of the mind and the heart before they can go to minister to others. Godly attitudes that the world will see in us when we go forth to share the gospel. We are to be salt and light in the world to bring people out of darkness.

Adjust Your Lenses

The church is called to action to go out to the community and bring the life-saving word of God. There is a major conflict going on with the divine and the human church. The mistakes that some Christians make is when their focus is no longer on God. They begin to see things through their human lenses instead of through their God's eyes. We try to do things like both the world and as the spiritual world, but it doesn't function right because we can't serve to masters, and one is going to influence the other. Most times we choose to listen to the culture.

In our Christian walk, we will always be challenged and have difficult situations. But it becomes more prevalent what we allow to influence us when we are following God from a distance leaving Him behind. We subtly deny God, and we deny knowing Christ.

There has to be a conviction in our hearts as our conscience reveals that we need to stop denying God and repent and cry out to Him for forgiveness. We must feel ashamed for offending God.

Christians must learn to integrate the reality of the divine and the human church by confessing Christ Jesus as Lord and see things as God sees them. Let us follow Christ closely and be a witness for him. The Bible is clear on that we are of one body – the body of Christ. God is preparing humans to do divine work to evangelize the lost souls without judging nor discouraging anyone.

We are to evangelize everyone and preach the gospel of Christ Jesus. God doesn't show favoritism but accepts everyone. But attitudes and behaviors can be discouraging, and it will create discord and push others away.

There will always be those who oppose God's correction and refuse to grow in His knowledge.

They are the ones that will come together to bring discord and discouragement to God's people. Christians must stay away from negative people because bad company corrupts good character. Some people in the church can be stumbling blocks in our lives. The enemy plants these people in the church to create doubt in our thoughts. But when you separate from them do it with love. Use wisdom when you minister to and witness to them, help them understand the plan of salvation, and pray for them. Be very astute when you have communication with negative people. Watch for those who cause division among the church members. Don't listen to their gossiping and stay away from speaking badly about a church member. These are people who harbor anger, bitterness, rage and go to get lengths to slander other members in the church.

God called us from among the heathens, and we need to control the way we act with one another and how we talk to each other. When there is no integrity in the church, the spirit moves.

Chew What is Good and Spit Out the Rest

The Church brought in a guest pastor in November to preach a word before the Thanksgiving holiday. But what a strange message he delivered to the church. He titled his message; "The Pipes are Clogged." He didn't reference scripture and did not commend the service to God but proceeded to talk about the Puritans and the Indians. I am expecting a thanksgiving service to speak on being grateful to God for all He had done for us that whole year but instead he talked about a massacre that occurred in May of 1629. He talked about how the Puritans had killed seven hundred natives in their camps and that they called it "Thanksgiving." He talked about the previous President and the current President and pipeline conflict that was making the news during that time and the wall going up. He said that we celebrate a holiday on the blood of others. At the end of the service, he asked the congregation to give a hundred dollars if they wanted to see a miracle in their life. That pastor appeared very angry during the entire time he gave his message. The message had absolutely nothing to do with God and/or being grateful. During the service, my spirit kept speaking to me that that pastor's intent was to create a division not just in the church but between Race. I didn't like it one bit what he was attempting to start in the church. It was enough that I had experienced being ignore now I had to contend with my Race being a factor. I feared that it would create a bigger chasm between some of the brothers and sisters in the church. God had created us just the way He wanted us, and we couldn't change.

"For those whom He foreknew, He also predestined to become conformed to the image of His Son, so that He would be the firstborn among many brethren; and these whom He predestined, He also called; and these whom He called, He also justified; and these whom He justified, He also glorified" (Romans 8:29-30, NIV).

I choose not to change whom I was born to be. I am not only proud to be called a Christian but also a Puerto Rican. We cannot ignore the fact that there are major Race differences in almost every country on this earth, but we do not need it in the church. In the church, we are God's children, and He commands that we love one another. I will choose to ignore someone else's prejudices and love my brothers and sisters in Christ as God has commanded.

The enemy throws these arrows at us to cause us to fall from grace. Satan knows our weaknesses and comes during our most vulnerable moments. The enemy will attack what we value the most and when we are in dire needs. Every time we experience a stormy situation in our life most times, we can see Satan behind it. Satan's attacks are so subtle that if we are not careful, we will fall for the lies. We must know when the thoughts are not of God and rebuke them before they turn into cancer and spread. Church members can't go on listening to the lies of the devil and continue to act like his offspring.

It's time that the true believers recognize who they are in Christ and think on things that are pure and pleasing. Our attitude should reflect Christ-likeness, holy and acceptable to God. Our God is interested in what is happening inside of our heart and mind.

CHAPTER NINETEEN

APOSTLE PAUL

The secret of the Apostle Paul's spiritual life was his strong attitude and pursuit to accomplish that which he made up his mind to do.

When I became a Christian for the first time at thirty-five years old, I didn't only fell in love with the Messiah Jesus, but I also fell in love with Paul of Tarsus. I would tell people that they should be like Paul because he was such an ardent follower of Christ Jesus after his conversion. I thought that if everyone who attended church would be more like him, there would more lives saved for the Kingdom of God. To me, he was such a great evangelist and missionary. The same way he went after the Christians to persecute them was the same way he went after the lost souls after his conversion. Paul was a zealot for the Pharisees in persecuting Christians. He was an Israelite and a descendant of Abraham from the tribe of Benjamin, (Roman 11:1.) Paul encouraged the followers of Christ Jesus to greet one another with a "holy kiss" (Romans 16:16.) Paul knew Jesus personally and intimately.

What do we have to do to have an attitude like Paul?

We must love Jesus Christ with all of our being like Paul did. We must change our attitude to reflect Christ Jesus. When the disciples heard that Paul wanted to meet with them, they were fearful because of Paul's reputation for persecuting Christians, but Paul proved himself over and over again that he was truly following Jesus Christ and that his desire to serve was great. So just like Paul, we must have a great desire to serve God in whatever He puts us to do. We must be devoted to God and serve Christ in what pleases Him. After Paul's conversion, all he wanted to do was to serve and help his fellow Christians stay safe. Paul wanted others to know Christ as he did.

Although he was a tent maker, his job did not become a priority, but his ministry to save souls became his main objective. We too must follow Christ, and our personal lives should not interfere with doing the work of the kingdom of God. There are too many lost souls for us not to go after just because we are too busy.

We must not allow ourselves to be distracted by the foolishness of church people whose only intent is to frustrate us and make us walk away from our calling. Paul was faced with church people's many issues but always encouraged the brethren to resolved them among themselves.

Paul had a new direction in life when God stopped him on his way to Damascus and detoured him to go after the lost souls and tell them about salvation. We must ask God to give us a new direction that we may keep our eyes fixed on His direction and not ours. If we are to do the work of God as Paul did, we need a change in our attitude. God promises to give us a positive and blessed future if we stay the course and not allow the people in church distract us with their ungodly behavior. Like Paul who was determined to "finish the race" put before him. We too should be determined to do the will of God and press on toward the goal.

When we come to church, let us ignore the negativity and seek God's face in prayer. Paul walked with God on a daily basis and so should we. Let us seek God and hear from Him daily. One good discipline that we should implement to hear from God is through our daily Bible devotional. The most important discipline to God is the Bible and prayer. I love Jesus Christ who is God in the Son. I liked Paul who was completely human and whose style of living for Jesus should be an example for us. He became a zealot for the gospel of Jesus Christ and so should we.

Paul is a former persecutor of Christians knew first-hand the evil and the wickedness that permeated in people's hearts. He knew what awaited him from the Roman Jewish Pharisees who continue to persecute Christians and later the Emperor Nero of Rome who took to slaughtering them in their 'Circus Maximus."

159

Paul served the Kingdom of God from the years 34AD to 66AD when he was martyred in Rome his place of birth. Apostle Paul had the intellect and attitude on how to elude the enemy in the different towns and cities he visited where he planted churches. Apostle Paul the tent-maker who became the greatest Evangelist and missionary of his time knew just how to respond to his attackers in every situation because he knew that his God had called him for such a time. Paul suffered great pain but refused to give up for he knew his end was to be heaven-bound. [16]

"For our struggle is not against flesh and blood, but against the rulers, against the authorities, against the powers of this dark world and against the spiritual forces of evil in the heavenly realms" (Ephesians 6:12, NIV.)

Every person who has been called into the Christendom has a projection of life, a purpose, a prophetic calling and a destiny to fulfill. Everything that has to do with our gifts and talents will be used to share the gospel of Jesus Christ.

Historically these figures in the Bible gave their best to God. Adam, Abel, Enoch and Elijah, and Noah. Noah built the Ark. Abraham followed God to where He wanted him to go. He believed and glorified Him. Jacob fought with God to bless him and didn't let go until God blessed him. Joseph kept on trusting God through all his trial and tribulations and gave God his best. Moses, he looked ahead to God and what he had to endure to get there. Moses put all his treasures and pleasures aside for only to get to God. Joshua believed God about the promised land and went to possess it. He decided in his heart to serve the Lord. Samuel was a perfect example of a servant who listened to God. David loved being in the presence of the Lord. Daniel and his friends in the center of all corruption and in the center of the infamous king in the entire world trusted God with their lives and didn't contaminate himself with his surroundings. Nehemiah was confronted by a fearful population, but he reminded the people of God and His greatness. Jesus Christ, He came to do his Father's business. He prayed to the Father and did what the Father did and went to where the Father went. Jesus Christ was in constant communication with the Father God. We must listen to the voice of God in the intimacy of our secret place. We will recognize His voice, deny ourselves, and seek the kingdom of God.

Like the Apostle Paul, we too must press for the crown that awaits us in heaven.

God's chosen people will always experience spiritual attacks, but it is how we respond to them that will win us the victory. The enemy lives to attack us, and we must understand that we will be attacked daily so don't be surprised. We must learn to identify the emotions (emotions are normal reactions) that we go through when we are attacked. We will feel fear, anger, pain, anxiety, restlessness, and sadness. What we should not do is let the emotions take control of us but to keep in mind that God is with us always, that is a promise. God has a plan for you and me, and we should not take our focus from that promise. Those church members who the enemy, the devil, uses to attack us do it to take our joy away and for us to get discouraged. That is why it's essential to put on the whole armor of God (Ephesians 6:11-18) every day and claim the peace of the Lord within us. Wake up every morning and declare the word of God and give God thanks for everything. We are to go before God and humble ourselves surrender every situation and concern to Him in prayer. You and I know that we are vulnerable at times so we must be on guard at all times and know that the enemy is around always trying to trip us. Like the Apostle Paul who remained faithful to the end you and I can do the same when we keep our focus on the Lord then will we mature spiritually and be established in the things of God.

"For though we live in the world, we do not wage war as the world does. The weapons we fight with are not the weapons of the world. On the contrary, they have divine power to demolish strongholds. We demolish arguments and every pretension that sets itself up against the knowledge of God, and we take captive every thought to make it obedient to Christ" (2 Corinthians 10:3-5, NIV.)

CHAPTER TWENTY

CULTIVATE SALVATION

Let me reiterate that not every person who attends church is cantankerous. There are some good people in the church. Regardless of how some folks in church act I concern myself with my salvation. I was saved by the grace of God and the faith I have in Christ Jesus. I had to learn to cultivate my salvation, and it wasn't an easy task for me, and I will refuse to lose it on account of people who are ruthless in church. I must admit that at the beginning of my conversion I had a rocky moment in which I thought I had lost my salvation but God rescued me and His power kept me. I now know that God had already established a foundation for me and that foundation was Christ Jesus.

God is always around those who call on Him, and He will have their back. God desires to maintain a relationship and partnership with those who seek Him with an honest heart. Proverbs 9:10 (NIV), instructs us that, "The fear of the LORD is the beginning of wisdom, and knowledge of the Holy One is understanding."

We must fear and tremble in His presence for respect of who God is. God is revere at all times. We discredit God when we watch movies and television programs with extreme violence, profanity, adult jokes (considered corrupt speech in the Bible) nudity and sex. Those things are not pleasing to God. We must suspend with arguing with one another and complaining in the presence of non-believers. Let them see the light of Christ shine through us by our godly attitude and behavior toward one another. We must be a beacon to the lost world and not be in darkness because of our own short-comings. We will never be perfect, but we can seek to remain a clean vessel that God can use. We must develop an attitude without complaints that will be pleasing to God.

If you still don't have it right and are having difficulty with your negative behaviors then come to the feet of Christ Jesus, He will keep you from falling. If you happen to be a recipient of someone's negative attitude, then come to the feet of Christ Jesus and receive His peace and love.

Take Responsibility

We may continue to be the recipients of such negative behaviors in our church due to the mere fact that the church refuses to take responsibility for their actions.

The church should take responsibility for their actions and Christian behavior. The church has a responsibility to help restore our church family when they are in trouble instead of judging and condemning. It is the leaders, the elders, and the deacon's responsibility to put those who have fallen from grace back to where God had first called them. The church can no longer ignore nor tolerate such behaviors but acknowledge it and help restore them. The church is responsible for helping lift up the spirits of those who are hurting in the church. We need to help with compassion, sympathy, empathy, humility, and gentleness. We are to love those church members who have been weakened by their sin.

The church must choose a member who has the fruits of the spirit and is more capable of helping restore that member who has fallen. The church family should never despise anyone who has fallen into sin. We should not think ourselves better than them.

However, the church can only do so much for those members, and if they continue in their ungodly behavior, His grace is sufficient. All we can do for them is pray and trust God will change them.

Since my conversion, I have seen the shift from reverence to God to idolizing the world of technology and social media. When a church transitions from godly to ungodly behaviors it is so gradual that they don't even realize the shift. But there are warning signs they just choose to ignore them.

We should examine ourselves to see if we are still in the faith. We need to combine the word of God with faith warnings which are not to go back to the old self and displease God. Our idols are the cellphone, uncensored television programs and movies, love for money by working 2-3 jobs. In addition, believers should not stop attending church gatherings and fellowship but stop attending worldly parties and clubs.

I know that it is a daily struggle to live a sinless life. We must daily seek God, and examine ourselves, and ask Jesus to help us remain faithful.

Indestructible Faith

Back thirty years ago I believe that the church had great and indestructible faith, but something happened that brought about a change. I look around and see it in their demeanor when they come to church on Sundays, and during Bible study nights.

We need to be more in prayer and fasting for repentance to occur in the church. We need to activate the power of God with much praying and fasting. Faith comes from hearing the word that activates the faith. When the church hardens their hearts, the word of God will not stay in their mind and will never go down to the heart. That is why the faith of the believer has been affected.

In every church I have attended the last thirty years I can say with certainty that the church is made up of good and bad people. Jesus Christ gave us the explanation in one of His parables which I have expounded on in earlier chapters. The weed and wheat grow up together, and they look alike. The church is the maximum reflection of God's kingdom. God is the one that plants the word. The problems in the church will always be there and may never end. Because when a member wants to be a good seed, there are bad seeds in the church trying to distract and cause them to stumble. When the church becomes the light of the world, then hades itself comes against the church. But hades will resist God's word and teaching. History has always reflected that. In the church, there will always be a problem because God created it like that so we can learn to rely on God. God will help us to be above the problem. We are the problem. When we come with the light, the darkness will rebel against us. If we come with the truth, the bad will not receive it.

I noticed that there are members you can't relate to because of the barrier they put up. They refuse to give entrance to anyone in the church. They are those who pretend they are the most popular and most attractive and ignore what is going on around them. Then there are the members who choose to deny there is a problem with their behavior because people have tolerated them for so long and never challenged them to change. The church leaders would choose to weigh the problem and pick their battles allowing the problem to fester and corrode the bunch. Church members choose to lose faith and face the problem with uncertainty, believe that nothing will change. And, the members with the problem of negative attitude and behavior will continue to repeat what is wrong.

In the end, the leadership and the church must be able to distinguish between the bad seed and good seed and by using discipline rip out the bad seed. There will always be sin in the church.

When the church promotes Christian spiritual growth then will there be less bad seeds to contend with, and the bad seed will have to change in the end with time.

All scripture is God breath and useful for teaching, rebuking, correcting, and training in righteousness. The Scripture helps to equip us for the good work.

The Pastor is the person who should teach, rebuke, correct, and train. There is a method to do this. "If our brother and sister sins against us," (Matthew 18:15, NIV.)

The method is to take the matter privately first and then publicly. Our attitude should be Christ-like, humble and considerate. The good seed seeks God's guidance and sponsors the vision of the church.

165

While I was going through these unwarranted experiences with some of the church members, I enjoyed God in the process. I continued to grow in my spiritual life even though I sometimes ended up in the valley. But I never gave up but continue to believe God.

Jehovah is with us even when others reject us. Jehovah is with us even when we are in the desert, in the valley, in despair, when depressed, and when everything seems to be going wrong. Jehovah is with us in times of crises. We should live like we have God in our lives and not become bitter, discouraged, nor angry with Him. Jesus had to go through His own process as well so He knows what we go through sometimes. We are not exempt from going through such difficult situations at times. Jesus went through it in the worse way. Jesus had been through the desert, the valley in despair and tempted.

Understand God

To understand the process, we must see in the Bible what God did. God raised a prophet during the Babylonian times. The Prophet Isaiah understood what God had spoken to him. In everything, God has the last word. Jehovah will give us new strength. Jehovah will do a new thing in us. We will rejoice in the Lord Jesus always. Jehovah will enlarge our territory. He will increase our faith and spiritual life and use us wherever He wants. He will send us across the water and land. We are to take steps of faith. The enemy will not prevail over us because Jehovah is with us. We must choose to be like Jesus and Isaiah who enjoyed God in the process and did His will without faltering.

In this day and age, the world's culture and its religiosity have come into the church. The members have opened the door wide through for false prophets to enter and false teachings. They don't know who they are serving, God or the world.

In my observation, the church members have chosen the culture of the day and want less of God. Joshua spoke to the new generation to choose whom they were going to serve, God or the culture (Joshua 24:14.) The church members will be held accountable for what they do and say against God. The reason that we are on this earth is that God extended our lives and this is the gratitude.

Even if we are having difficulties with the culture attempting to erode the very fabric of Biblical truths that we hold dear to us we should always rejoice and be glad in God who keeps us and sustains us. God will allow it to only go so far until a revival breaks out.

Jesus Christ went to great lengths and at a high cost to give us life and that more abundantly. We should continue to thirst for spirituality and honor God. We need to stay focus so that we may be successful in our spiritual walk and in our personal life because both go hand in hand.

It wasn't easy for me when I was still a babe in the church to be treated badly by the same people who profess to love Jesus Christ, or when I changed churches to accommodate others. These were major distractions for me. I had allowed distraction to keep me from doing what I had been called to do. Even though I went through difficult moments I had to continue to thrive toward my goals, press on and not let the distractions stop me. I kept right on seeking the Lord until the Lord heard my prayers and answered them. In the parable of the judge and the widow, she demonstrates persistence. If we are persistent God will be just, and He will answer our prayers and meet our needs.

Don't give up because our victory is at hand. Everything worth having requires persistence no matter what. I can say with certainty that I will not allow myself to be distracted again. Try not to get distracted by any of these emotions and thoughts.

> Do you think about past betrayals?
> Do you blame yourself or others?
> When you are struggling with something, do you quit?
> Are you fearful about the future?
> Are you easily discouraged?

The real question is who has all the power in the world? God still has all the power.

There will be times when we feel overwhelmed and frustrated with the church, but it's alright because that is when God shows up and gives us His grace to help us move beyond the situation. It's during those times we need to pray, fast, and speak to God about our situation and he will answer us. God's grace isn't to be taken for granted but it is offered to His children.

Never be anxious for nothing, because we have power over the devil. So, we will rejoice and cast all our cares on God. He will give us peace in the midst of the situation. Pastor John Hagee says, "worry is like a waste of time." As soon as we become children of God, He is our Father and will take care of us and provide a way out of every unpleasant situation.

Form of Godliness

Some church members have a form of godliness they subscribe to. They are neither hot nor cold for God. They attend and participate in church activities and events but are not truly walking or talking the same language as God. There were several ladies in the church in Midwest that were odd. I call them odd because they attended the church year after year and didn't get love meant. The word of God doesn't say love only the ones you want and ignore the others. Every time I saw them, I would greet them because if I didn't greet them, they would ignore me and that would be awkward. They rarely spoke to anyone unless someone initiated the conversation. As customary I would embrace my sisters in Christ with a godly kiss and hug and most of them reciprocated. But with these two, it was like hugging a corpse. I think it bothered them to return the greeting (my estimation). Several times I made attempts to have a social conversation with them, but it was like pulling teeth. I began to feel uncomfortable with them because it was hard to engage them and they would not budge. I was afraid to appear to be unsociable by the other sisters if I didn't keep trying to engage them. One of them made me feel like an idiot because whenever I said something to her, she would turn it into a question, "do you mean to say this?" She would turn what I say around and use her own words to explain to me what I was saying. Sometimes I didn't want to talk to her because I would feel intimidated by her. I think she did that on purpose so that I would not talk to her (my estimation.) In the three years that I knew her, I never felt any genuine love pour out of her for anyone, but I didn't let up on her because I was told by my God to love her regardless of her behavior toward me. The other female actually yelled at me in front of everyone. This incident happened after being around her for about three years. She never greeted anyone when she walked in, at least while I was around. Most times, she would have a sour-looking facial expression and most of the other sisters stay away from her.

One of the Latina sisters told me a story about the time she and two others share a hotel room with this female. The Latina spoke very little English. The Latina told me that this sister made her cried because she screamed at her so loud that the other roommate felt so sad for her. She kept on ranting about the Latina not speaking English until the Latina left the room with all of her belongings. I got to see her anger that one day she screamed at me "I DON'T WANT TO HUG YOU." I walked around and gave every one of the sisters a godly greeting, and when I reached her, I did the same, and her arms were down by her side, and I gently and quietly said to her hug me back and she screamed at me those words. Everyone in the place stopped what they were doing and stare but then they chose to ignore the incident, and it was business as usual.

Know whom you are walking with and make sure that you are not going to counsel with the ungodly. Without love, we are not walking right. We should be known for our godly behavior and attitudes. Wherever we go in this culture, they should know that we are Christians. Whether it's our place of work, church, home, and in our social relationships, people must see a Christ-likeness in us. We should be edifying and loving one another. We should be operating under the word of God at all times. I choose to walk with God. Who are you walking with?

The wicked will be picked up by God and tossed in the fire. Bless is the one who doesn't sit with the wicked. Watch where we have been walking, who we have been walking with, and see what we have done. "We must delight ourselves in the law of the Lord" (Psalm 1:1-3, NIV.)

I have chosen to feed on God's unconditional love and not worry whether any of my brothers and sister in church love me. They didn't deliver me from my pagan lifestyle God did. They didn't shed their blood for the forgiveness of my sins Jesus Christ did. God loves you and me so much, and I know He will not withhold anything from us. We should get so excited just knowing that even if no one else loves us God loves us, and to know this is to live in peace. As God loves us, we should transmit that love to others.

> "Who shall separate us from the love of Christ? Shall trouble or hardship or persecution or famine or nakedness or danger or sword? As it is written: "For your sake, we face death all day long; we are considered as sheep to be slaughtered." No, in all these things we are more than conquerors through him who loved us. For I am convinced that neither death nor life, neither angels nor demons neither the present nor the future, nor any powers neither height nor depth, nor anything else in all creation, will be able to separate us from the love of God that is in Christ Jesus our Lord. Who should separate us from the love of God." (Romans 8:35 39, NIV).

Righteous Conscience

My story is to help create a righteous conscience and what it's like to be righteous. Righteous means to have a moral compass that reflects Christ Jesus, the son of God. Unrighteousness means to have a hardened heart to the things of God.

Righteous people give thanks to the Giver of life and are passionate about blessing others with the gospel, their time, and love. The righteous don't have anything to do with those who blaspheme the Lord, who gossip about others, and who like to get over on others. Instead, they seek peace and are pacifiers and are not around trouble-makers or problematic people.

The major crisis in the church today is that people are living the unrighteous life and are faking godliness. An unrighteous person is a liar and justifies their lies and has made it a state of mind by attending church and all the church activities and events.

I know that that we all come short of the glory of God, but some of the Christians are trying to live right before God in a culture that has gone immorally mad. I believe that church people can live in this culture and still be righteous if they truly follow Biblical sound doctrine and stay true to God. All we basically have to do to be a righteous person is seek the presence of God in the temple of the Lord and bow down to God. Humble ourselves before the Lord. Share our blessings with others. Share with the sick, afflicted, sad, hopeless, and considered worthless and lift them up.

The righteous should not fear but believe and trust in He who moves the stones out of our way.

I choose not to depart from the presence of the Lord no matter the craziness around me or the maliciousness of church people that may impede my walk with Him.

Church people believe the culture that thinks it's crazy to believe that Jesus lives and they forget about God's promises and are blind to what Jesus had done for them before.

We must never forget that God is the one who moves distractions that are getting in the way of His plans from going forth.

We should not be sad, miserable or in distress over things that the ungodly are doing in the church. We must be in prayer and fasting for the redemption of their soul and do whatever we can in the kingdom of God. I will pray that their eyes will be opened and that they will have that burning in their heart when they first loved Jesus and felt His spirit.

I know that God has His eyes on you and me even when church people overlook us.

CHAPTER TWENTY-ONE

WHERE IS THE COMPASSION?

Like my friend Cecilia who was completely ignore by a female church member who sat to the right of her in a church that one evening I was also over-looked almost every time, I attended church. For the most part, I had to force the greeting from church members.

Every now and then I would take my grandchildren to church with me and believe it or not they would also receive the same treatment as I did. No one would take the time to greet them as we entered the building or when approaching the pews. They are children, so they don't notice things like that, but it's still hurtful.

My son was visiting me for the weekend, and I invited him to the church that Sunday and I regretted it to this day. When we got there the pew I usually occupy was taken, so we sat several pews back and maybe five seats in toward the center. I had registered his name as a first-time visitor (even though he had been at the old church fourteen years earlier) and even put my name as the one who invited him to church. When the minister called out the first-time visitors, they mispronounced his name and when it was time for the church to come to welcome the visitors with a godly greeting no one came over to greet him. He was completely ignored (and they were greeting others for at least five minutes.) I wanted to cry because it hurt me so much that my son (a grown man) was overlooked by the church ministers, deacons, and the rest of the members. No one stopped by our pew to greet him when they were greeting others around him. My son didn't want to come to church, but he did, and that was how he was treated. He was not blind to see that every new visitor was being greeted except for him. I had been so excited that he had come to church with me that I even asked him to stand up so everyone can see him (I am very proud of my son, a Marine) but I was soon saddened by the behavior of the church.

I remember the day the Shepherd of the house presided over my son's wedding. My son had just returned from the Marines Corps Bootcamp. He told me about having a conversion with one his Marine Instructors about the girlfriend and baby he had left behind to join the Marines Corps and the issue about marriage came up. My son came home thinking that it was his responsibility to marry his girlfriend and raise their child together as a family. As soon as he came home from Parris Island he and I spoke with the Pastor about setting the wedding date. The Shepherd met with my son and his girlfriend, and the date was set. It was a private wedding with only the immediate family. My son was married at my church, and the reception was at the bride's parent's home.

I thank God for people like my former pastor (went to be with the Lord). Like him, there will be no other. He was truly a man of great integrity and compassion who knew how to love people.

Integrity is what God wants from those who profess to be Christians. That even when we falter in our Christian walk, we can come to God and ask "create in me a pure heart, O God, and renew a steadfast spirit within me" (Psalm 51:10, NIV.) The Lord is looking for people of character who will seek him and follow His commands.

Change Your Attitude

Anything that is not pleasing to God we need to change. God didn't spare us and preserved our lives so that we may continue to behave like the devil's offspring. The church will continue to create dysfunctional members while the divine order is in chaos. God will in the latter days turn the hearts of people toward Him. But in the meantime, He is looking for godly men and women who will put their trust in Him that He may guide and instruct them in the way they should treat one another in their family, in the church, and at their place of employment. There has to be some kind of order in the life of the believer for God to show up. We do not know the day or the hour of our death, but we will die, and there are only two places that await us on that day, it's either we rest in heaven and feast in the presence of the Almighty God, or we live in Hades for eternity.

When the Prophet Elijah went to Hezekiah to tell him to get his house in order because he was going to die. Hezekiah was distress by the news and chose to pray to God and remind God of how he was living his life for the Lord. This prayer moved God, and he gave Hezekiah fifteen more years of life. God had a change of plans. (2 Kings 20:1-6a, NIV.)

Take the example of King Hezekiah who was on the verge of death and prayed to God and reminded God of His promises. As believers in the Almighty Savior, we must not stay down when we are faced with challenging times but get up and focus on the one who made us. Christians must be established in God. In whatever state we find ourselves we should be content. When our pastors and church family are not available, we must speak to the Lord who can make a way out of any situation. We will not fret because no situation is too difficult for the Lord. Difficult situations will always be around but know that God in whom we trust is in control.

We should not be moved from trusting God regardless of how much we are hurt in the church. It takes confidence in the true and living God to have joy and be stress-free when circumstances around us seem to be contrary to the belief. My Bible, tells me to come to the feet of Jesus when I am drained and torn between what to do in a given situation (Matthew 11:28.)

In our walk with the Lord, there has to be a period of rest and know that God will provide a way out of an uncomfortable situation. I was not called into God's kingdom to go through so much stress especially caused by the members in my own church. Stress is not of God because it brings sickness and diseases. It's the number one silent killer and something to be considered as very serious. The National Institute of Mental Health (NIMH) shares this report about stress;

"Routine stress may be the hardest type of stress to notice at first. Because the source of stress tends to be more constant than in cases of acute or traumatic stress, the body gets no clear signal to return to normal functioning. Over time, continued strain on your body from routine stress may contribute to serious health problems, such as heart disease, high blood pressure, diabetes, and other illnesses, as well as mental disorders like depression or anxiety." [17]

I am not implying that attending church causes people to get stressed out but what I am saying is that certain situations can be stress producing. How many times did I hear the members complain about needing more member participation for certain events, but only the same group of people would show up. In a congregation of three to four hundred, only thirty to forty volunteers to do the work and I would see the frustration and disappointment in their face and hear it in their voice. Before I came to the realization that it's not my job to worry; I did worry. But I will choose to rest in Him even when I don't understand the reason for my troubles because God's promises assure me that this too will come to pass.

Follow the Instructions

The scripture is written for instruction and guide so that we will not sin. The scripture is full of God's compassion to remind us that Jesus is our strength in our weakest moments. Jesus understands our sorrows and pains because he himself experienced these same emotions in the Garden of Gethsemane. "Then he said to them, "My soul is overwhelmed with sorrow to the point of death (Matthew 26:36-46, NIV.) Jesus is our friend who loves us, restore us, and returns us to our place when we fail.

When we rebel against God, we are telling God that we want our independence from Him. It's a mistake that Christians make when they try to manage their lives without God. There will be negative results. The moral values will fall into degradation. We end up doing things that are not pleasing to God. We will never be happy, and misery will creep in. We lie to ourselves and begin to descend into the pit of destruction. We end up alone with our failed condition when we don't listen to the voice of God calling us to stop our sinful behavior.

Regardless, of how callous some Christians in the church have been to you and me God still loves them and desires that they repent and turn from those ungodly behaviors. But as for you and me, we must stay the course and trust that God will work it out for us. We will never stoop to their level and act as they have acted toward us. We must understand that they have lost their way, but God will restore them as well as us.

It's at our lowest level that we are restored. We begin to be restored when we remember who God is in our life. We must go to the Father in prayer and supplication to heal us and those who have hurt us. We must confess our sins and confess that Jesus is our Lord and Savior. We must acknowledge that we are not worthy to be in the presence of the Lord so who are we to judge. But at this time, we can receive God tender mercy and love if we come to Him. Real restoration comes from God, but the Holy Spirit will return us to the place we should be spiritual. God wants to be the manager of our lives. He will protect us, provide for us, and gives us a successful future. We must trust Him, and all His promises will be yours and mine.

> "The son said to him, 'Father, I have sinned against heaven and against you. I am no longer worthy to be called your son.' "But the father said to his servants, 'Quick! Bring the best robe and put it on him. Put a ring on his finger and sandals on his feet" (Luke 15:11-22, NIV).

PART THREE

LOOKING AHEAD

CHRIST JESUS OUR LIVING HOPE

Praise be to the God and Father of our Lord Jesus Christ! In his great mercy, he has given us new birth into a living hope through the resurrection of Jesus Christ from the dead, and into an inheritance that can never perish, spoil or fade. This inheritance is kept in heaven for you, who through faith are shielded by God's power until the coming of the salvation that is ready to be revealed in the last time. In all this, you greatly rejoice, though now for a little while you may have had to suffer grief in all kinds of trials. These have come so that the proven genuineness of your faith—of greater worth than gold, which perishes even though refined by fire—may result in praise, glory and, honor when Jesus Christ is revealed. Though you have not seen him, you love him; and even though you do not see him now, you believe in him and are filled with an inexpressible and glorious joy, for you are receiving the end result of your faith, the salvation of your souls.

...Therefore, with minds that are alert and fully sober, set your hope on the grace to be brought to you when Jesus Christ is revealed at his coming. As obedient children, do not conform to the evil desires you had when you lived in ignorance. But just as he who called you is holy, so be holy in all you do; for it is written: "Be holy, because I am holy."

Since you call on a Father who judges each person's work impartially, live out your time as foreigners here in reverent fear. For you know that it was not with perishable things such as silver or gold that you were redeemed from the empty way of life handed down to you from your ancestors, but with the precious blood of Christ, a lamb without blemish or defect. He was chosen before the creation of the world but was revealed in these last times for your sake. [21] Through him, you believe in God, who raised him from the dead and glorified him, and so your faith and hope are in God.

Now that you have purified yourselves by obeying the truth so that you have sincere love for each other, love one another deeply, from the heart. For you have been born again, not of perishable seed, but of imperishable, through the living and enduring word of God.

1 Peter 1:3-9, 13-23. (NIV)

CHAPTER TWENTY-TWO

LIFE WORTHY OF GOD

I understand that nothing is new under the sun. The church has always been a mess, and it will continue to be that way until Jesus return. Meanwhile, we have a responsibility to live a life worthy of God if we are following after Christ Jesus. I could not have worded it any better than the character in this movie titled, Sheffey. He touched upon the condition of the church in such a way that it broke my heart. The church was headed toward the direction of insensibility in the 19th-century. Much can be said about the 21st Century church in that seems it too have arrived at the station of insensibility. This movie is based on a true story. I don't think it was coincident that I found this movie on YouTube one night after I had done some writing for this book. I was captivated by a conversation the Evangelist Sheffey was having with a young man in the revival tent after everyone had gone home. With sadness in his voice, Sheffey tells the young man the following,

> "Do you see the new attitudes creeping up among your leaders? They want to call themselves Christians because it's respectable, but they try to tear down everything that Christianity has ever been based upon. They say that Christ is not the Son of God, but they try to support a religion that's based on this very fact. They claim that the Bible is only a human book but everything they know about religion is based on it. They claim to follow Christianity and deny everything that Christianity has ever taught. [There] are many good men but they seem to have less influence. It's always the liberal attitudes that are attractive… My choice

is easy, or rather it's already made… But I am determined
to follow the leading of the Lord anyway."[18]

We can live godly, upright, and self-controlled lives by the grace of
God. His grace brings salvation and redemption through the Blood of
the Lamb. Christ Jesus has washed and redeemed us to live for God.

However, there are those in the church who have stopped loving
God, and they don't respect Him any longer. They feared God when
they were first saved and baptized, but after some time they became
complacent, and at that point, they have lost the fear of the Lord. But
they are fooling themselves when they ignore the sins they commit
because God is not blind. Whatever has come upon the church God
has allowed it, and we will be bothered by it, but God will bring us
out of the depths of it.

> "For the grace of God appeared and offered salvation
> to all people. It teaches us to say "No" to ungodliness
> and worldly passions, and to live self-controlled, upright
> and godly lives in this present age, while we wait for
> the blessed hope—the appearing of the glory of our
> great God and Savior, Jesus Christ, who gave himself for
> us to redeem us from all wickedness and to purify for
> himself a people that are his very own, eager to do what
> is good. These, then, are the things you should teach.
> Encourage and rebuke with all authority." Do not let
> anyone despise you" (Titus 2:11-15, NIV.)

The church in America and in other nations have chosen to
ignore the fact that God is real. And as they turn from the truth they
then chose to become the servants of the deceiver, Satan.

John Bunyan was an evangelist who was incarcerated several
times for preaching the gospels. He wrote the *Pilgrims Progress*. He
writes about this character in his book named "Shame." Although
written in 1678 it still holds true about mankind and their secular
way of thinking. This man Shame "believed in his mind that for

a man to follow after religion was to be" unmanly." Mr. Bunyan wrote this truth about the church back in the late 17th century and how people were ashamed of being a Christian, especially the male figure. Today over four centuries later the church members are still ashamed of Christians, especially the male.

In the church, there are members who are ashamed (male & female) of the gospel. They come to church on Sunday for form and fashion, and to inflate their ego and act self-righteous, but the rest of the week they live like the heathens they are. No one in their neighborhood, place of employment or any place they frequent know that they are Christians. I am talking about people who grew up in the church from birth. Their attitudes and their behaviors tell a different story.

"Ignorance of the Law is No Excuse"

Like some of the characters in Pilgrim's Progress, there are members in your church and mine who are ignorant in their belief regarding Christendom. Mr. Bunyan writes about a man named Ignorance. Ignorance had come out of the Country of Conceit. Ignorance follows the religion that he thinks to be the one true religion of his country. And does not believe that the narrow way is the only way to come into the kingdom. He believes that good works are going to get him in and Mr. Bunyan writes this about him.

> "Let Ignorance a little while now muse
> On what is said, and let him not refuse
> Good counsel to embrace, lest he remains
> Still ignorant of what's the chiefest gain.
> God saith, those that no understanding have,
> Although He made them, Them He will not save."[19]

The ignorant Christian thinks in his/her mind how to get to heaven. They looked at the true believer as if they are the ones making up stories about heaven. These people fool themselves believing their own theology. Ignorance of the Bible will get you in trouble all the time. The Bible could not state it any clearer, "The fear of the Lord is the beginning of wisdom, and knowledge of the Holy One is understanding (Proverbs 9:10, NIV.)

God is warning His people to let go of the carnal stuff in their life and their form of godliness because there is no time for foolish behaviors. We must be spiritually prepared to do God's will.

So, the church must begin by truly repenting of their sins and live holy as God is Holy. God desires we walk in the straight and narrow. He guarantees to make our crooked way straight. In my Christian, I have taken several detours from God's path, and have led a crooked path, but He made it straight for me. I know he can do it for you as He did it for me. All we have to do is be in the will of God and stop playing church. We need to live holy before the Lord. There is nothing better than letting God direct us and guide us. We must be put in a place where God is in charge of our every move and receive His permission for everything. We must aim for something that is larger than life.

It goes back to what kind of people are we affiliating ourselves with that is causing us to sin. We need to study ourselves to show ourselves approved to God. As long as we seek God, we will have goals and strive for perfection. The Scripture reminds me that what God started He will finish it. The goal must be to do great things for God. Ask what we can do for the kingdom. Don't do anything without the Holy Spirit. God is in our future and has plans for us. If we are going to be successful, we need to focus our eyes on Jesus and direct our attention to Him.

In the novel by William Golding, *Lord of The Flies*, written in 1954, it depicts a group of young British schoolboys during WWII who are stranded on an island after the plane they were on was shot down by an enemy plane and what happens on that island is frightening. When these boys ignore every principle of humanity, they have learned to engage in barbaric behaviors toward one another it demonstrates the lack of moral leadership. They were following the wrong leader to guide and instruct them who failed to have a moral compass.

The most important walk with God is when we live right after we leave the church on Sundays or Bible Study group and go into the world. To know how to act outside of the church, we must know the word of God and put it into action. We have to give an account to God for every word we speak and every negative action against our brethren.

We should not be gossiping or creating division among the church members or against anyone in general. We should not use the same tongue that we praise God to curse anyone. We must surrender our lives, our thoughts, and our lips to God on a daily basis. We must be watchful of what we say and do so as not to offend God nor anyone else. The tongue is an evil member of the body. The tongue can kill the joy of a newcomer to Christendom. The tongue can't be tamed but disciplined by God when we determine in our hearts to walk and talk like our Lord Jesus.

God is not only a disciplinarian, but He is also a life preserver. Through God we are sanctified, strengthen, and made holy. When we are saved, we are separated from the world's way of life.

In the Bible passage found in Numbers 14, it reads about those who died in the desert for not believing that God was able. So, in His anger, He told Moses that those who were over 21 years of age and older would die in the desert and that those who were 21 years of age and younger would live and God would teach them of Him and His kingdom. These people had lost their opportunity to be saved and save their families. The same will happen to us if we continue to put God to the test with our ungodly attitudes and lack of belief.

But follow the example of Caleb and Joshua, they never lost their hope and faith in God but believed, and God preserved them. God is our Preserver. God will preserve us if we want to be preserved so that by His strength, we will help preserve others in our churches, communities, and the nation.

God called us to intercede in lamentation for the salvation, deliverance, and redemption of others.

Lamentation

Lamentation is to cry out in great sorrow whether it is for someone or something. The church should be grieving for their lost family, for lost relatives, neighbors, friends, and co-workers.

God called Jeremiah to prophesize to the people of Judah of the impending doom that was coming because they did not turn from their wicked and sinfulness. Jeremiah cried out to God for mercy, and he cried out to the people to stop their rebelliousness toward God and stop worshipping other gods. Jeremiah cried out to the nations to repent and pray for their nation and its people, but only a few listened. So, as believers in the word of God and followers of Christ, we must pray for this nation because the children are being lost to the world.

The way I see it instead of the church fighting among each other we should all be lamenting for a change to occur within ourselves, within our families, the communities, as well as, the nation.

We don't have to look far to see what is happening in our nation today with the school killings, the prayers not allowed in the schools, the Ten Commandments being taken out of government buildings, the infestation of the drug abuse and addictions and drug dealing in our streets; the legalizations of recreational Marijuana (a gateway to other drugs), the senseless killings of young men, especially Black men. Just look around, the Department of Children separating the families by removing young children from their homes, parents losing control of their children's discipline because the courts have interfered in the child-rearing, euthanasia, assisted suicides, killing of unborn babies.

In the arena of the moral decline of our nation, in our homes, and in our churches. The disrespect of the elderly by the younger generation, and the rampant increase of dishonesty and deceitfulness in our church, and the government in our homes. As a people of the Most-High God, it is our obligation to cry out to God to save this nation. We must pray from the heart. Pray that God will save our children and their families. Pray that God will save the people who run the systems of this land, starting with the government. Christians are called to serve and lament on behalf of one another in church and on behalf of the unsaved.

We have not been called to serve for just a little while as Christians but to serve for life into eternity.

Don't be included in the breaking away from Biblical moral standards as the culture has been flagrantly doing. It is sad to say, but the reality is that the culture of the secular world is becoming more appealing than God.

Keep It Sacred

I couldn't believe what I was hearing from the pulpit one Sunday morning because it sounded like something one would hear in a secular protest rally. I know that at times the preacher would use the pulpit as an opportunity to get an important point across to the congregation pertaining to their health, security, and social well-being. But this was more like bashing pastors from other churches and making derogatory statements toward the membership of that church. I felt the tension and heard the anger in the preacher's voice. I didn't think it was appropriate to address such hostility at that time or in that place. The pulpit is the altar of God it's not a place to curse nor condemn anyone. The preacher was looking for his members to agree with him against another church family in condemning them for whatever reason (my estimation.)

Sometimes in our lives, we want to take revenge against our enemies. We want to take revenge against them because we are so fed up with the stuff, they have done to hurt us. We have been hurt in the past, and we want it to stop. We mustn't do things that will hinder our spiritual walk and our work in the kingdom. If we allow ourselves to be driven by our emotions, we will cause our walk with God to falter and ruin our reign with God. Let us be extra careful how we react to the hurts inflicted upon us in church and guard ourselves against ourselves.

In the story of David and the landowner, it is clear how easy it's for a people to lose control of their emotions when they are deeply hurt and want to retaliate. He had been foolish and wicked in David's site, but Abigail goes to David and tells him, "do not give yourself grief if you take Nabal's life." Abigail (the wife) went out to save her home and family and also had a concern for others when she met with David and spoke with him as she shared her food and other items with his men. Nabal's name means 'fool,' and he behaved as such by his actions when David sent his men to ask him for food to feed his men, and he refused. (1Samuel 25:23-33, NIV.)

Who is the Nabal in your life? Behind this person, there are people like Abigail who love God. Be careful what we say to the fools in our life because we will hinder our future with God. Don't take revenge but be at peace with yourself.

During that service, I was so appalled at what I heard that I got up and left the service because his ranting went on for a while. I realized that I didn't want to sit through the barrage of insults against another church and against his own members.

The service had nothing to do with scripture or with God. If we know there are members doing foolish things in our church, we must let them know. But we must wait on God who will send us to this person to speak His words. It is because of the foolishness of some church members that believers find reasons to turn away from God. They also refuse to believe the preachers because of their outright hypocrisy. The Priesthood is a very serious calling of God, and some preachers are giving it a bad reputation.

People are violating the laws of God in the church by using the church as a social club where they can do whatever they want, even bash people in the pulpit. There is a spirit of lawlessness, iniquity, and rebelliousness against God stemming from the church.

Those who are rebellious and stubborn are spirits that don't listen no matter how much God speaks to them because they don't want to live according to God's will. They will not even listen to their Pastors. People in this culture don't want to live right, and the church is following right along-side with them.

But you and I will not be afraid to say yes to the Lord, and we will trust God to take us where He wants. You and I will be in the place where we say goodbye to the self and yes to the Lord. Saying yes to the Lord is to prepare us for our enemy who is coming. You and I will allow the Holy Spirit to inhabit this body and transform it to please God. You and I know that our body is not our own, it has been bought with a price when Christ Jesus died on the cross at Calvary.

You and I will stand in the freedom and confidence that God is with us always. We should not be afraid to speak what God wants us to say because God will bring us out victorious every time. Victory is in the power of our mouth, and God will let us speak ourselves into a blessing. You and I will be on trial because we believe in God, but we will not be moved. You and I will not be included in the break away from the truth of the gospels.

God need people that will serve Him with sincerity, integrity, and honesty.

Keep Legalism Out of It!

The problem is that there is too much legalism in the church. In the Old Testament, the Pharisees created their own concept about the law – Judean Law. It was their own interpretation of the law. They were very religious and judgmental. Pharisees believed that God looked at the external. In our day and time legalism is found in people who refuse to change their old way of thinking and of doing things.

They also refuse to become a new person and don't see beyond their own concept/interpretation of the law. They adopt ways that are their own, which makes it difficult to change when change is necessary for growth. Legalism is man fallen from God's grace. Legalism is what smothers the fire of the believer and push away people who are hurting.

Jesus reminds us that God made the Sabbath for a man to enjoy it. That it was God who brought Evangelism. He did it to free us from being slaves to sin, to give us victory over the enemy and restore in us new growth. Jesus came to save us from our sins and heal our wounds.

Legalism is here to silence the truth about Jesus. Legalism looks at people with indignation, anger, and harden hearts.

Legalism confabulates and seeks to hurt and devise ways to do just that. But Jesus looks at us with merciful eyes and heals us. The religious leaders of the time wanted to silent Jesus and conspired together to stop Jesus from speaking the truth. But Christ Jesus wanted to restore us to the Father in Heaven. The church of today has been breaking away from the Biblical truths and adapting their own way of delivering the Sunday message. <u>Tolerance is the new legalism in the church</u>.

Christians must be careful not to fall for the legality of the church but follow the way the Bible teaches. If it's not in the Bible, don't follow it. The church is adopting the new morality of the culture. We must walk like Jesus Christ did and not concern ourselves with what society is doing. Again, society has a way of civility, but we follow what the word of God tells us.

The Evangelist is the person who teaches the recent converts to lose their burdens. Deliverance is getting rid of the burden. When we are in the world, we don't feel the burden of sin until we realized as a child of God that we are sinners headed straight to hell. I reiterate legality does not set anyone free.

In the book *Pilgrim Progress* the character Christian is asked by Apollyon (symbolic for worldly things and the opposite of all that is good) where he is coming from and where is he traveling to. When Christians tell him, Apollyon responds to Christian with, "you must be one of my subjects because everything in that country is mine. I am the prince and god of it." Satan is the prince of the air and earth and if we are not serving Jehovah than we are serving Satan.

But you and I will keep right on sowing the seed of the gospel whether the world wants to hear us or not because there is someone out there who needs to hear and it is our calling to do it. They want to know who the God of the Universe is, and we must continue to be a witness for God and share Christ with them. There is a change when Jesus is in our life. Jesus helps us to get our thoughts and our lives in order when the things of this world come to bound us.

Most times Believers are bound by demons, and that is one reason they break away. There are principles we can learn from to protect ourselves from being bound by demons. The demons are manifested by violence, hostility and anger, and an attitude that threatens our moral judgment.

Demons bring their victims to desperation and despair. They bound them to promiscuity, altered lifestyles, addiction, and pornography. Demons cause us to hurt ourselves physically through, self-mutilation, and suicide. But Jesus came to rebuke demons. Those unclean spirits festering in some members.

Jesus came to heal the emotionally, mentally, and physically sick. Jesus came to offer salvation to everyone. You and I must go in the name of Jesus into our homes, to the place of work, into the grocery store, to our relatives, school, and even church to remind them that at the name of Jesus demons tremble and flee. (Mark 3:11) You and I will help restore the church to be a place of strength and growth to help our family.

Keep the Heart Pure

Another reason a believer may break away is that of a heart problem and not the physical kind. There is a hardness of the heart in some of the believers, and they are being deceived to tolerate the things of this world. The heart represents our person, our emotions, and our thoughts. The heart is also the center of our personality.

Our heart will guide the course of our life. Many conflicts come from our heart when we allow our thoughts to influence it. The most wicked and polluted things come from within the heart. When we entertain the sinful thought, we let temptation have its place, and it begins to fester in our heart. The heart can be deceitful. A member who carries around a hardened heart will come to church to sit and continue to leave unchanged. This is being religious which has nothing to do with having a relationship with God. Religiosity will not cleanse the heart.

> "Both Christians and non-Christians use the term "religiosity" to refer to those who have replaced their God with their religion. In Christianity, religiosity occurs when people focus on church activity, rules (which often go beyond actual biblical commands), tradition, and pet doctrines rather than on a relationship with God. Religiosity is characterized by a lack of grace, love, and true enjoyment of life. Religiosity for Christians is neither becoming nor appropriate. We are called to follow Christ, not promote a religion." [20]

God Jehovah will change our hearts and guard over it because He wants to live in it. We must choose not to go on living with a heart that is polluted and unclean.

The Book of Daniel is a perfect example of a believer who didn't allow himself to be contaminated by the culture and the gods of the world. "Shadrach, Meshach, and Abednego answered, "Your Majesty, we will not try to defend ourselves. If the God whom we serve is able to save us from the blazing furnace and from your power, then he will. But even if he doesn't, Your Majesty may be sure that we will not worship your god, and we will not bow down to the gold statue that you have set up" (Daniel 3:1-30, NIV.)

The decision to change our heart is ours when we believe in our heart and confess it with our mouth. Ask Jehovah God to cleanse your heart and guide you.

I learned a valuable lesson when I made a choice to path my own way and stepped out of the will of God. I had made a choice to marry someone God had warned me against.

Sometimes it may appear that God is not with us, but God is always observing us. God provokes us to see how we can manage what He has called us to do and wants to see how we respond to His calling. When our heart becomes hard, we have a difficult time understanding who God is. And, we also need the heart to understand who Christ Jesus is in our life.

Back then I thought I had a heart who knew God until I had that awful experience. But now I do have a heart that knows who God is and I will not go back to that awful place. Jesus has to be the heart of my life and your life.

CHAPTER TWENTY-THREE

TO MAKE THINGS
RIGHT WITH GOD

Are we going to believe in God or in the world?

I chose to believe in God and have a relationship with Him. I will no longer oppose God as He molds and makes me more into His likeness. I have a God who helps me as long as I believe in him.

"But because God was so gracious, so very generous, here I am. And I'm not about to let his grace go to waste" (1 Corinthians 15:10, MSG.)

Believe!

You and I must speak to God with passion believing Him for strength and blessings.

Let us determine in our hearts to learn to hear God and believe that He will always give us the victory from our enemies. If we truly believe to be faithful servants, then we must be submissive and obedient to our Sovereign God.

I have been able to survive the many trials throughout the years because of God's comforting love and sweetness as I feel His peace. The Bible tells me that, "In the same way, I tell you, there is rejoicing in the presence of the angels of God over one sinner who repents" (Luke 15:10, NIV.)

God is happy with us even when we don't deserve it. God saves us for His name sake and not because of anything we have done but because He is good and His mercy is forever. God's mercy is better than life. God's mercy and grace are expressions of His love toward us. The characteristics of God's mercy are expressed through His love, righteousness, and justice. God's love is steadfast as He blots out our transgressions. You and I must be a witness of His love to everyone around us, especially to our brethren.

God is watching us how merciful we are toward one another as well as to strangers, more so to them. Don't make God sad with our negative behavior toward each other. Remember that we should, "… not grieve the Holy Spirit of God, with whom you were sealed for the day of redemption" (Ephesians 4:30, NIV.)

Therefore, we must learn from God how to be merciful toward one another. Let us be kind and helpful to one another and forgive each other as God has forgiven us. Being merciful toward others is liberating for us.

There was a period in my life where I had a difficult time forgiving God, others and myself. I was bound for years not realizing that I had the key in my hand to free myself. It wasn't until I forgave that I was liberated. The liberating mercy is what we all need to express. You and I need freedom from negative attitudes and behaviors,

Believers should be empathic and put themselves in the shoes of the person who needs help and see what they want not what we want. Help should be genuine and honest, uplifting and edifying. Mercy facilitates forgiveness. We should never be in the business of judging but of building up. God sees the entire picture, and he is looking for a radical change in the church that will reflect His mercy and grace to all who visit. When church people are unkind and hurt people, God is displeased with them.

God knows our sins, and he establishes that we should present ourselves without sin before His presence for He is holy. We need to know God's characteristics, principles, and glory to understand that unkind treatment of any kind toward anyone is unacceptable to Him. When we violate the law knowing His Statues, the judgment is great. Let us strip ourselves from the sin nature, the old self that is corrupt. For the will of God is that we consecrate ourselves – set ourselves apart and be pure and remain holy. We have a God who knows us, sympathizes with us, and knows our proclivities and weaknesses. So, remember, if

God is holy, we too must also be holy. We must cleave to God's law and rely on Him through Christ Jesus who will intercede for us.

Many are called, but few are chosen. Matthew 22:14. When we are called, there is sanctity and a new wardrobe that God furnishes us with. The chosen will wear the clothes of worship, wait on the Lord, and put on humility. They will follow God and be faithful. God will offer us mercy, forgiveness, and a clean spirit to walk upright before Him. Jesus died that we will be made the righteousness of God to walk in humility, peace, and love.

Purposeful Living

Take the example of Joseph who was considered a faithful servant and made the minister of Egypt, second in command to the Pharaoh. His life was exemplary of a person who depended solely on God no matter the circumstances. He remained faithful to the end, and God blessed him beyond whatever he could have imagined. God chose him and gave him a vision in a dream.

Most if not all of God's chosen have a vision that He will bring to fruition if we remain faithful and stay the course of our calling. Like Joseph, if we remained faithful to God, He will make our dreams become a reality. I am writing my vision, and I see more to come. How about you? Will, you remain faithful and see your vision become a reality? I pray you will stay the course.

All God desires from us is to offer Him our complete obedience and let His purpose be our purpose. When God promises us supernatural blessings, He means to do just that. The purpose of God in our life is to do His will. The question we must be asking God is, what do you want us to do, Lord?

When we ask God for our purpose in the kingdom, we are to prostrate ourselves before Him and listen to what God wants us to do and through the Holy Spirit God who will speak to us.

We must not become restless waiting for God to use us because we won't be able to hear Him. Stay the course and do not deviate from it. In the Bible, there are instances of people God called, and they had to wait on Him to prepare and send them out. It took Paul three years to prepare for his ministry. In the book of Galatians Paul writes of having received his preparation from Christ Himself. "I want you to know, brothers and sisters, that the gospel I preached is not of human origin. But when God, who set me apart from my mother's womb and called me by his grace, was pleased. To reveal his Son in me so that I might preach him among the Gentiles, my immediate response was not to consult any human being. I didn't go up to Jerusalem to see those who were apostles before I was, but I went into Arabia. Later I returned to Damascus. Then after three years, I went up to Jerusalem to get acquainted with Cephas and stayed with him fifteen days.

I did not receive it from any man, nor was I taught it; rather, I received it by revelation from Jesus Christ" (Galatians 1:11-2:10, NIV).

God calls us to bear His name before the pagan world, but we must wait for God to send us out to do the ministry. God expects that we will remain obedient in our wait. Here are some examples from the scriptures of complete obedience to God. God is still looking for people like these in this present time. "God testified concerning him: 'I have found David son of Jesse, a man after my own heart; he will do everything I want him to do" (Acts 13:22b, NIV).

Noah was called to build the ark.

> "This is the account of Noah and his family. Noah was a righteous man, blameless among the people of his time, and he walked faithfully with God. But I will establish my covenant with you, and you will enter the ark—you and your sons and your wife and your sons' wives with you" (Genesis 6:8-22, NIV).

Abraham was called to move to another country. "The LORD had said to Abram,

"Go from your country, your people and your father's household to the land I will show you." "I will make you into a great nation, and I will bless you; I will make your name great, and you will be a blessing. I will bless those who bless you, and whoever curses you I will curse, and all peoples on earth will be blessed through you" (Genesis 12:1-3, NIV).

Moses was called to go to Egypt to free his people.

"Now I am sending you to the king of Egypt so that you can lead my people out of his country." But Moses said to God, "I am nobody. How can I go to the king and bring the Israelites out of Egypt?" God answered, "I will be with you, and when you bring the people out of Egypt, you will worship me on this mountain. That will be the proof that I have sent you" (Exodus 3:10-12, NIV.)

Queen Esther was put in the position to save the Jewish people for "such a time as this." "...And if I perish, I perish" (Esther 4:14-16, NIV.)

Mary was chosen to be the birth mother of Jesus, the Savior. "I am the Lord's servant," Mary answered. "May your word to me be fulfilled" (Luke 1:38, NIV.)

Jeremiah was called to call the people to repentance. "But blessed is the one who trusts in the LORD, whose confidence is in him" (Jeremiah 17:7-8, NIV.)

John the Baptist was called to Baptist the Savior – Christ Jesus. John replied in the words of Isaiah the prophet, "I am the voice of one calling in the wilderness, 'Make straight the way for the Lord" (John 1:23, NIV.)

Paul was called to bring the gospels to the Gentiles. "But whatever were gains to me I now consider loss for the sake of Christ.

I want to know Christ—yes, to know the power of his resurrection" (Philippians 3:7-11, NIV.)

Deborah was called to be a mighty warrior in battle.

> "Now Deborah, a prophet …was leading Israel at that time. … She sent for Barak. …The LORD, the God of Israel, commands you: 'Go, take with you ten thousand men of Naphtali and Zebulun and lead them up to Mount Tabor …Barak said to her, "If you go with me, I will go; but if you don't go with me, I won't go." "Certainly, I will go with you," said Deborah. "But because of the course you are taking, the honor will not be yours, for the LORD will deliver Sisera into the hands of a woman" (Judges 4:4-9, NIV.)

As you can see throughout the Scriptures, God has been calling on warriors who will take a stand and fulfill His purpose here on earth. You and I are the warriors that will say yes to Him with their whole heart, soul, and mind. God is not done looking for warriors in this day and age. You and I can be the warriors God is looking for this time.

I Want to Be Like Deborah!

When I was living in the Midwest, my friend Darla (one of the ladies in my dance team) is a tabret maker, and she made one for almost everyone in the team that requested one. Three months before she brought mine, I had this vision. I saw this vision three times in a span of several months. In the vision, I was told that I was to be a Deborah for this Century and almost every time I heard the voice fear would creep up on me. I would tell myself, "be realistic, people are not going to believe you are a Prophetess and they are not going to believe anything you say, and you're going to be embarrassed and ridicule." The night Darla gave me the tabret she handed me a handwritten card and asked me to read it before I saw my tabret. I opened the envelope and pulled out the card and read it. I couldn't believe what I read, "You are Deborah. God is calling you to be the Prophetess Deborah." I began to tremble with excitement and tears welled up in my eyes. I felt the presence of God, and I worshipped Him at that moment. The tabret was made with earth tone colors of beige and brown with gold. Darla and I never talked about my favorite colors nor did I share my vision with her. But God will call whom He so chooses to complete His purpose.

The vision is for the female warrior in you to awake the Deborah in you. God is telling the women in the church to wake up. God is calling the women of Zion to wake up and do His will. He is calling most of those women who have been in the Evangelistic ministry and those just beginning. Like Deborah, we must go and do what God wants us to do. You and I must decide to obey and follow God. Women in the church are called to be victorious in everything they put their hands to do. The single women are made to serve God until their helpmate is given to them by divine selection.

We must learn how to sit in peace like Deborah and forget those things that cause stress and anxiety. Let go of those things that will bring you down, and let God handle them because we have more pressing things to do for the Lord. The secret of Deborah was to be at peace. Philippians 4:7 reminds us that, "...the peace of God, which transcends all understanding, will guard your hearts and your minds in Christ Jesus." (NIV)

We need the peace that will empower us to go to battle. When things come to attack our home, family, health, job, we must not break down but stay calm and clear-headed to receive a word from God as to what to do. Confidence and peace can help the woman govern her life and those who surround her. Deborah knew who God was and so should we.

God wants to lift up women no matter the age for His purpose. Deborah heard the word of God and got into action mold awaiting His orders. She knew that with God on her side all things were possible. We must activate the Deborah in us. Our battle is not in the church. We come to church to be fortified and receive a word from God to go out and conquer the enemy in the community, in the nation, and in other countries.

We must activate all the women in the church, and God will give us strategic plans to go and do what He has called us for. We must first be saved and healed to serve the Lord and have a relationship with Him. Be a Deborah and stop being fearful and know when we are with God He will protect and keep us safe. Every gift and talent God has given us must be activated to be used in the church, the community, and in the nation. God wants to use valiant women in action.

In my former church, the intercessors would get together every Saturday from 9 AM to 12 PM. The majority were female members including the Pastor to pray for the family, the community, and the nation as well as other countries and Missions. I want to share with you my observations and estimations about the group's faith in God and their willingness to do kingdom work.

I sat in that group for six years and heard many prayers and conversations to form my opinion about the members desire to leave the four walls of the church to reach the lost. I also gathered the resistance to leave the four walls of the church. Like in the few churches I have attended the consensus of those who want to evangelize and those who do not want to change is almost the same.

In this particular group I concluded that most of the older members are complacent seeing visions for others to fulfill but don't see themselves going out into the community nor the nations to evangelize. The thirty-something and forties are comfortable being grateful to God for what He is doing in the church and in others, and they have yet to see the big picture because they are waiting for the leader to activate them. They talk about what needs to be done to evangelize and are willing to get involved but not on their own initiative. They will do the work, but someone else has to ignite the fuse. Some feel paralyzed to do anything perhaps because they are not fully equipped to take on the responsibility of a ministry. Others are comfortable giving God praise and worship in the sanctuary that will move mountains and hope something will miraculously happen to bring in the loss from the streets without they having to go out and get them. Some talk about being humble and obedient to God because it is the thing to do but offer very little to help the vision move forward. The others in their late fifties and early sixties make the decision to move out of the country believing God has told them to move but do very little to expand God's kingdom. Yet, there are those who allow the afflictions and difficulty of this world to strangle their dreams and visions for the church and God's kingdom. They are all godly men and women and want so much to see God's kingdom flourish here on earth but are too comfortable where they are.

They are called Comfortable Christians. Those people are comfortable with the way things are. Some church people just run Jesus out of town because of their "let things take their own course" attitude. God is telling the church that it's time to leave the comfort of the pews and the four walls of the church.

God's Agenda

I agree that we need much intercessory prayer in the churches, but we also need to activate and put those prayers into action. The church needs to get and stay connected to God and trust Him completely. The church members have been very disobedient, and it is time that they repent and get back into the word of God. They need to be equipped to share the gospel of Jesus to everyone.

The decision is ours to stay the course. God is getting ready to raise a new generation of warriors for such a time like this who will say yes. You and I should be telling the Lord to reveal His plan for us.

The Lord commissions us to go out to the four corners of the world and share the gospel with the lost souls. The Lord has prepared His church by giving us the gifts and talents to assist in our ministry. To some, He has given the role of the Apostles which is to be a spiritual leader and plant new churches where God sends them. To others the role of the Prophet who reveals the will of God. And, to the Evangelist the role of proclaiming the gospel to the people and the nations. The pastor's role is to take care of his church and teach them doctrines. The teachers are to cultivate the relationship that goes deeper into the issue and seeks explanations. Through our ministry, we will edify the church.

In one church I saw how the pastor took the lead role he was given and reactivated his church to go out into the towns, cities, and the nations and thus far he has planted several churches. This pastor saw the vision and began to equip his ministry leaders to accept his vision and help him bring it to fruition. He didn't allow his church to sit on their hands behind the four walls but moved those who were willing to get the work done. Like many churches, there is always a remnant that will say yes to the will of God and serve the kingdom. Imagine if every church member would follow the will of God how much more lives would be saved for the kingdom and how many more visions would come to fruition.

We must pray to God to reveal His plan for us. God wants to equip us to work in the ministry, but we must be willing servants. The church will reach unity in faith and become mature. Whatever we do let it be for the glory of God and let the church reflect His love unto everyone. Whatever we do is to edify the Lord. We should never be a hindering block to the church. There can only be one agenda in church, and that is God, and His kingdom and anything else will not work.

The agenda of God will always be greater than the enemy. Can there be two types of agendas operating in church? Sure, Satan is always on the prowl looking for someone who has not been delivered from the flesh. Those are members who are mean and cantankerous who displays such negative attitudes toward other members and newcomers.

God's agenda is to anoint us to be blessed, to bring us freedom, justice, and restoration. Satan's agenda is to seduce us and cause us to sin. Church members should always be vigilant and not ignore the agenda of Satan and his mechanics. Don't be caught unaware of his agenda. Satan wants to destroy what is of God in us. Every time we are moving to do something that God calls us to do Satan gives us a spirit of jealousy, envy, gossip, and hostility. He tries to destroy God's purpose in our lives. The pattern that the enemy uses is when the church is doing something for the kingdom of God, he will he creates conflicts, especially in leadership.

Satan will use his strategies to detour us from God's purpose in our most vulnerable moments when we are in pain, physically, mentally, and emotionally.

CHAPTER TWENTY-FOUR

THE DIVINE PRESCRIPTION

The church that God is looking for must humble itself in the act of humility, recognize their faults and their short-comings. This church must be transformed from worldly ways, behave godly toward one another and do the will of God. "If my people who are called by my name…" God will hear us, forgive our sins, and bless us and our land" (2 Chronicles 7:14, NIV.) This message is for the people who profess and confessed Jesus Christ as their Lord and Savior but are not living godly lives. God desires to have a church that will put Him first above anything and anyone.

The Church God Desires to Have…

The church that follows after God's thoughts is the church God desires to have.

The church that prays and looks for God with their whole heart, soul, and mind is the church God desires to have.

A church that will humble itself pray and seek God for every decision and plan they make in life is the church God desires to have.

The church that will seek God's ways and be transformed into His will is the church God desires to have.

Confession Is a Start

If we confess Jesus Christ for our lives, then we should be transformed from our sinful way and stop once and for all offending God the way we do. The church must stop all acts of sinful behavior, sexual immorality, impurity, debauchery, idolatry, witchcraft, hatred, discord, jealousy, fits of rage, selfishness, drunkenness, and corruption.

The Bible is clear in that the wicked will not inherit the kingdom of God. The church must put off falsehood and speak the truth in love. We are to work to feed ourselves and others from God's word and not from the world's immoral menu. It is the will of God that the church rid itself of every bitterness, rage, and anger, fighting and arguing among each other. Stop lying and slandering one another. Stop all malicious behavior because if we don't do it, God will give us over to our wickedness.

They are not secular people that God is admonishing but church people who know God and His laws but continue to do bad things. It has to stop! The church people who insist on being stubborn and unrepentant are storing up wrath for the day of judgment. God will not be mock. He gives us all according to what we have done. We need to repent while God can still be found.

When I was going through my disobedient stage after my conversion, I kept believing I was all right and that what I was doing was not bad. But my mind began to torment and accuse me of being a shameful sinner that I thought God would never forgive me for walking away from His will. It was not until I cried out to God to free me from my unforgiving spirit and repented, that I was liberated. Our conscience control by Satan's lies will hold us captive as long as we don't seek change.

The church has to change not the government nor the school system. The word of God instructs us, "If my people who are called by my name…" The church needs a spiritual revival because it is going through a spiritual crisis.

We must make a godly conscience decision whom we will serve Baal or Jehovah. God is calling the church to repent. "I am the light of the world. Whoever follows me will never walk in darkness but will have the light of life" (John 8:12, NIV.)

There is famous painting by Holman Hunt, *"The Light of The World"* that epitomizes the following scripture verse of Jesus' love for humanity and how He stands at the door of our heart waiting to be let in. The artist explained that the reason he didn't put a lock on the outside of the door in the painting was that we are the ones who allow Jesus to come into our lives if we are truly serious about Him. "Here I am! I stand at the door and knock. If anyone hears my voice and opens the door, I will come in and eat with that person, and they with me" (Revelation 3:20, NIV.)

Walk By Faith

Jesus is the same yesterday, today, and tomorrow. When we walk by faith, we trust and believe Jesus regardless of our problems, doubts, worries, negative influences, fears, and limitations. He will help us. I'm a living testimony and a recipient of His love and grace.

However, the option to believe and have faith is ours. So, let us give our lives to Christ and take that step toward the kingdom. Jesus is calling us to do something. We should never make it about us but about reaching those who will die in their sins because they don't know Him.

In the Old Testament, God called on Isaiah, and by faith, he went to prophesize to the people about the judgment of God. Ezekiel was called and by faith prayed for the lost souls and in a vision, he saw the dry bones come alive. Bartholomew was called by Jesus and by faith responded. The woman with the issue of blood came to Jesus in faith-believing that He would heal her. The Sanhedrin who asked Jesus to heal his daughter. Jesus told him to believe, and he believed.

God offers restoration daily. The church members need to be restored and reconciled to God, or they can choose to stay where they are. You and I will choose wisely and follow Jesus Christ, the savior of the world.

You and I must keep from being polluted by the world's culture but follow after righteousness. Let God cultivate the potential that is in each one of us and strengthen us with His power. Remember that God created the humans and had a purpose for them. Jesus will make that purpose flourish within us if we stay connected.

Therefore, let us continue to attend and stay connected to our local church. If God is calling us, we need to stop our excuses and go and evangelize. Speak with people everywhere we go and invite them to the party of salvation, deliverance, and redemption. You and I will go to everyone and tell them about the gospel of Jesus Christ and invite them to come for we know that God also has a purpose for them. In the parable in Matthew 22:1-14, Jesus tells this story,

> "The kingdom of heaven is like a king who prepared a wedding banquet for his son." "...The wedding banquet is ready, but those I invited did not deserve to come. So, go to the street corners and invite to the banquet anyone you find.' So, the servants went out into the streets and gathered all the people they could find, the bad as well as the good, and the wedding hall was filled with guests." (NIV)

When God calls His people, and they don't come, He then calls on the lost souls of the world. One of my former pastors made this declaration, "God doesn't accept excuses and never cancels His party." If my people...will stop making excuses, I will bless them.

Submit to Authority

If we want to follow Christ, we must deny the self.

It appears that for some people it's quite difficult to submit because their interest is more important than God's interest. What interest do we put before the kingdom? The Lord will put us through a test to see if we will deny ourselves and follow Him.

Jesus uses the parable of the rich man to illustrate this point of view. (Matthew 19:16-30, NIV.)

We must give up our pride and our personal gain and adjust

our lifestyle to what God wants without questions. God's goals and plans for us is what we should be looking forward to accomplishing.

Let us submit our dreams and aspirations and goals to God and see them come to fruition. Jesus submitted His will to God at the Garden of Gethsemane, and we have reaped the benefits of His submission. We need to say not my will, but God's will be done for a better future and for better results.

When I widowed, I was so upset with God that I made decisions without consulting Him, and that proved to be disastrous for my family and me. But God who loves me restored me to Him again. I love God more now than ever before because He loved me more and did not allow my disobedience to cloud His judgment.

We must pass through difficulties to get to where God wants us to get to, which is total dependence on Him. During those years where my head was on backward, and my priorities were backward. My perspectives were different, and I began to worship, (without realizing it) other things more than God.

When I finally came to my senses, I began to give God my undivided attention and destroyed all those idols and stumbling blocks. God deserves the best from me. I stopped my blaming and complaining instead I trusted God to take care of me for the rest of my life here on earth and for eternity.

The church needs to put God first in everything and change their "stinking thinking" attitude and see how things will work out. The church should know that God sees the end in the beginning.

We are called by God to be servants first, do good, and no harm, and above all give thanks to God for everything.

CHAPTER TWENTY-FIVE

FATHER ABBA HELP!

The church must return to the Father as the prodigal son returned to his father in the parable found in Luke 15:11-32, that points out that facet of God as the loving father who welcomes his lost, wayward church. God is our Father, and like sheep, we have strayed away, but He is waiting with open arms to receive us.

Our Father Knows Best

Fathers are an important figure in the home, especially if they are godly and righteous men.

It's important to understand that not all men make for a good father, but men can be good fathers with the help of God. To be a father means to accept their children the way they are. A father should supply their children's needs. Fathers should discipline their children without using excessive corporal punishment, and they should know when to comfort them and forgive them. A father should comfort their children and let them know that they can come to him for help when they need it. Father's should celebrate their children and love them for being their children. God created both fathers and mothers for a reason.

I am not a Family Therapist, but I do have a Master degree in clinical social work, and I can say with certainty that the absence of a father in a home may cause some disruption in a child growing up. I respect the single parent homes, and I don't make light of it because every situation is different. I am an expert in having had that sort of experience myself with absent parents and what it did to me and my siblings. In my opinion, both parents are equally as important.

But when we talk about our heavenly Father, we can say with certainty that he loves us unconditional but will not spare the rod when we are disobedient. The Father will chastise us because he loves us and desires to keep us on the path to His kingdom.

Those who serve the Father and obey His commandments will be protected by the Father in the end days. There will come a time when the church will be persecuted, mocked, laughed at and shut down. And, those who come to church and don't do anything or commit themselves to God will have to face the consequences. The church should take responsibility to go out in the world to tell the lost souls the truth about their corruption and oppression. But instead, the church goes out into the world and befriends and tolerates their behavior. The Father will reward those who have revered Him and who will take up the baton to speak to the oppressed and corrupt to repent.

The Father is Not Mocked

In my observation, the one thing missing in the members is the fear of God. There are many churches falling apart and pastors leaving the churches because members have become incorrigible. Church members are looking for a 'feel good' church where the word of God is 'candy-coated," and they do not want to hear about 'fire and brimstone' anymore. Some of these churches are raising up a generation of children, adolescents, and young adults who don't fear the Lord because they are not taught sound doctrine. They are also learning from the adults in the church to accept the things of the world as good. They believe the secular world's standard of thinking, such as that, "good is bad and bad is good." "All Scripture is God-breathed and is useful for teaching, rebuking, correcting and training in righteousness, so that the servant of God may be thoroughly equipped for every good work" (2 Timothy 3:16-17(NIV.)

In the last fifteen years, I have noticed a radical change in the way church members tend to imitate more of the secular worldview than a Christian view. Let me explain it this way, Christian women more so than men have outdone themselves with the tattoo phenomenon and the sensual clothing that accentuates every 'nook and cranny' in their body. The dress or skirt hemline is thigh-length that when they bend over, others can take a sneak preview. I am not exaggerating. This is why when they have praise and worship some women walk around with sheets tied around their waist, just in case they fall on the floor they will not show their underpants. The sisters are wearing low-cut dresses and blouses that show half of their bust. The brothers in the church have adopted the secular new look of wearing their pants on their hips showing the sisters their underwear as well as wearing tight pants that also accentuates their body. The church has become a runway for worldly fashions. In 1 Timothy 2:1-10, Paul writes the following verse pertaining to the use of clothes for women,

> "I also want the women to dress modestly, with decency and propriety, adorning themselves, not with elaborate hairstyles or gold or pearls or expensive clothes, but with good deeds, appropriate for women who profess to worship God." (NIV)

In contrast, the characteristics of a healthy church are God's vision, the fear of God, and last but not least, unity. We must recognize that God is the creator and sustainer of our life. Having a fear of God is to realize that God is Holy and deserves reverence. We should fear God simply because of who He is. God is the Alpha and the Omega. He is the Great I AM. "Let all the earth fear the LORD; let all the people of the world revere him" (Psalm 33:1-9, NIV). We must recognize that we have been separated from the rest of the world for His purpose and His glory.

The Bible Scripture's tell us that even the pagans and the demons feared God. The fear of God is to acknowledge who He is in Creation and in the Universe. We must remember that He gives us everything we have. God is the peace that the church needs to bring tranquility, freedom, harmony, and joy. God will hear our prayers and help the church resolve their problems. The fear of the Lord is to love Him and want to always be in communion with Him.

Talk to Your Father…

What should you and I do to be in communion with God always? We should dedicate ourselves to God daily and talk to Him God about all of our burdens. The many ways that God let us know He is with us are through our convictions which makes us sensitive to Him. God reminds us He is with us through a hymn and the scripture we read. Prayer is another way we can laugh with God and enjoy His company. Prayer also helps us to quiet the other voices as we spend time in meditation with the Father. Fasting is also another way we communicate with God. We need to give up certain things like television programs, computer/internet time, music, food, and shopping at the mall because these things interfere with our communication with God. When we are in covenant with God, we are transformed to be a beacon of light in the darkness. God is resurrecting us to go where the darkness is to proclaim new life to those dead to Christ Jesus. Our worst battles have been fought and won on our knees, and God has promised to fight them for us, and He never loses.

Hope in the Father

When I moved to the Southwest, I went on nothing but hope. The hope that I would find an apartment I could afford in a decent neighborhood. The hope that I would find employment immediately. The hope that I would be happy in my new surroundings. I didn't know what awaited me there, but I depended on God to help me all the way.

A few months earlier my church had invited a guest preacher, and he delivered a message related to being released from bondage. I didn't think it was coincident, but I felt that God was telling me

213

that I was going to be all right because I had been released by what had me bound. The preacher was sent to tell the church and me that, "It is almost over." He told the church that we were out of our bondage. I was still struggling, but I had reasons to celebrate coming out, while I was still in it. Wow, am I grateful that God's love covers a multitude of sins and He gives us an early release from bondage.

> "Comfort, comfort my people, says your God. Speak tenderly to Jerusalem, and proclaim to her that her hard service has been completed, that her sin has been paid for, that she has received from the LORD's hand double for all her sins.
>
> "And the glory of the LORD will be revealed, and all people will see it together. For the mouth of the LORD has spoken." "…but those who hope in the LORD will renew their strength. They will soar on wings like eagles; they will run and not grow weary, they will walk and not be faint" (Isaiah 40:1-31, NIV.)

The Prophet Isaiah preached about their bondage and that they were almost out of that bondage. The preacher continued to share God's message with me, and he talked about how the attacks were only a test I had gone through and that the devil had put an attempt on my life because he didn't want me to be about my Father's business. The enemy, the devil is always trying to stop our vision and our dreams. The preacher said, "Satan has a hit on your hope." In the end, what the devil meant for evil, God turned it for my good. I had new hope for the new help that was coming.

God's children must never give up but keep hope alive no matter the attacks, for they are only a test.

The next message I received came the following month, and God spoke to me to be ready for a transition, to make a move, to make the change. When I made the transition, I immediately found the church I was going to attend. Whenever you are going through a transition, believe that prayer will move mountains, heal your wounded heart, and rebuke the demons that come to torment you.

In our Christian walk, there will be people who will attempt to stop us from where we're supposed to move – where God wants us. People of God it is time to walk in the word. Somethings come to force us to move and force us to transition, and we just have to move with it. Whatever God has for us is all good. Stop being afraid. Those things that make us cry, feel sorrowful, hopeless will move to make us stronger, and we will receive joy and peace. It is time to get up and move. It's time to have peace in our life. We have the authority to speak to our life, prosperity, and success. We can't feel strong without a transition. I listened to God, and I am moving forward at a supernatural speed like never before. Godliness living makes a big difference in life because God will move mountains for us.

Godliness separates us from the world's habits. The body of Christ must be holy for God is holy. We must be morally upright and pure and built good holy habits. Spiritual discipline allows us to be in a place with God where He can make us holy. But we must persevere and decide to let God change us.

Father Loves Us Just the Same

We are the children of God. "Yet to all who did receive him, to those who believed in his name, he gave the right to become children of God" (John 1:12.) We are connected to the Savior. "I am the vine; you are the branches. If you remain in me and I in you, you will bear much fruit; apart from me you can do nothing" (John 15:1-5, NIV.)

Church people must give up the competition with one another, and stop their feuding with one another long enough to enjoy time with God. "He brought me out into a spacious place; he rescued me because he delighted in me" (Psalm 18:19.) Get God's name for you and stop calling yourself the names the devil has chosen for you.

We are not only His children, but we are God's friends. "I no longer call you servants, because a servant does not know his master's business. Instead, I have called you friends, for everything that I learned from my Father I have made known to you" (John 15:15, NIV.) We have made joint heirs with Christ Jesus. "but those who live in accordance with the Spirit have their minds set on what the Spirit desires" (Romans 8:1-5, NIV.) We are the saints of the most high God.

> "Accept one another, then, just as Christ accepted you, in order to bring praise to God. For I tell you that Christ has become a servant of the Jews on behalf of God's truth so that the promises made to the patriarchs might be confirmed and moreover, that the Gentiles might glorify God for his mercy. As it is written: "Therefore I will praise you among the Gentiles; I will sing the praises of your name." Again, it says, "Rejoice, you Gentiles, with his people" (Romans 15:7-10, NIV.)

Keep simplicity in your life and just get down to the basics by being submissive to the things of God and serve the church and the church family in everything. Have solitude time with Christ Jesus and confess your sins. Worship God all the time. Use anytime as a time to worship and be grateful to God and look for ways to praise Him. Pick a verse to meditate daily and get together with someone to share the gospel and pray with. Let the church do more praying together and less bickering amongst themselves because there is work to be done and souls to go after. Seek guidance from your Pastor and the Elders in your church.

Follow the Father

Let the Believers think outside the four walls of the church edifice to where the real ministry of saving souls is, the streets. Thinking outside of the church walls becomes a journey that will change the lives of the people they encounter. When the church steps out, there will be a shift in the way they see the world. When the church makes up its mind to think outside the church, God will move some folks that are a hindrance to their Christian walk. The mission of the church will be for salvation to become a germ that will be used to infect the world – rub a little Jesus on. The church will be shifting the atmosphere without them knowing it. The church should make up their mind to walk by faith and allow God to order their steps in every way. If the Lord is not the head of the church, it will not work because only God can soften the hardened hearts of the ones we are to preach to in the streets. He is the only one that can open doors for our ministry to flourish. Let us keep in mind that God is the author and finisher of our life and communication with Him has to be right if we are to be about our Father's business.

I believe that the church has to fall in love with Jesus Christ and the things of the kingdom of God once again. The only way the church will gain spiritual perspective is when they get the wisdom from the spirit of the living God. The church needs God to be the light in their darkness and the Savior to rescue them from themselves. Church members must take heed and stay away from people who are stumbling blocks to doing God's purpose. These people do not know God. They look for ways to entice the believer through a false sense of friendship. They flatter the brothers and sisters with their lies. Church people must not be going to people whom they know do not serve God but are running from God. What help will they be to a Christian in trouble? None! What they need to do is ask God for help and stop running from Him. Talk to Jesus about yourself, and He will tell you things about you. God is trying to give us His thoughts, receive it, bath yourself in them, and experience His goodness and love, just you and Him. Love Christ Jesus and only Him.

In the book "*The Practice Of The Presence Of God,*" written by Father Joseph Beaufort he describes Brother Lawrence as a lay brother at the Carmelite Monastery in the 1600's whose many saying were published in that book. This is one of his saying that I thought it is befitting to share,

> "Men invent means and methods of coming at God's love, they learn rules and set up devices to remind them of that love, and it seems like a world of trouble to bring oneself into the consciousness of God's presence. Yet it might be so simple. Is it not quicker and easier just to do our common business wholly for the love of him?" "...I began to live as if there were no one save [else] God and me in the world." [21]

CHAPTER TWENTY-SIX

...THIS MAN NAMED JESUS

"Doing the will of God is a style of life," my former pastor once told the church.

When I converted, I was so much in love with this man named Jesus the Savior. All I wanted to do was talk about Him to everyone I spoke with. But then something happened, and that enthusiasm wore off after several years when I neither saw it in other church members nor heard Him in their conversations. I began to treat church like any other thing in life, as ordinary. But I disagree with my former pastor; God isn't just like another style of life, He is life. Styles come and go, but Jesus Christ is forever. I can't just take Him off and tuck Him away in the closet like last year's fashions.

We must be wise and intentional in everything, especially when we are talking about Jesus Christ. He is the one who gives us a purpose in life. I realized that my way of living was not working for me and I wanted more even if others had settled for less. I wanted more, and it was only by following this man name Jesus Christ that I would get all my needs met.

I implore everyone who is reading this book to allow God to take the reigns over your lives and fall into His arms. He will give you the direction you need to live a purposeful life. Let God take control of you and listen to His advice and counsel for the betterment of yourself and those around you. Living in the will of God is better than going to the best well-known counselor in the whole entire world. Don't be so proud that you can't take His recommendations and suggestions for your life. God sends blessings to those who live in Him and in unity with others, especially those in the body of Christ.

If you have never had an encounter with Christ, then today is the day. Here is how you can have an encounter with Christ. You must prostrate yourself first before Him. Pray with supplication, wail, moan, and groan before His presence.

Allow God to choose your friends as well as those in church. We all need people who have faith, and we can trust. Always have an environment of peace. Dismiss people who tend to ridicule Christ Jesus in heaven and laugh at you because you chose God over the things of the world. I challenge you to have an intimate encounter with Jesus by believing Him and only Him. Do not fear the circumstance nor the situation around but give God the reigns he knows what to do.

Jesus Died That We May Be Forgiven

> "He was despised and rejected by mankind, a man of suffering, and familiar with pain. Like one from whom people hide their faces he was despised, and we held him in low esteem. Surely, he took up our pain and bore our suffering yet we considered him punished by God, stricken by him, and afflicted. But he was pierced for our transgressions; he was crushed for our iniquities" (Isaiah 53:3-5, NIV.)

The church has made a shift to live the way of the world because they have stopped reading God's word and listening to Him. God's word is the Rhema word, and it has principles that He wants us to live by. We need specific directions so that we will do the work of Him who sent us. This word is the illuminated word of God. The word of God prophesizes to us. When we search the word of God, we are listening to God. God speaks and reveals His will to us.

As I continue to mature in years, I am able to delight myself more in Him and in His will to be done in my life. How do we get to delight in His will? God desire to change our priorities and desires. When God sends us to do something, we can't be indifferent to it the calling of the Lord. The fruits will show us if we are called by

God. There should be peace and patience when it is of God. We must have faith, and the Spirit will give testimony. The Spirit sometimes gives us the testimony not to proceed. We should allow the Spirit of the Lord to lead us, not by this world's culture.

When I couldn't forgive myself and those who had hurt me God rebuked me and said, "who are you not to forgive yourself if I forgave you?" I was ashamed that I had done such a thing that I apologized to God and asked Him to forgive me. I also forgave myself and those I needed to forgive. I had a long list, but I am now free of them. Thank God.

We must learn to forgive ourselves and others because the only person it hurts is the one who refuses to forgive. We must know that forgiveness brings healing and a sense of freedom from sins.

Unforgiveness is a sin because we harbor animosity against another person.

God is our Fountain of all healing. God forgives and heals our wounded hearts. You and I have to recognize that God is a Forgiver and a Healer.

There is no guaranteed that we will not be hurt by others but know that God is a healer and all healings come from Him. The forgiveness of sins is up to us, but the healing is up to God. God took us out of the world's slime and grime and gave us a new life. He forgave us our transgressions.

Endure for the Gospel of Jesus

The word of God challenges us to go to the world and bring the gospel of Jesus Christ to the lost. The church must not be afraid to go out into the world. The world is waiting for converts to help the unsaved receive Jesus Christ as their Lord. These lost souls do not know the word of God, and they are caught in a place of darkness. They don't see a way out of their wretched lives. The harvest is ready in this present time, and we need to go out because God will bring them to us. God is waiting for the church to say, send me Lord.

221

Our challenge is to talk to the lost souls about the good news about the Living Savior found in the word of God. We can give our testimony with the expectations that it will bring them to want to seek God. God challenges us to do what we are called to do, which is to plant the seed of salvation to the lost souls in our families, in the communities, and in the nation.

For the love of the Father, and for you and me, Christ died on a cross. There is no bigger love than that of Jesus Christ. Isaiah wrote about the coming Messiah 700 hundred years in the past. He wrote these words, "Man of pain and sorrow" is Christ our Lord (Isaiah 53:3, NIV). Born in a manger and died on a cross. No one really understood Him. Despised and rejected. He was tortured, spit at, beaten, crowned with a crown of thorns and crucified. He remained humble and at peace. Christ Jesus persevered. He was compassionate and concerned about His people.

Christ had to know what suffering was so that He would know our own suffering. He can identify with our pain of being rejected, mistreated, and hurt. He is familiarized with our pain. Through Christ, we can be effective in the things of the Lord and grow in these things. Through the spirit, we can be convicted of how we are doing and how we should be in Christ.

I have met people who have been hurt in the church and have walked away, professing that they would never return. I try to encourage them to return by sharing that we should never go to church looking to make friends. But that we go looking for God and His love and guidance. That we ignore the antics of the members. But there was a time when I myself didn't believe what I was telling them. Being hurt is being hurt, and there are no two ways about it. Especially, by people who should be loving each other, since they are learning about the Son of God, who epitomizes what love is all about. Why would anyone want to go to church to get hurt? It would be ridiculous!

Our role isn't to allow others to provoke us to anger regardless of the situation but have control. We are to accept and manage it with patience. We are to remain faithful and refrain from taking vengeance or revenge. I have decided to seek God constantly with my prayers and supplications and to grab hold of Him and not let go until He fixes it.

When we persevere and pray for things that are important, God will answer our prayers. So, waiting patiently on the Lord should be our everyday motto, as well as, being ever grateful to God for giving us the peace to endure those trials and sufferings.

Pain and suffering should not come as a surprise for Christians. There have been others before us who have endured worst. We will also have many problems, concerns, and worries during our walk with the Lord. But in the middle of our situation, we have called on God to help us. Only God can help us from our church issues and concerns. God can take us out of any difficulty. Let God deal with the church issue, and we just stay focus on God. Patiently we will wait for God to do it His way. God will rescue us from the situation and give us new strength. God will put new praise in our heart and a new song in our mouth, and we will testify to others of what God has done for us. God will bring order into our lives and make it stable, as well as, give us strength. Christ Jesus is the stability we need. You must be confident and trust in God that He will help you, and He will change your situation for the better.

Believe in Jesus

The presence of the Lord should never be rejected but celebrated. Because of Christ, I can confront everything that comes my way with authority and assurance that God is with me. He will be with you also if you believe. Believers in Christ means that we do the will of God, trust in His faithfulness. We must have love with understanding, insight, awareness, and discernment.

We should forget the past hurts and press to what lies ahead. How we manage our past reflects what happens in the future. God will do a new thing in our life when we look toward the future with Christ Jesus at the helm. And, let us challenge ourselves to not be around those who practice gossip and create discord for they are wicked and crooked. Our main goal in the church is to know Christ Jesus and the sufferings He went through, and the hope to be molded into His image more and more. In that way, you and I will be a light to the world. Believers in Christ Jesus agree to work in harmony which is God's will for His children – the Gentiles. Gentile means good, unselfish, and considerate.

What God desires is that you and I let the unbelievers know that we are considerate.

The unbelievers and newcomers are to see us working together in harmony. People working together produce a better mental health environment.

Every believer must practice what they are learning from the word of God.

As Jesus believers, we are to think positive and on things that are pleasing to God.

Every church member (no one is exempt) should have an attitude that reflects God.

The men and women who profess to have been called into the ministry must unequivocally possess good model leadership skills that will teach others the positive things that will impact the church members in a positive way.

Therefore, let us celebrate and give tribute to God who gave us His Son, and to Christ Jesus who is the reason for our being.

Because Jesus was born, we have eternal life, and our sins are forgiven.

Because Jesus was born, we have received the Counselor, the Holy Spirit, and the mediator to God. Because Jesus was born, we are healed.

Because Jesus was born, the evil one can't hurt us.

Because Jesus was born, we are hopeful that our families will be restored.

Because Jesus was born, we have the hope and the faith that we will have the victory forever and ever.

Because Jesus was born, we have a Redeemer, Lord, and Savior. Blessed be the Lord.

Reflect the Love of Jesus

I have a few emotional scars that were caused in certain churches. Sometimes I feel a little bit of anxiety rise up in me when the thought pops into my mind of going back to that church. I had to endure much negativity from those members in that church. But I must not allow what happened to me interfere in my walk with God. I have learned to have patience with church members. In Romans 12:12 (NIV) the Apostle Paul writes, "Be...patient in affliction..." For some of us this is easier said than done but for God, Paul did it and so can you and me. Patience means to be under the auction of the Holy Spirit and how we interact with each other. There is no question that, in our lives, we will experience pain, hurt, diversities, and disappointments. But in having patience, we show kindness toward others. We must learn to have patience with people who are hostile.

Again, Paul reminds us that it is better to wear our hearts on our sleeves. "Let us not become weary in doing good, for at the proper time we will reap a harvest if we do not give up" (Galatians 6:9, NIV.) But we are to follow sound doctrine and, "Refrain from anger and turn from wrath; don't fret—it leads only to evil. For those who are evil will be destroyed but those who hope in the LORD will inherit the land." (Psalm 37:7-9, NIV.)

In the book of James, we read that trials in our lives come to produce patience and that patience produces character. A good character produces benevolence which is the ability to act with gentleness to those who abuse us. Treating people with kindness, gentleness, and goodness nurtures a good relationship. This should be the type of attitude that the church needs to be kind with one another. The believer must repent and admit their sins and must go to the person he/she has offended and reconcile themselves to that person and ask for forgiveness.

I can't remember the many times I wanted to share my thoughts with some of those who offended me. I wanted to let them know how they had offended me, but instead, I would go home cry and complain to God about them. I wanted God to intervene and convict them of their offense against me and in the hope that they would change their behavior.

People in the church can be convicted of their sins only if they are serious about their belief in God and in his word. In the culture that we live in, not too many have deep confidence in God or are faithful to Him. The Christian of this era needs to have faith in God to live a righteous life.

As much as I like volunteering in the church, there were certain people I couldn't be around without being made to feel like an intruder. And, that was like a major distraction to fulfilling God's goals.

He wants us to bear fruit by being disciplined and doing His will, but when we allow people to be a hindrance, it stops us from moving forward.

But you and I are called by God to use our gifts and talents that He blessed us with to further the Kingdom of heaven. You and I are called to live a life that is good and beneficial to us and others.

I have resigned myself to be very passionate for the Lord, do His will, and go where He wants me to go and do what he wants from me. God wants me to be fruitful, and bear much fruit, and that will be my intention moving forward. God will decide what things He wants to take out my life. I am hopeful that God will take away what distracts me from bearing fruits.

Brothers and sisters do not resist the Lord but let us rely on His will for our lives. There are too many church members coming to church in sin, leaving the church in sin, and returning back to church in sin. There is no way that people who despise other people can be in the spirit of God. We must love all of our brothers and sister in the church.

We All Have Sinned…

When I was in the world living the secular lifestyle, I was serving Satan and dead in my sins.

And thirty-one years ago, I accepted Jesus Christ into my life and was born again. When I received Him, I was given power and authority, and I was a changed person. Through attending church and reading the scriptures, I was convicted and convinced that sinning was out of God's order. I was told that I had to consecrate myself to God to be more devoted, pleasing, and holy in serving Him. I was told that I wasn't to conform to the things of this world any further and to allow God to transform me, and renew my mind and my attitude that I would be pleasing to Him.

At the beginning of my conversion, I wanted to walk in the spirit and do things right before God.

But after three years I changed churches as mentioned in the beginning chapters and something happened where I went back to living in the world, but I was no longer happy there. It was different, and I could not enjoy what I was doing because I knew that it was outside of the will of God. One day after being fed up with my old lifestyle I humbled myself before God asked Him to help me come back to Him. I had been lost in sin since my birth but was saved, and I felt that I wanted to remain saved because the world no longer had anything to offer me. Now, I want to share my testimony with the lost to bring them to the loving arms of my Savior Jesus Christ. "But God demonstrates his own love for us in this: While we were still sinners, Christ died for us" (Romans 5:8, NIV).

CHAPTER TWENTY-SEVEN

SERVANTS

To be effective in evangelizing every believer must give of self and be Holy Spirit-filled. The church must take on the attitude of a servant, as Christ Jesus. Our purpose in sharing with the lost souls is to speak about our own liberation from sin, about our life. We must be genuinely caring, loving, and show concern for them. This way we will establish a relationship and eventually they will come to us for the word.

The night that I left crying and prayed to God to release me from that church, I didn't know that it was God who had placed me there. But when I heard a faint voice say to me, "this is where I want you," I knew in my heart that it was that church and with that pastor where God wanted me. I was to receive my evangelistic training there.

Serve Unto the Lord

The Sovereign God hears our cry and will take us out of whatever desperate place we find ourselves in if it's His will. He will give us a new understanding of our purpose. We will not focus on the opinions, attitudes, and philosophy of others but have confidence in God. God will guide us and order our steps so that others will see us bearing fruits and that His glory is in us. God knew that I wanted to live a life pleasing to Him. We will be tested. Where does God want to take you?

I had no choice but to immerse myself in the word of God and do His will with delight. I internalize the word within me because the word teaches, guides, and instructs. The word restores and helps make us wise. But not only do we need the word of God we also need a pure heart within us. We must read the Bible daily and saturate our entire being with it because it's alive and full of power. I developed a love for the word of God. I started reading from Genesis to know everything there was to know. I deliberately read daily devotionals to learn more Scripture. I meditate on it, and it helps me stay focus. In my opinion, if everyone in church read the Bible daily, they would be more loving and caring one for another.

In the parable of the sower, Jesus speaks about the four types of soil which represents the hearers of the message. The people who represent the different soil can either be believers or non-believers, and they have the choice to receive or reject the word of God. They can either serve in the kingdom/church or not. I am going to share this interesting contrast on how the different characteristics of church members can help or hinder the church's mission and vision.

These are the types of church people we may encounter in the church. I have attended several churches, and I have observed some of these distinctive traits.

The people who are the more liberal in church tend to be arrogant, self-absorb, create division, their life is disorganized and are judgmental based on their outlook on life.

The people who are more Christ-centric tend to be humble, harmonious, seek peace, have a passion for God, for the Scripture, tend to be more stable and seek to evangelize. The true believer has to be steadfast, endure, and have patience.

Secular society has nothing to offer the believer but the pagan lifestyle of the world and the lies they themselves fall for. When we tolerate immorality and say nothing about it, we must not be sure of who we are in God. Tolerance demands that we accept what others are doing even when it is a sin. Some Christians pretend to serve God, but they are serving the devil and continue in sin even when they call themselves Christians. We can't disguise our sin and lie to God. He knows our sins.

But those who follow God's doctrine will be saved. God wants us to focus on the unsaved and witness to them. New people in the church should be made to feel comfortable and appreciated. This is equally as important when giving out tracks to someone in the street. We leave the person feeling unappreciated and unwanted (put yourself in their shoes). We must take the time to ask them for their name instead of walking away from them after handing them a track. We should at least try to have a conversation with them and get to know them if they allow us the time. In the church environment, we should take the time to have a chat with the visitor and the new members every so often. Invite them into your world because they have been lost in their world far too long. We must have a heart like Christ Jesus.

This is Not Self-Service

The talk in the twenty-first century is that people are leaving the church in record numbers than ever before. They have been enticed with the latest tattoos and latest cell phones. They are enamored with their hairs, nails, and body image. The sexier, the better they think. Did I forget to mention that I am talking about Christians aka Believers?

God wants that all His followers be vigilant and know what type of spiritual life they are living. We must remember the Biblical teaching that we have learned at the beginning of our walk with God. We must never forget the word taught to us because the days are evil. Let us repent of all our sins. Keep in mind that the Lord will come like a thief in the night and we will not know or suspect the date and time (Revelations 3:3). There is still a remnant of church members whose spirit of the living God still moves in them. God will keep those who continue to do His will, and their name will be written in the Book of Life. We will all be judged by the evidence that is recorded. If our name is not in the Book of Life, we will be thrown into the lake of fire (Revelation 20:15). You and I will stay awake and know that we are not dead in our spiritual walk.

God is trustworthy and faithful and a true witness to His word. Either we love Him or not.

God will continue to love us, but we must change our mindset and attitude. He is knocking at the door of our heart – let Him in.

In the book of 1 Samuel, it tells a story about a man who said yes to God when he called him. Samuel said, "speak that your servant hears" (1 Samuel 3:10, NIV). The first thing God saw in Samuel was his obedience to the word of God. That he was humble, had a clean heart and did not allow the world to contaminate him. He was a sincere man, and there was no malice in him toward anyone. God choose Samuel because he was groomed by Him and had observed Samuel from birth. Like Samuel, we also should be willing to listen to God.

We must wait in expectation that God will speak to us. Let God know that we are willing to listen and go where He wants us to go. We must have a humble attitude and a dependency on God.

When God called me to Christendom, He chose the church and the pastor because he had been observing the pastor for years. God knew that I would be taught the word and be prepared for the ministry under that particular pastor. There was a purpose in that church for me but being so naïve I didn't know what. The purpose of God is to shape our lives according to His way. God has already preordained us to complete His purpose. Can you even imagine? Can you even fathom that the God of the universe foreknew us and predestined us to serve Him? That He would bless us beyond what we could think? How then should we not seek him with all of our heart, soul, and mind when He first sought after us.

I want to share my excitement of how much in love I was (still am) with God. One night while I prayed, I asked Christ Jesus just to let me touch Him. Suddenly I'm on the floor with my face to the floor, and I saw His feet right before my eyes. My arms had been by my sides when all of a sudden, they reach up and I am touching His feet. His feet were big, and He had big toes with thick (clean) toenails, and He wore a pair of huge brown sandals and the straps were made of thick leather.

He wore a white (not quite white) tunic made of a thick material, and it covered His ankles and draped onto His feet. I could only look at His feet for a while before I put my face down on the blush carpet but still able to touch His feet for a while longer until they disappeared. That was some experience that I shall never forget.

There was another time that I was concern about having cervical cancer, and I asked Jesus in prayer to heal me, and I laid down on my back on the floor in my bedroom and felt a hand touch my abdomen, and it was like something was being surgically removed from me. The next day I felt good, assured that everything was all right. I felt like a heavy load had been taken out of my insides. I had my regular GYN checkup, and the medical report was good. To God be the glory.

We will know the purpose of our life when we have an intimate relationship with God. A relationship with God means that we submit every area of our life to him. God has given us divine endowments to use for the benefit of others. God has a calling on our lives and if for a brief moment we fail Him it's not over. His grace will take us back. We are the works of His hand, and He will not forsake us. God will continue to work His purpose for our life. We must be grounded in the word of God at all times. Whatever we do for the kingdom of God just be vigilant because Satan is relentless. He works incessantly to distract us from our mission. But, Jesus has the last word in our lives, and He has authority over Satan.

CHAPTER TWENTY-EIGHT

IN MIDST OF DARKNESS

As followers of God, we are to put on truth, integrity, morality, and peace.

God defeated the dark forces at the Cross at Calvary, but the war goes on. I had been serving the Lord for over seventeen years and thought I had it all under control. But I was wrong?

It's easy to be overpowered by the enemy even when we are serving God. We give the enemy entrance with our behavior. We give place to the devil when we do things such as quarrel and scream at each other, by being resentful, by being religious, by gossiping, being deceitful, refusing to forgive one another, and deliberately creating conflicts among the brethren.

Don't Let the Sun Go Down...

"In your anger don't sin." Don't let the sun go down while you are still angry" (Ephesians 4:26, NIV).

I remember on several occasions seeing church members express their anger with one another in the church. I saw this young female storm out of the church with such anger in her face that I didn't dare say goodbye to her as she walked out. I had observed everything that had happened in the sanctuary which made her angry. On another occasion, while the pastor was teaching Bible Study, a teenager screamed at the top of her lungs at an adult, "LEAVE ME ALONE." The church was in complete silence, but the pastor continued with his Bible lesson. I witness this pastor use such harsh language when talking about former members, other churches, and those in political office. In my opinion, we should never use the church's pulpit as the forum for insulting the brethren or anyone for that matter.

I get it! Some of us were transgressors and lived according to this world and the forces of darkness. But there has to be a transformation when a person receives Christ Jesus, the Prince of Peace as Lord. Don't think for one moment that Christians can't be influenced by the enemy and that they can't open the door to the enemy to come into their lives. Think again. The attacks of the devil are real. He is a liar, an accuser to make us feel guilty and puts doubts in our mind about our godly life. He puts bad thoughts that are against God and tempts us to sin against God.

I know the damage Satan can cause if allowed him entrance into your life. Satan will not mess with the heathens because they are already serving him, but he comes after the church people. We must not argue with one another because the one behind those conflicts and behaviors is the devil. We must seek God when the enemy is tempting us and allow God to fight our battles.

The church parents must also shield their children from Satan. In the Scripture, Eli's sons didn't listen to their father, and they brought judgment to their home. The reason for their disrespect for the father was in part that they didn't have a relationship with God. Parents must reinforce the teaching because children will stray from the word of God. Eli's behavior allowed his sons to act the way they did (1 Samuel 2:22-25).

Fathers are the Priest in their homes and must instruct and teach their children the word of God. It's the parent's responsibility to not only meet their children's physical needs, and their emotional needs but also their spiritual needs. It's the responsibility of the primary caretaker if the father is not available to see that those needs are met. But for the most part, fathers must model a Christ-like behavior for their children, or they will learn to be ungodly from the pagan world. Teach your children the different ways the devil will try to tempt them. The devil will use the Scriptures to tempt them.

They must know the word of God to protect themselves against the devil's temptations. Share with them that Christ Jesus defeated the devil's temptation with the word of God and so can they. Let them know that the devil leaves us for a moment and comes back so that they are always vigilant in their prayer life. Let them know that God will send angels to keep them. Parents must be godly models in their home that their children may grow up to possess godly behaviors. They should foster love and care toward their children and discipline. It is imperative that Christians have a healthy relationship with Christ through their prayer life.

Jesus used prayer before starting His ministry. The prayer is important to focus on Christ. The church should be a house of prayer, thanksgiving, and praise.

While living in the Southwest, I participated in a prayer vigil every last Friday of the month from twelve midnight to three in the morning. I looked forward to attending. I also to ministered in dance with the church's praise team. It was a time to speak with God and allow God to speak to us. In those prayer services, there was nothing I couldn't ask God for in Jesus name and in faith-believing that He would not grant it to me. The prayer is the best way to conquer everything since we are praying in the name that is above all names, Lord Jesus. Prayer should be like breathing, you need it to survive.

Love & Peace Conquers Evil

When the praise dance team would come together for the midnight vigil, we would always pray before ministering in dance. The lead instructor would ask us to form a circle, and everyone would be touching the feet of the person to the right and to the left feet as a sign of unity. The instructor would start by praying and anoint each one with oil. The prayers were always about God being glorified through our dance and for the people in the pews to be ministered to and edified.

The church is a dedicated sanctuary, consecrated and sacred

where people come for help and healing. God expects the members to be receptive to those who come to our church. In order for us to help others, we must edify ourselves in love. Then and only then can we edify our brothers and sisters in Christ. Edifying is used to benefit them. We are never to offend our brothers and sisters because it is not about us but them. We should not be selfish and think just about ourselves. We are not to say negative things against one another or use harsh words to hurt.

The dance ministry has a set of 'Core Values" that we have to adhere to and they are not an option. It should never be about us but about God in us, which means that we must operate in integrity at all times. If we can't say anything good about someone, then we should say nothing. I have been guilty of that and have repented after doing it, but I have learned, that the only person it convicts, is me. And, I don't want to walk around with that conviction. Edifying should be intentional. We should be comforting to each other. Don't reject the person in need of encouragement, especially if you know that they are new in your church.

When we are joined together with Christ, we have no choice but to want to encourage one another. Strengthen and build up your brother and sister in Christ and encourage them to grow in the things of the Lord. Be at peace with all your Christian brothers and sisters. Peace helps foster edification of people. We must be well-balanced Christians. I remember my pastor saying to the church, "be sober, be vigilant and cautious, be firm in your faith and have self-control." He was talking particularly about caring for each other and their families, as well as for the stranger who comes to the church. As Christians, if we profess to love God but it is equally as important also to love one another, there are no ifs, and buts about it. Learn to cry with those who are sad and laugh with others who are happy. Love everyone but be careful whom you have as an intimate friendship with, that they are respectful of your faith. A major problem among people, in general, is the interpersonal relationships especially if you are a believer. You and I are not of the world as the others, and the world hates those who belong to God. Satan hates that we have been delivered and redeemed by the Lord and Savior. Be as wise men in the middle of the enemy and innocent without falsehood that they will not have something negative to say about you. Let you, and I be kind in our actions and attitudes toward everyone.

I have no qualms about telling everyone about what God has done for me throughout my Christian walk and even my backsliding years. I tell them about His mercy and grace. The Scripture tells us about going to the four corners of the world because we are the salt and light of the world. I have been restored to God through the Blood of Jesus to restore others to Him.

God has restored you and me to restore others. And, He has called us not just so we can receive blessings but for others to have the same blessings. When we are negligent with the lost souls, we are also negligent with God.

Seek God…

We must search our hearts and ask this question of who needs restoration in my family, in my job, and in my church? What situations are they going through that we may be able to help them with? For example, resentment, a broken marriage, past negative experiences, addictions, an illness.

Sometimes people don't know what restoration means to them, and we may be able to alleviate those distresses and guide them. We can share with them that a prerequisite for restoration is repentance from the inside out and that they need to make a choice to accept Jesus as their Lord and Savior. Many of us have lost our way at one time or another and have needed to be restored. For some people, religiosity has been a part of their wandering away from the truth.

Jesus illustrates for us just how easy it is for us to get lost. Remember the parables of the lost sheep, lost coin, and a lost son. The sheep symbolizes us in our fragile stage; we are ignorant of the things of the world and Satan's snare. We are dumb and stubborn and want to do things our own way even when it isn't working right for us. We are neglected, lost, and careless; and need direction and guidance. God Jehovah, Christ Jesus, and the Holy Ghost will find us and restore us to Him. Jesus comes searching for us because He loves us so much. All God is asking of us is to allow Him into our lives and to do His will. He will take the responsibility to care for us. No matter what has happened in our lives and the mess we have made of it, turning to God Jehovah is the only way. We must never be ashamed to admit that like sheep we have gone astray (Isaiah 53:6). But know we can be restored when we repent and say yes to His will.

God has called you and me to repentance and forgiveness. And, the calling of God is irreversible. We should want to know everything about God since He called us. To me having been called is the best thing that could ever happen to me. Do I know God personally? I want to believe that I do.

Some of us think we know Jesus, but we don't and we should. We should be telling Jesus, "I want to know you." King David said these beautiful words, to the Lord and I want to echo them,

"One thing I ask from the LORD, this only do I seek: that I may dwell in the house of the LORD all the days of my life, to gaze on the beauty of the LORD and to seek him in his temple" (Psalm 27:4, NIV).

I want to seek God's face daily to see His glory and power. Being in God's presence to me is better than life. Knowing Christ and being intimate with Him should be every Christian's goal.

The Scriptures are a great reminder in that we should cast all of our cares and concerns on the Lord because He cares for us. All we have to do is just wait on Him, and He will stabilize whatever is causing us to fall behind, in our Christian walk. But whatever the situation is we must not lose heart but wait. Just do what is right, remain holy, and trust in God in your wait.

Jehovah God is all we need, really. Jehovah forgives, redeems, and heals us. Jehovah provides all our needs, renews our strength, is merciful, graceful, slow to anger and never holds a grudge. We must give Jehovah all of our issues and concerns.

Before I began to write this book, I had made up my mind that I was not going to keep anything from God, not even my cares and concerns. He must have several file cabinets filled with all of my cares and concerns because I refuse to hold on to them or try to solve them myself. The minute a situation I knew would be difficult for me I would tell God you handle it and He would.

Be Not Conform to This World

We must lose ourselves for the sake of He who preserves and saves us. Because I know who God is in my life I refuse to conform to the things of this world or love the things of this world more than Him. This world's philosophy and environment cause us to sin when we imitate their world and their fashion. When we follow after those things, we are following the prince of this world – Satan and his demons.

Followers of God must never follow after the flesh with its passion for sin nor rebel against him. We are to destroy the strongholds of the enemy with the word of God. We must always, daily be on one accord with God as we read the sacred words. You and I who are followers of God must always let the word dwell in our hearts. In Deuteronomy 6:1-8 are instructions on how to value the commands given by God to the Israelites.

The present-day Jewish people have a Mezuzah affixed to the doorpost of the main entrance of their homes to remind them of these laws. This is the Scripture engraved in the Mezuzah, "Tie them as symbols on your hands and bind them on your foreheads" (Deuteronomy 6:8, NIV). The prayer they recite when the mezuzah is nailed or clued to the doorpost. "Blessed are You, Lord our God, Ruler of the universe, who has sanctified us with His commandments and commanded us to affix a mezuzah." [22]

We should take heed and allow the church to train us in the

spiritual things of God to gain the wisdom and revelation. We are to read the word and gain knowledge of the word of God because it is good, pleasing and perfect. The word of God gives us the authority to change the atmosphere wherever we proclaim His word.

Take authority and speak the word of God to those spirits that are trying to destroy you and your family, your relatives, in your jobs, your homes, in the world and even in the church. Rebuke and dismiss all the assignments from Satan by using God's word. Remember that Christ defeated Hades and the grave and had smashed the head of the devil to give us the authority against him.

Jesus gave us power and authority to preach the gospel of our Lord and over demons.

We must align with the agenda of the Living God and have the same attitude that is in Christ Jesus. God will continue to work in the willing believer until our attitude is like His.

I have to confess that after being treated like a stranger in my own church I had decided to only speak with those who had been kind to me. I thought I'm not here for them I'm here because God wants me here. But I didn't feel comfortable in my own skin and felt convicted to the core. God rebuked me and told me, that is the wrong attitude.

In Jesus, we have the peace and the confidence that things will work out. God isn't the creator of bad and suffering. He does everything well. He gives us the freedom to choose and most times we have taken that freedom and have chosen wrong. We all have sinned and come short of the glory of God. The Scriptures informs us that wicked things come out of the heart and that we are born sinners, and that is precisely why we sin. I knew it was the wrong attitude to take, but it was my frustration that caused me to think in that way. I had to leave it up to faith that things would turn out for my good.

"The righteous shall live by faith [alone]" (Romans 1:17, NIV). Faith is confidence and trust in God. Faith that is living in the natural man and believing that God gave us our gifts and talents.

It's having faith the size of a mustard seed that can move obstacles preventing us from living holy. Faith always starts small. Faith is the hope (being sure of) and the certainty of what we don't see (Hebrews 11:1). "And without faith, it is impossible to please God because anyone who comes to him must believe that he exists and that he rewards those who earnestly seek him" (Hebrews 11:6). I am so elated that God came after me. I would not be alive today if it were not for God saving me from dying of a drug overdose or killing myself and another motorist the times I drove home drunk. God, I love you!

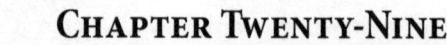

CHAPTER TWENTY-NINE

CAN I GET A WITNESS?

I am so glad that Christ Jesus is on my side. Jesus prays for us day and night while we are going through the trials that may cause us to lose our faith. Jesus wanted to warn His disciples of the trials they would face because He knew their weaknesses. Satan will test our faith like he is testing the church. Satan receives permission from God to test our faith. Why was Peter chosen for Satan to sift? Satan knew that Peter's leadership would lead to great missionary work. We can't believe to be invincible. But we have a powerful intercessor. Satan will tempt us always, but he doesn't have the power or last word. All we have to do is rebuke the devil in Jesus name, and he will flee. Sometimes our faith has to be tested, especially if we are arrogant and selfish.

I was tested, and it was not a good thing. I would encourage those of you reading this book if there is the slightest of arrogance, selfishness, thoughts of you being better than anybody, please choose to change and quick. God will sift us until we can be Christ-centric. We all need to be cleansed before God in order to be used by Him. Our failure should not have the last word in our life.

Peter wept bitterly and repented and so can we. Peter went on to preach to the people, and 3,000 were saved. Peter was restored and returned to his home and church. Let God heal you, restore you, and trust in His provisions.

Let There Be a Testimony…

Daily allow God to examine and search your heart and see if there is anything in you that offends Him. God will seek out whatever is there that hinders our walk with Him. Because we allow God to guide and lead us nothing will be able to harm us.

For too many years, I have observed the church and its ungodly behavior detour people from seeking refuge in the church. I have seen people leave the church and when I see them in the community, it's always the same story. They say things like, the church is in chaos, and the members are callous.

One day I needed to ventilate about how horribly the people treated me at the annual Holy event and mustered the courage to speak to an older sister in church. She and I had become friends at work back in 1992 before I even visited her church. She was in the supermarket, and I stopped her and began sharing my frustration about my negative church experience. Her respond didn't surprise me at all. She went on to tell me that when she also felt shunned by the church after she began to work for the pastor as an office assistant. She told me that the wife was not too please and rarely spoke to her and that there was murmuring and complaining among the members. She continued to share with me that although she knew members didn't like her, "I kept right on coming to church regardless of their behavior."

The church needs to have a sincere heart and let our testimony be our witness. Do whatever you find to do in the kingdom regardless of what others will think. We must be collaborators with God and disciple others and ignore everything that is foolish and ungodly. Let our behavior, our testimony, and our prayers, connect the unchurch with a community church which is what we are called to do. Be good examples of Christ. Be Christ-centric. Forget about the haters in church. God's truth should be invested in people who truly want to hear it. Go and witness to others in different areas and let God do miracles. Regardless of how things may look in our church we just need to respond to His call.

We are God's workmanship to do good work. We must pray for those whom we will disciple, and they will not be treated as we were. Protect them because they are fragile human beings who have been hurt and abused. We definitely, don't want those hurting souls coming to church to get the same treatment they received out there. We need to sit with them and teach them the word.

Let you, and I run the race God has prepared for us and proclaim the good news. This is our calling to preach the gospel everywhere and to everyone. Many times, the church forgets that it's not about us but His Son's business we should be about. "For God so loved the world that He gave His Son" (John 3:16).

In the book of Matthew Jesus tells Peter "Get thee behind me, Satan: thou art an offense unto me: for thou savourest [sees], not the things that be of God, but those that be of men" (Matthew 16:23, NIV). The name Satan means adversary, stumbling block, scandalous and entrapment. Peter had become a stumbling block to the agenda of God. And like Peter, the present church has become a stumbling block for ministry and evangelizing. The devil is invited by us according to our thinking. Satan knows when we have our vision on the things of man instead of having our vision on God and His kingdom. It's about time that we take our eyes off the things of man and move into the things of God.

There is a colloquial saying in the urban neighborhoods, when a person is acting in a silly way that is frustrating to another person, "act your age not, your race." That is in no way meant to insult someone's particular race. There are customs within our culture that we assimilate throughout life and "bad habits are hard to break" they say. It's how we see life and how we interpret it. It's our own opinions and our beliefs as we grow up in a certain environment.

"Stinking Thinking"

Because the church is made up of many different cultural backgrounds and economic status' everyone will see things differently than others. But when we are in the church, there should be one way of doing things and that way is Christ-centric. We must put everything in a heavenly kingdom perspective.

A commission that isn't Christ-centric is dangerous because it leaves room for Satan to come. We need to move on in the kingdom. Change everything that keeps our eyes on mankind and the things of this world. We must resign to look at what God wants from us and what He wants us to do. We need to change the way we think that causes a stumbling block to doing kingdom work.

Throughout the years I have heard statements made by members that are from godly thinking.

Those statements sound something like this, "I felt like smacking her", "I had road rage, I screamed out the window" "I hate that woman" (talking about a supervisor), "I want to hurt somebody", "well I'll do whatever I want", "I gave them the bird" (give middle finger at someone), "sometimes a cuss word comes out" "I'm not going to do nothing for him", I don't want other churches coming," or they scream at you and tell you "I don't want to hug you."

That kind of thinking is called, "stinking thinking" or negative thinking. That type of thinking comes from years of living in an environment that fostered negative behaviors. I should know, I came from such an environment where profanity was the norm among adults. I witness many unfavorable things that children should not be privy to.

The moment I heard one former pastor preach on generation curses I knew that I had my work cut out for me. I know that both my parents had been intentional sinners and had no interest in changing their ungodly behaviors. It was up to me to pray to God for me, my children, grandchildren, and great-grandchildren to spare from the curse that was on my parents and their parents.

Past generations have brought a curse onto future generations until the fourth generation for their disobedience to serve God. We suffer the sins of past generations. We have to cancel every sin our ancestors have committed against God. We must confess the sins of our antecedents whether it was witchcraft, jealousy, dysfunctional behavior, drugs, envy, gossip, fights, and alcoholism. We must pray and believe and cancel every negative word that had ever been spoken against us, and our family. Even those sins that we have committed against ourselves have to be confessed and forgiven.

We must stop that "stinking thinking" and know we belong to our Father, Jehovah.

We Have an Advocate

When I came back from the Southwest, I had big plans to start a dance ministry and do full-time evangelism. I had high hopes, and I approached the pastor with my plans, He told me who to see and made suggestions about how to get things started. My first contact was with the evangelistic minister and was quite disappointed that there was no evangelism taking place at the time due to lack of participation from church members. When I tried to get, the dance ministry started all the avenues were closed to me. I could not get anyone to help get out the announcement on church media. The drama director caught an attitude with me and stopped talking to me, and the former dance instructor decided she was not interested.

When people can't appreciate the effort a member makes to work for the kingdom then it's up to God to do something. Anything that is aligned with God is not impossible. We all have dreams, and God gives a vision in those dreams. Always think God's vision whenever we want to be blessed. When God gives us a vision for the church, it's His vision, and we just have to wait for God to bring it to fruition. When we believe in God's vision, nothing will be able to prevent it or stop it from coming to fruition. We might be small and insignificant, but our God has called us to do great things for His glory and honor. Jesus says, "Very truly I tell you, whoever believes in me will do the works I have been doing, and they will do even greater things than these because I am going to the Father" (John 14:12). Because He goes before the Father, the Father will do whatever we ask in Jesus name so that His Son will bring Him glory. We must believe whatever vision God gives us is a miracle waiting to happen. We must believe in the miracles of God and His visions.

Live in the expectation that we will receive great things from God. The old man Simeon lived expecting to see the Salvation of the world – Christ Jesus). The day arrived when he saw Jesus and even touched Him (Luke 2:25-30). We have to live in the supernatural and expect something supernatural to happen.

When God begins to interact in our situation, it means that He wants to place us somewhere to use us. Do not limit yourselves in God's kingdom. When the presence of God is manifested in us take action, it's time to help change the environment and the people. The book of Ruth is about God interacting in our lives and in our problems. Ruth meets Boaz, a man who is sanctified, provides security and is wealthy. Believe that God chooses people to save others. If God did it for Ruth and Naomi, He could do for you and me.

Some of the struggles the churches are experiencing are because of their disobedience to God.

They have the spirit of ambivalence and unbelief that are bringing the church under.

The church members have been weakened in their spiritual life because they want to have one foot in the church and one foot in the world. They and are listening to the lies of the secular culture. The church needs to receive a spiritual cleansing to avoid polluting themselves with the world.

Thank God that He knows our heart, and will put covering over us. He will send His angels to keep the church from further harming themselves. God will make sure that the church gets to where they should be going. The Scriptures reminds us that we win because we have an advocate.

CHAPTER THIRTY

IT'S A NEW SEASON

"You foolish Galatians! Who has bewitched you? Before your very eyes, Jesus Christ was clearly portrayed as crucified. I would like to learn just one thing from you: Did you receive the Spirit by the works of the law, or by believing what you heard? Are you so foolish? After beginning by means of the Spirit, are you now trying to finish by means of the flesh? (Galatians 3:1-3, NIV)

Paul called the Christians in Galatians foolish people and implored them to stop being fooled by Satan. There is a time that God will say to those who insist on sinning; enough is enough. The only way we will get out of our mess is to say yes to the will of God and live holy.

We are making excuses not to serve God or to being obedient to His commandments. We worship the material things God gives us but not the God who gives it to us. God is calling His people, and they refuse to come. But yet Satan calls them, and they run to him.

Time to Shift

You would think that the church members would want to be delivered from their pagan behavior. This is not the time to give up or the time to retreat. It's time to say no more flesh. God is going to shift some things in our lives, and we have to start thinking what new thing he has for us in the future. God is about to shift the years, and we should be ready. We have to learn to intercede for ourselves and others and watch God restrain the devil. The time has come to move and take another step the waiting is over. Make every day your new season and moment with God and believe that He will visit you in your hour of affliction. "You are the salt of the earth. But if the salt loses its saltiness, how can it be made salty again? It's no longer good for anything, except to be thrown out and trampled underfoot" (Matthew 5:13, NIV).

Take Another Step

It was September when I decided to plan my retirement from the State of CT and had made arrangement to move to the Southwest. The message I received from God that last Sunday in Eastport, He told me not to worry that everything was going to be alright. I prayed to God to embrace me on my new journey, to a place I had only visited once, and not to let me go. And, in the three years, I was there He never let me go. When I say that God embraced me, I truly felt Him every day and night. It was supernatural.

I was living in the Southwest attending the church where I learned so much about many things besides Scripture. The pastor not only taught us about the Bible but he also talked about social justices and about his love for America and that touched a chord with me because I too love this country. Because the future of this nation is in the hands of the church we must act and ask, God what should we do? To raise the standards, we must worship God, teach the Scripture to our family members and friends.

God is still the standard of how we should live our lives. To raise the standard in this nation we need to start with ourselves, the body of Christ. In order for us to be effective in rebuking unclean spirits and setting free the captives, we must start by praying and fasting. Jesus can deliver them, but we must first go to Him in prayer and fasting. This isn't a season for us to sit back and watch the devil throw our beloved family members into the fire to burn.

The church must come out from behind the church's four walls and be more aware of what is happening in the nation. Christ followers are God's ambassadors to the world and representatives of the kingdom of God and thus, must walk in the integrity of God. We are to be the voice of salvation to the lost in our family, community, and the nation. We must teach the Bible, and what the Bible calls sin we must call sin. We must rally against abortion, pornography, nudity, and sex in public media. The church must stand up for the children and tell the liberals to stop taking God out of the schools.

When the church observes the nation living in such deplorable sin, we should be bold enough to express it and not hide in the church. Salvation comes from the hearing of the word and through the blood of Lamb, Christ Jesus. So, let us teach the unsaved that once they are baptized, they will also become an adopted child of God and a brother and sister in Christ to you and me.

When God calls us to be baptized and disciple, it's because He is getting ready to send us out to disciple others. We are the team of godly men and women who are to represent the kingdom of God here on earth. We are being commanded by God to make disciples. Our duty is to make sure that they get baptized and are taught the word of God. We are to stay with them until they are ready to declare the word on their own and are attending church regularly. Because when a lost soul is saved the heavens rejoice over that one (Luke 15:10).

In the church I attended in the Southwest they had group baptism once a month with up to as many as twenty plus people being baptized. The church would celebrate with praise and worship.

The church must continue to monitor its behavior and not lose sight of what is important to God and also, for the benefit of those around us. The words we speak and our actions play a huge role in how the unbelievers receive us.

God is still the standard of how we should live our life. To raise the standard in this nation, we need godly men and women following sound doctrine. Because the future of this nation is in the hands of the church we must act and ask, God what should we do?

To raise the standards, we must worship God, teach the Scripture, and share the love.

We must consider everything we do for God because He deserves our devotion, loyalty, love, and passion for rescuing the lost and unsaved for the kingdom. And, don't stop whatever God has put in your hands to do for him.

CHAPTER THIRTY-ONE

MY RELATIONSHIP WITH GOD

What is our relationship with God?

Our relationship with God should be unequivocally different than the relationship we have with humans. God desires that we be totally dependent on Him. We are expected to have a positive attitude in and outside of the church.

It's imperative for me that others see me as a servant of God. I will continue to persevere in my relationship with God.

There should be nothing better than attending Bible study and Sunday school and learn more about God. We must learn to fast and pray to be in agreement with God. And, no matter how bad things get we must never complain but trust Him in everything. This is how our relationship with God should be like.

Renews

There was a time in my life when I doubted whether I was going to complete God's work, and thought since I had made such a mess of my life, there was no way I would bring to fruition God's plan. Until God reminded me of His words, "For those God foreknew he also predestined to be conformed to the image of his Son, that he might be the firstborn among many brothers and sisters" (Romans 8:29, NIV).

God had predestined us to do His purpose. God saw in us a potential since before our birth. Don't count yourself out, you and I have a celestial potential, and we were born for excellence. The enemy may know everything about each and every one of us, but he can't cancel what God has predestined for us. We have been chosen and given the authority to rebuke and bind everything that is ungodly. God can't use us unless He cleans out our minds of all the junk of the past and the present that affect us from moving forward with His plan. Get rid of all negative thoughts because they don't serve any other purpose but to make you sin against God. We must ask God to renew our minds and take captive every thought that is not pleasing to Him. Every one of God's children needs a renewal of the mind in order to have a new attitude.

Reach Out

The church is admonished to go back to a time when Christians reached out and talked about God and His love for others. Jesus said, "love your neighbor as yourself." But how can members love one another when the real love of God is missing in them and in the altar. God desires that we go back to the "first love" - Christ Jesus. The church should recall when they were first "born again" to rekindle that fire they had for Jesus.

The time for turning back to God is now! Let us start praying without ceasing that God will turn our hearts back to Him. Why fight it!

We are God's chosen generation, and we need to position ourselves to fight the adversary the devil and stop fighting among each other. The devil wants to kill this and the next generation. God has destined us, and we will be given the power and the capacity to evangelize the lost souls, and all we have to do is obey the laws and commands set before us in the Bible.

Understand that we are in this place and this time as it is written in the Bible. We are a living witness of the gospel of Jesus Christ, and the only thing that will change the minds of this lost generation is our witness. We must not waste any more time being mean to one another but let us get serious and evangelize the unsaved.

You and I are not of this world, and our life was given to us by

God for a bigger purpose. You and I are to establish a redemptive plan and continue to proclaim the name of Jesus the Messiah.

If I can forgive those who have hurt me in church so can you. I have come up with this logo "Forgiveness is Key" to remind myself and others of the importance of forgiveness.

It also serves as an ice-breaker to start the conversation about the 'Good News.' I have no time to be angry or upset anymore with my church family. There is so much work to get done before the coming of the Lord. And, you and I have been sent for such a time as this.

In the book of 1 Samuel 16, he was sent by God to anoint David as king while he was still an adolescent and in his father's home. God chose David because God saw his heart, not the outward appearance. God saw that David was "a man after God's own heart" (Acts 13:22, NIV). David was someone that would do everything that God wanted.

We are in a time of making a serious decision. This isn't the time to be hiding inside our church walls, but it's the time to prepare ourselves. We have been hiding from our calling and purpose far too long. God is now calling us all, those He has predestined from birth, to listen. He is telling us to go to battle that He will be with us. God will go first and make way for us to do what He has called us to do. God is very much interested in this generation – even this depraved generation.

The church has a covenant with God and will be anointed by Him to fulfill His purpose. For the battle belongs to God and He will give us the wisdom and the spirit of discernment.

There will be times that we will feel weak to do battle but God' is our strength. We will not allow anyone to try to intimidate us or make us feel that we are nothing. Realize that we have been called by the Great I Am.

This is it! There will be no more living outside of the will of God. The King has called you and me and the rest of His anointed children, and we will say yes Lord send me.

Believe it or not, I was a shy girl growing up and still have some of the residuals of shyness in me. I am sociable, but I have to muster up the guts sometimes to "break the ice." But once I introduce myself, I have no problem talking up a storm.

Most times God would give me an opportunity to speak with someone about salvation, and I would have a reservation about doing it. It would take me some time before I could say anything and at times missing that window of opportunity because the person would walk away before the words would come out of my mouth. I had to ask God to free me from that type of fear because I was losing too many people I could have witnessed to. What I did to help testify to the unsaved was buy the 'Pocket Testament' booklets with the book of John and give them out to certain people saying something like, "God loves you, and this is a letter from Him to you." Sometimes I would put the tip in it and leave it sitting on the restaurant table for the server. But I have come to realize that evangelizing that way is not right.

I still have a smidgen of reservation about witnessing to people especially in this day and age when Christianity is frowned upon by the liberals, but I'm confident God will take the reign for me.

God will choose the person and give me just enough word to share with him/her and walk away feeling hopeful that something God said penetrated their thoughts. I believe that God is speaking to the church of this day and age. When God gives us instructions, we need to go and take advantage of that window of time. This is the season we need to go after God and listen to the words He is speaking into our lives and obey them. The only way we miss our window or season is when we are not righteous and in sin. There are things God wants to manifest on earth if we can turn from our sins and be obedient to Him.

Rescues

Keep in mind that we are living in evil times, but God will give us favor. God knows that there are people and situations that are hurting us because He allows it. The pain is a way of preparing us for the harvest because it is about ministering to hurting people and we will be able to empathize with them. You and I are being challenged. I say to God, bring it on!

God had commanded Noah to build the Ark. Before Noah started building the Ark, he was ministering, and he preached for 103 years about the salvation of the Lord in a land that was so wicked. People committed atrocities. In our own day and age, there such atrocities being committed daily in the abortion industry with the killing of unborn babies, mass murders in the schools and other areas of recreation and occasionally in special events, and in places of employment. The sexual explosion in America and around the world where there are no censors on what can be viewed in public television, such as constant nudity, profanity and vulgarly in the social media. The lack of respect for authority figures, and the obvious corruption in government. The vicious attacks against Christians in the free world and slaughters of them in the Muslim countries. Sin is consuming this nation's moral and Biblical standards, and it's not being confronted by the church. When God calls us to do something how committed are we to do it? The last time I checked God is still the Great I Am.

There have always been conflicts in the world. Our Savior knew conflict first-hand. You and I can choose to raise a standard of righteousness or compromise with the world's immorality.

I am reminded of the logo that came out in 1988 which became a national craze, "What Would Jesus Do (WWJD)? Dan Seaborn was the youth pastor at the Central Wesleyan Church in Holland, Michigan who got that logo started. This logo was made into bracelets and other items, but the bracelet was unique in that it served a spiritual purpose. I brought into the craze and bought many of those bracelets to give out especially to the youth. My purpose in giving those bracelets out was two-fold, one to minister Jesus Christ as Lord and Savior and two to get them to think on how to respond in certain situations. Which made them think how Jesus will respond? [23]

We are the children of God, and we need a Jesus mindset to be consistent in our ministry and in our standard of living. The church of the Living God endures and never surrenders, and we are not excused from the battle, but we must speak the truth, and raise up the banner of righteousness. We can't live for Christ Jesus and keep silent. We are here today to be standard bearers. Christ Jesus started a movement to save the sinner, and we will stay the course.

As I mentioned before, I am the praise dance team leader at my church, and before every practice and every dance ministry I pray with my team and anoint them and myself with oil. I tell my team that we must dance with excellence because we are dancing for the King. Whatever we do for the kingdom of God must be done in excellence.

The church is to serve with excellence in everything because we serve the "King of kings and Lord of lords. I get glad when I sing the song, "Oh, what a mighty God we serve…" If we believed that we should serve with excellence then maybe this pagan world will believe that our God is a mighty King. We must stop making excuses for not witnessing about Jesus Christ. Having the spirit of excellence is a choice like anything else in life. The same thing goes for choosing to become a Christian. Why choose to become a Christian if we are not going to live like Christ followers. The pagans must see a distinction between them and us.

In the book of Daniel, King Darius thought that Daniel was ten times better than those in his kingdom realm because of his God (6:25-28). Daniel had no issues about serving God with excellence, and for doing so, he got the attention of the king. People will bless God simply because they see us blessing and obeying Him. We must stop walking around like we are on the defense all the time and be nice to each other. We want that when the people hear us, they hear our God talking and our behavior reflecting His. Let us choose to be faithful to God by living out the Christian life and let us be bold about our Christian walk.

> "Is not this the kind of fasting I have chosen: to lose the chains of injustice and untie the cords of the yoke, to set the oppressed free and break every yoke? Is it not to share your food with the hungry and to provide the poor wanderer with shelter—when you see the naked, to clothe them, and not to turn away from your own flesh and blood? Then your light will break forth like the dawn, and your healing will quickly appear; then your righteousness will go before you, and the glory of the LORD will be your rear guard. Then you will call, and the LORD will answer; you will cry for help, and he will say: Here am I. "If you do away with the yoke of oppression, with the pointing finger and malicious talk, and if you spend yourselves in behalf of the hungry and satisfy the needs of the oppressed, then your light will rise in the darkness, and your night will become like the noonday. The LORD will guide you always; he will satisfy your needs in a sun-scorched land and will strengthen your frame. You will be like a well-watered garden, like a spring whose waters never fail. Your people will rebuild the ancient ruins and will raise up the age-old foundations; you will be called Repairer of Broken Walls, Restorer of Streets with Dwellings" ((Isaiah 58:6-12, NIV).

CHAPTER THIRTY-TWO

MY REDEEMER LIVES

It never occurred to me to think that Christians can be so non-Christ-like. This is what Mahatma Gandi had to say about Christians, "I like your Christ, I do not like your Christians. Your Christians are so unlike your Christ." [24]

Common sense tells us that if we confess Jesus Christ as our Lord and Savior and receive Him unto ourselves, as well as, receive the baptism, and attend church regularly; pray and read the Bible, we should be living like saints and talking scripture. Christ followers should be living peaceably with their church family and those in the community.

The church with no question needs to get their roles in order and act like the redeemed of the Lord. You and I profess to have received Jesus as Lord and Savior than we should spend the rest of our lives loving Him. I understand that life is not as tidy as we would want it to be so that we can focus our entire time on being spiritual. I get it! Life happens! I know for a fact that during difficult situations God is not the first thought in our minds, it's always the situation. But it is during those heart-breaking moments that we need to get spiritual.

He Cares...

When I thought about leaving the churches because of how I was being mistreated emotionally, I didn't think God first. All I wanted to do was scream and call them "you bunch of hypocrites." As you have read, I jumped from church to church because I didn't like what I saw in those churches or the behaviors of the people. I didn't think to have God fix it, instead I ran away.

Some of us are in church hurting but afraid to leave the church because you have family members to think about, you like the pastor and the preaching, or you do not know where to go. We all will have problems and troubles but God, He cares for us.

It wasn't until I gave all those concerns to God that I got my life back. Give all of your troubles and problems to Jesus. You can do it, I did. Cast all of your cares to God (1 Peter 5:7).

I am writing this book for you and for myself to be reminded daily of what a mighty God we serve and that he loves us. Just humble yourself under His mighty hand and see Him work in your life as He has done in mine.

Most of our worries are lies that we believe. Because if we know that "nothing is impossible with God" why do we worry about this and that. I am not assuming that life's difficulties are not real because they are, very real. What I am saying is that with God on our side things can be a little easier and better. God will always find a solution for our situation if we believe. I have believed God (intentionally) for everything for the last six years. Prior to these six years, I believed my late husband for moral and financial support; then it was my employer of twenty years for more financial provision, my secular friends and my family for loving relationships and myself for my exceptional health. When my husband died, I was devastated, to say the least. I lost my support system, my friends and family, my properties, my finances dwindled, and my health began to fail me.

Those people I believed in were of no help when I needed them the most. I say all this to say that Satan is a liar and the father of all lies. I told myself all those lies. I did everything a Christian was expected to do. I thanked God for everything I had, but I believed and depended on humans.

When I say that our worries are lies, it is because Satan is telling us that our situation has no solution because he had already explored our weakness and knew that we will panic, which is natural. He will make us think that our situation is bigger than God to overwhelm us. We are children of God and God will fix our mess. I know He did it for me so 'no worries.' God will break us loose from the bondage of Satan's lies. I refuse to believe Satan's lies. I will walk with the truth always and believe only God.

We should not complicate things by trying to do it on our own when God's instructions are to help us. He always has our best interest in mind.

I heard God say to me plain and simple, "get away from him, run!" I told God, NO. I lost fourteen years since that NO! Not that I wasted those fourteen years but they could had been more productive in the kingdom if I had used them wisely. This is why now I do what the word tells me to do, and I do not debate it.

We are living in a time where wasting time is not an option. We must be ready to do what the Bible tells us to do and trust that God will bring it to pass. We must never listen to our words.

So, when we hear from God don't bring our own agendas from our formal life. But remember that we are saved and been cleansed of all our past sins. They should be no murmuring or using defeating words, and definitely no complaining coming from us. Our walk with God should produce a change in us that transforms us that others will see the God in the things we do and say.

God wants to send us all to the nations of the world, and we can't take our old self with us. People should be able to see Christ in us. We should look like a family whose father is God.

I had never intentionally played church or had one foot in the church and another in the world. I might have slipped a few times but have regretted so much to the point of wanting to bury myself so far from God's face. I have felt so awful about it that have seriously vowed never to do it again.

He Provides

Since I rededicated myself to Christ, my commitment has been long-standing. I believe that God will help me in time of trouble and I trust that I will be victorious in everything I put my hands to do. All my friends, family members, and relatives know that I am a Jesus follower.

Everywhere I have worked my co-workers have known that I was a Christian. I would share Jesus Christ and His gospel to as many as would listen. Even the clients I worked with knew because as soon as they opened the door for me to talk to them about Jesus, I didn't hesitate. I have been very transparent about my faith everywhere I go. And. I am a staunch believer that with God all things are possible. I believe in His healing power. I believe in His provisions. I believe that I will lack for nothing and that His plans for me are great beyond what I can imagine and think.

Unfortunately, there are those who still doubt God and don't believe in His powers but still attend church. They know the Bible but make up their own doctrine. Then there is the one who can't believe beyond their problem and will not trust God to help solve it for them. There is the sinner who doesn't believe God can forgive them or the sick who refuses to believe in God's healing power and will take medication on top of more medication and remain sick.

The true believer trusts God and is committed to the things of God. They have the faith the size of a mustard seed and believe that Jesus will help them in every circumstance. He will make a difference in their lives and receive the victory.

Christians can't be warm Christians, or God will vomit us out. We have to believe that Christ Jesus is the truth, the way, and the life and that nothing is impossible for those who believe in Him.

In John 14:12-14 (NIV) we read,

> "Very truly I tell you, whoever believes in me will do the works I have been doing, and they will do even greater things than these because I am going to the Father. And I will do whatever you ask in my name, so that the Father may be glorified in the Son. You may ask me for anything in my name, and I will do it."

He Restores

If we continue to behave ungodly Satan will slander our character with the non-believers, and we will have no credibility. We will embarrass God and ourselves in our attempt to share the gospel of Jesus Christ.

The enemy is taking advantage to distract us by pinning us against one another. The Christians are not taking the things of God seriously when they continue with their petty behaviors. The word out in the street is that Satan is enlarging his territory not just for the pagans but for the Christians with their constant fighting among one another. This kind of behavior should be left to the ungodly.

I realize that we are humans, and we are far from perfect.

What do you suppose should distinguish us from the non-believers?

It's our Christ-like behavior which demonstrates love, kindness, and respect for everyone, not just some. We are to show the world who we are and how we live for God and that Christ Jesus is apparent in our lives by the respect we show to our brethren and for those who hate us.

We are to be a model of morality and hold a high standard that reflects God. We are to carry ourselves with humility and simplicity. Christians should never be heard using profanity or displaying acts of violence toward anyone. I always say that the world is watching us to criticize and contradict us. Keep in mind that the non-believer can spot falsity a mile away. I know how pagans think when a Christian approach them to witness about Jesus and salvation because I was a pagan once.

When I was younger, my parents would tell us kids, "don't open that door it's the hallelujah people." When I was a young adult, I would walk on the other side of the street and get away from them fast. As a mature woman, I would open the door, and listen to what they had to say but politely say to them, "I'm not interested, thank you." I share with you in the beginning chapters about my encounter with my friend who was a Christian. I ran into her about two or three times in the same block crossing the same corner and every time I wanted to run from her.

Anyway, I recall that every time she stopped me, I would feel strange like I wanted to run from her because she knew I was a sinner, (my estimation) and that bothered me.

At the time, I liked my lifestyle and was not interested in joining a church. I was friendly and would stop and say hello, ask her how she was doing and the family and then say goodbye and walk away. She would not be done talking when I was already turning to walk away, that is how uncomfortable I was. It wasn't that I didn't believe that God existed but that He was too heavenly for a sinner like me.

Most people that I know believe that God exists and very few questioned it. But like me (back in the days) they don't want to hear about it. I admit that it was foolish of me to run away from my friend who was only trying to save me from going to hell. But when I was in the world, I didn't quite have a concept about sin. I liked what I was doing. It was not until after my conversion that I realized what sin was and who Christ Jesus was and what He did for me on the Cross.

Many people are walking around without a clue about Christ Jesus. I tell people that my encounter with God is real. I tell them that the only way to God is through their conversion. Some are receptive when I speak to them about my conversion, and others just want to run from me, and I understand.

I had one young female, (my granddaughter's friend) say to me, "I don't believe in God." I said to her He is your Creator and the Creator of everything in the universe. She didn't know what to say after that and I left it alone. Several weeks later I asked my granddaughter about her, and she made me understood why she made that statement.

I can understand a non-believer make such a claim but when there are people in church walking and acting like God does not exist, there is a problem.

It's exactly those people who walk around with a chip on their shoulder, in the church, waiting to take it out on someone. They have issues that they have not resolved. They are the fools that Paul writes about in Galatians 3:1-3(NIV),

> "You foolish Galatians! Who has bewitched you? Before your very eyes Jesus Christ was clearly portrayed as crucified. ² I would like to learn just one thing from you: Did you receive the Spirit by the works of the law, or by believing what you heard? ³ Are you so foolish?"

The Webster dictionary definition of a fool is, "an imbecile, an idiot, and someone who lacks judgment." The scripture tells us that a fool is someone who says in their heart that there is no God. Like this young female, she had it all wrong because she had not met my Christ yet but she will.

But what excuse do some of my brothers and sister in Christ have for their foolishness? Christians must stop acting like God doesn't see their ungodly behaviors. We know He is alive but yet we don't behave like He is.

The last time I checked God is still sitting on His throne being faithful and trustworthy, willing to carry our burdens, heal us, and provide for us. I'm a witness to what God had done in my life even when I was lost and headed straight to hell.

When I was told by a doctor, we need to do further testing my God canceled whatever it was, and I was given a clean bill of health. My prayer nowadays is more for the Christians than for the sinners because they have double the trouble for acting like heathens. My Christian family needs to get it right that God is very much alive.

True God followers must hear His voice and adhere to His laws and forget what others are saying. What is happening in our churches today is that they are listening more to the world than to God's messenger, their pastor. They have lost their way and have been enticed by the world's latest craze and have put aside their Bibles, prayer life, and holiness. They know God and His Son and even the Holy Spirit, but they have forgotten who they are in Christ.

There was a time that walking with God was the most cherished desire for Christians but now they have settled to walking with worldly people. They have become self-centered when they should be Christ-centered.

I pray that for the sake of the next generation they will be awakened from this bewitched state they are in.

He Reconciles

God will be here for you and me day and night. The moment we received Jesus, we were reconciled with Jehovah God. Before our conversion, metaphorically speaking, we were like sheep without a shepherd. After our conversion, God through Christ Jesus resurrected us who were dead in our sins. The circumstances of the world will try to remove us from where God has put us to do kingdom work. That is why we must daily be about the things of God and not on the things of this world. If we have been seated in heaven with Christ, no one can move us from there, except for ourselves. We are a holy priesthood because of what Christ Jesus did on the cross at Calvary. We must never leave that place God has purposed for us for anything the world has to offer.

In the book of 2 Samuel we read that King David had taken his focus off of what God had positioned him to do. Just like King David whom God had to refocus, we too need a prophetic word that will bring us back to God's focus.

I believe God to use me and you in a mighty way to blow the top off of the secular world. God will turn everything around for His good. God is about to do something we will not believe. The enemy is trying to discourage us, and we need to shut down those things that are not productive or are a hindrance in our lives. God is in control, and the church will come of out their sleep, and God will get the glory.

I want to end this chapter with an excerpt from a song I like to sing in Spanish titled that has inspired me to seek more of my Savior,

(Mi Cristo Vive, by Danny Berrios) "My Redeemer Lives" (English version by Nicole C. Mullen). [25]

> "Well I know my Redeemer lives
> I know my Redeemer lives
> All of creation testifies
> This life within me cries
> I know my Redeemer lives."

Do you have a favorite song or a favorite Scripture that will inspire you to stay the course?

CHAPTER THIRTY-THREE

SPIRIT, PRAYER, BIBLE

"May the fire on my altar never down, May the fire on my altar never burn down…" This is the verse to the song, "House of Prayers," written and sung by Eddie James. [26] I am partial to this song because I never want my fire for the Lord to burn down. We should be on fire for the Father, the Son, and the Holy Spirit continuously.

The Fire Has Died Out

Born-again and veteran Christians must have a passion for the gospel and for doing the work of the kingdom of God. They should not let the things of this world enter into the hearts of those professing to be Christians. Let the fire of your altar burn continuously. The church must be on their knees praying that God will give them the courage to influence others with their words, as well as, show them that they Jesus in their hearts. We must lift up an altar in us to God.

There were so many prophets from the Old Testament and disciples from the New Testament who had a great passion for serving God no matter the consequences. What excuse do we have when we have received so much from God and have not been persecuted like they were.

Let the church take up their cross and persevere to keep the fire burning and serve God. No matter what happens let you and I continue to draw closer to God, that He may draw closer to us.

I saw and heard the shift from 2014 to 2016, and the preaching that came from the pulpit. The theme was for the church members to straighten up their mess, love one another and get right with God. The preachers talked about how messed up the members were and how their mess would trickle down to others not only in the church but in their family and friends.

I am a witness to the mess occurring in the church in the New Millennium.

There is a war going on in the soul between good and evil. We are battling to stop the flesh from taking over the spirit. We definitely need more of God and less of the flesh.

It's time that we go down to the Potter's House so He can fix our mess. There is a Spanish song title, (Al Taller Del Maestro by Alex Campos) [27] "To the Masters Workshop" and the song is about the need for the Potter to fix us because without God what good our life if He isn't there." I like the song because it reminds me that without God in my life is nothing. I hope that every Christian will feel this way.

Bishop T. D. Jakes has no qualms about telling the church what is right and wrong when Christians lose their anointing. Bishop Jakes was the guest speaker at my former church, one Friday evening and he preached about the church losing their fire for the Lord. He used the example of the first disciples who were filled with the anointing of God, "the early church was on fire on the day of Pentecost. They had the anointing power. The Spirit of the Lord was fresh in the early church. Prayer couldn't be kept out."

Some of us have smothered the fire of the Holy Spirit and wonder why things are going from bad to worse in our lives. The early church wanted nothing more than to be in the presence of the Almighty God and soak in His beauty and glory. They knew about His power and grace. They knew that He was in the business of setting captives free and delivering them from all kinds of infirmities. He whom the Son set free is free indeed (John 8:36).

We all are faced with the choice between good and evil every single day. But our response will determine who we will serve, God or Satan. God will allow us to go through certain situations in life as a test of our faith. For the most part, the source of our temptation is the worldly things and materialism. The media also plays a major influential role that starts the juices of our cravings to flow through our flesh. When we lust after those worldly things that's when sin enters our mind, heart, and body.

The temptation in and of itself isn't the sin but when it's activated by the person who is seduced.

There's no doubt that we all will be tempted, but it is how we respond to that temptation. We have a perfect example in Jesus who was tempted but didn't sin because the Father was in Him. He was proactive and was never tempted by the sin nature. God will make a way out of our desire to sin. When we are preoccupied with the sin, the spirit of the living God will convict us and will not allow that sin to fester anymore. When we love God more than we love sin, we will run from it.

In one of his sermons, Pastor Hagee preached on the anti-Christ and share the following,

> "That the immorality infiltrating the church today is to oppose the doctrines of the Bible inclusively Jesus Christ. The Church of Christ must be careful because they are the target of this mass-movement to create a new heathen nation. So, Christ-followers take note if you are not for Christ and all His teaching you are for the anti-Christ."

In the book of James, it reads, if you are a friend of the world you are an enemy of Christ. The pastor went on to say that,

> "the Holy Spirit is calling the church all around the world, but some of these churches have a fake gospel that produces no changes in the people's lives. They lie to their congregation about abortion and same-sex marriages, and tattoos."

In the book of Leviticus, it specifically states that people are not to tattoo themselves because the body belongs to God. The Bible makes it perfectly clear to the followers of Christ Jesus that it's either you serve God or Satan, but you can't serve two masters. America has become a cesspool of debauchery as evidenced by what we see in the media where there is no censorship as to what children and young adults can watch on television such as nudity, sex acts, profanity vulgar displayed of affection among the same sexes. The music they listen to with its illicit expressions of violence, gangs, drugs, and guns, and vulgar use of the female anatomy. There is a real demon problem in the television, theater, and music industry.

The Spirit Has Moved Out

One of my neighbors when I lived in the Southwest introduced me to a Christian couple who were her son's neighbors. Several months later, I needed work on my car, and I remember her son's neighbor who was a mechanic and I called this young man to make an appointment to have him check out my driver-side headlight. I had to leave the car, and his wife drove me home, we talked and became good friends after that night. One day she invited me to attend the Wednesday Bible study service at her church. When I got there, she and her husband were sitting in second to the front row, and she waved me to come over and sit with them. They were deacons in the church. She had told about the many problems they were encountering with the members in her church, and most of what she said had to do with jealousy from the other members because she and her husband had been long friends of the pastor. She mentioned that the pastor had taken a two-week cruise on church money, but because of the friendship, they never said anything to him.

I had been to many churches and had witnessed many oddities in these churches, but this one went beyond strange. I walk into a tiny foyer that leads into the sanctuary. The music was so loud it hurt my eardrums. There were two huge projection screens in the front walls behind the altar that was announcing the best ways people can tithe to the church. An older female member stood up at the altar to pray to start the service. What I found strange was that the screens continued to flash the announcements and she could not be heard over the loud music, and the people having full-blown conversations; and children running around. After a few minutes the pastor came from the outside, and as he reaches the altar, he yells out at the media person to play dancing music to liven up the service. I then witnessed what I thought was blasphemous. Several church members got up to dance as if they were in a club scene. One of them was the Elder of the church who had walked in with the pastor, and he started dancing with one of the females. He was about to do a dance called "the bump" as his hip moved toward her hip and I heard him say, "I almost did the bump with you." I couldn't help but laugh. I am writing about this because some members have lost their sense of shame.

People were actually dancing even the pastor, and it was not in the spirit. My friend and her husband just sat there as so did I. Really, in church? I remember the pastor taking a while before he spoke on the message. He began to cry, and these words came from his mouth, "I don't know why God has me asking Him for forgiveness, but I feel a heavy burden to ask God to forgive me and to ask the church to forgive me." These words came spewing from his lips. I saw in his demeanor a fear of being exposed in front of the members (most were family and friends I was told by my friend), but he looked scared (my estimation).

Several weeks later she invited me to a prophetic service at a different church. She mentioned that the pastors of the church we are going to visit are sincere and honest people. The invited guest was her church elder. Out of curiosity, I decided to attend. I was not surprised at what I witnessed that night. While the Elder was prophesizing to some of the attendees suddenly, the spirit of the Lord told me to go outside of the church and pray for the angels of God to encamp around the church and cover those who were in the church, including myself of course.

During the service, he prophesized and prayed for the people. I noticed there was a young male recording the service with his camcorder. In one instant the Elder turned to him and asked "did you get that" the young male told him, "no, the battery died" he took his right hand and smacked him on the right cheek and then made it look like he was laying hands on him. I sat and witnessed all that was taking place. The spirit of the Lord also revealed to me that night, "he is a charlatan."

My friend confirmed my suspicious since the spirit had also revealed it to her. The following evening my friend and I spoke, and she had known that he was a charlatan and that they had tried to tell the pastor, but he was not listening to them. My spirit had revealed to me that the pastor had not been called to pastor and he used the church to make a salary out of the tithes and offerings. She had the gift of prophecy but had to keep it hidden because her pastor would not allow her to use it in his church. I believe that God used me to witness everything and encourage this young couple to pray about those things and listen to God's direction for their lives. Both she and her husband have a gift, and they are using it for God's glory and honor. My friends have since left the church and have their own ministry.

The followers of God must know their purpose and not allow the secular world to stifle it. The enemy will present thing which we are not supposed to do in order to and keep us from our true ministry. Like my friends mentioned above, the pastor had them sitting in church attending meetings, but they had no real say about anything. We can't share what purpose we have been called with everyone because the enemy is listening and will take us off focus our vision.

The enemy knows that purpose-driven people are prepared to go to work and choose God's direction rather than their own. And, that they also have a heart of love for the lost souls.

Come Holy Spirit... Light the Fire

The church needs people to pray, intercede and begin to rally for revival to take place in their nation. But for revival to happen the church must have like-minded people who have a passion for changing the generation and their community. The church should wake up and go after their vision even when no one else sees it. Ask God to let you see your vision and why you are here.

There is a difference between the early church and today's church when it came prayer life. In the early church, they believed and had the faith that they would receive what they prayed for. Their faith and prayer went hand in hand. They prayed with the power to shake up the heavens here on earth. The true followers must believe that their promise is at the door and God is ready to give it to them. Everything that we have asked God for will come to fruition if only we believe and trust Him.

Karen Abercrombie played Miss Clara in the movie "War Room," and she inspired me to start my own prayer war room. In the movie, there is a young female who is having marital problems, and she visits Miss Clara's home on Real Estate business. As the young woman is walking through the home, she enters a room Miss Clara calls her prayer war room (specific prayers written on paper are taped to the walls). The young female turns around and says, "you wrote prayers for every area of your life," and Miss Clara responds, "prayer strategy." As the movie progress, Miss Clara continues to share prayer strategies with her, "you need to plead with God so that He can do what only He can then you got to get out of the way and let Him do it. You need to do your fighting in prayer." In one scene Miss Clara is praying by herself, "Lord we need an army of believers, raise them up Lord, raise them up." [28]

We must believe that we can move mountains with prayers because it's the power given to us from God.

If things are not happening, it's because we have not taken dominion over the sin or the situation in serious prayer. When we pray our prayer should enter the spiritual realm where the angels are sent to us to take authority and rebuke all manners of unclean spirits. We need a manifestation of heaven in our prayer war room.

On the day of Pentecost (which is 50 days after the resurrection) in the upper room, the church was gathered and God's spirit set upon everyone in the room. As believers we also have an invitation to come to Him and be filled with His Holy Spirit. When we are empty, (which can happen from time to time) come back to that upper room in fasting and prayer and get another spiritual refill.

Pastor Dr. Sharon Nesbitt calls this power given to us by the Holy Spirit to be the "Rhua" (Spirit in Hebrew) Power. The power that changes the atmosphere when we allow Jesus to inhabit our homes and honor the Holy Spirit. You and I must pursue after the presence of the Holy Spirit, and the Lord will arise in our lives once again. Dr. Nesbitt shares that,

> "the reason we play church is because the members don't see the glory of God. We should not get so comfortable in the church. There is a need to get into action and help those in the church and change the atmosphere both in the church and in the world. We must realize that we have the authority to change because we have the Rhua power of the glory of God. We must be serious about God and His business." [29] Let the Holy Spirit have his way in you and glow.

"Ripley's Believe It or Not!" Was the name given to a television show started back in the early 1950s. My family and I began to watch a revised version in the early 1980s hosted by Jack Palance. It featured strange and unusual things and supernatural occurrences. We don't need to watch a television show to know that we serve a supernatural God that is more than happy to bless His children supernaturally. When we ask God to watch over us, He will put a supernatural covering from above to keep us safe from harm. The Old Testament calls this supernatural occurrence the covenant when

He covered His children in the desert with a cloud by day and a pillar of fire by night (Exodus 13:21). With God's covenant comes supernatural blessings of hope, prosperity, and help from above. In the New Testament covenant, we are under the Blood of the lamb, Christ Jesus. All that is required of us to retain these wonderful supernatural blessings is to maintain a relationship with Jehovah.

Jehovah will raise those who are dead in the church and eliminate everything that is a hindrance in fulfilling God's divine purpose. He will take us out of our dead situation, and by His power alone God will raise us up again. We are no good to anyone being dead in our spirit. They need to hear that God isn't dead but very much alive and that we are His breathing witnesses. You and I are the prophets for the New Millenniums. We are to prophesize life to our family, friends, neighbors, and strangers by sharing the truth and let God bring them to life.

Our Foundation...The Bible

In 1944 God used President Franklin D. Roosevelt to bring life to the soldiers during WWII having this statement printed in Bibles to be handed out to everyone in the armed forces,

> "To the members of the Army:
> As Commander in Chief, I take pleasure in commending the reading of the Bible to all who serve in the armed forces of the United States...It is a fountain of strength and now, as always, an aid in attaining the highest aspirations of the human soul. Very sincerely yours, Franklin D. Roosevelt" [30]

> The President recognized that the Bible, the word of God, is where our greatest source comes from. "If the foundations are destroyed..." (Psalm 1-7, NIV). The church must get back to reading the Bible, our foundation. The quality of our life depends on our

understanding of the Scriptures for it is good for all the reasons found in 2 Timothy 3:16-17 (NIV),

"All Scripture is God-breathed and is useful for teaching, rebuking, correcting and training in righteousness so that the servant of God may be thoroughly equipped for every good work."

We need to claim God in our life for every situation, especially if we are regressing to what we use to be. We sometimes don't understand God's grace and forget that He came to cleanse us of all unrighteousness and to bless us in the process. If we read the Scriptures, we will understand God's character. God does nothing randomly, but He always has a plan. For those who have been in the church long enough, you know that we can't get to Christ Jesus unless God calls us.

Like Ezra, I too am appalled with what I am seeing in the church of Christ today. Ezra was bothered with his people because they were living like the heathens when they should have separated themselves and remain holy. If I can recognize a problem in the church, I am sure so do the pastors, and it's their responsibility to tell the people to stop doing things God's word explicitly prohibits.

It appears that the Shepherd of the house of God needs to take accountability for the straying away of their members, their sheep.

"What has happened to us is a result of our evil deeds and our great guilt, and yet, our God, you have punished us less than our sins deserved and had given us a remnant like this. …Would you not be angry enough with us to destroy us, leaving us no remnant or survivor? LORD, the God of Israel, you are righteous! We are left this day as a remnant. Here we are before you in our guilt, though because of it not one of us can stand in your presence" (Ezra 9:13,14B-15, NIV).

I get up every morning and pray for God to give me His wisdom and revelation to follow His every cue on that day. I surrender my very being. It may not go as perfect as I want my day to go but it could be worse if I didn't commend myself to God daily. I pray, "let this day be a production day that God may get the glory and honor." Every day we should get up to seek God's guidance and direction as for how to proceed and have a successful day.

We must understand that God will tolerate only so much before He chastises us if we refuse to get it right. We have been bought with a high price to be playing dangerously and carelessly. "God is not mock" Galatians 6:7). God's mercy and grace liberated us from the sin of death through the shedding of Blood through His Son, Christ Jesus. It is by God's grace that we can receive mercy for our sins, not for anything that we have done (2 Timothy 1:9, NIV). We must continue to follow God's laws and believe that through His grace we will not die in our sins.

God made us, and we are not a mistake. That we are prone to make mistakes, yes, absolutely, but God can fix them. You see, God chose us before we were born and we have a reason to be where we are now, it is no coincidence. We must be confident of this one thing, that He will never abandon us.

Our assignment is so unique that only we can do it. So, we should not concern ourselves with what others may say or do to us because God has a purpose for us, and He will remove all the obstacles from our way. Claim what God has for you and believe that it will come to pass.

For many people having their first baby is a gift, buying their first home is like a gift, and getting their first brand new car is a gift, but the greatest gift we can receive is the gift of life in the name of Christ Jesus.

In John 15:5 Jesus illustrates the purpose of the vine and the branches, and He tells everyone who will hear,

> "You are already clean because of the word I have spoken
> to you. Remain in me, as I also remain in you. No

branch can bear fruit by itself; it must remain in the
vine. Neither can you bear fruit unless you remain in
me. "I am the vine; you are the branches. If you remain
in me and I in you, you will bear much fruit; apart from
me you can do nothing." (NIV)

The victory that you and I claim today is because of the shed
blood of Christ Jesus, and we should eternally be grateful to Him.
We must remember always to thank God for Christ Jesus.

My cousin Elsa is a Messianic Jew who converted to Judaism
about twenty years ago after she married a Jewish fellow. They
were both attending a Christian church when she decided to attend
a Messianic synagogue. My cousin told me that she first had to
learn the Hebrew language and take a series of courses. I value her
devotion to the Scriptures and to God. I had the privilege of staying
with her for a few days as I had mentioned before and I saw her
collections of books and how she had read the majority of them. I
do not see myself being that devoted but I should. She believes that
in the Christian-Judeo faith it's okay to have the Torah which is
meant for teaching, it is an instructional book that contains the law.

Maybe this is why she has been to Israel several times because
she is enamored with God, His land and His people. "I love the land,
I love the people, and the more I visit Israel, the more I love being
there, and I see how good God is to His people. God gave them
Israel because they are His people." She breathes and sleeps the Holy
Scriptures, especially the Old Testament. When she talks about the
Messiah, her eyes lit up, and there is no stopping her from talking
about God once she gets started on the conversation. I definitely
saw her gratitude toward God. "I know how faithful He is. When
we know what God has done for us, that is why I love my Messiah.
My life is complete when I have God's love. We need to have a first-
century mentality to understand the scriptures", she goes on to say.

Gratitude is a great attitude in response to what God has done
for us and will continue to do.

Remember that God has been faithful. He will bring solutions to our dark days. When no one else cares, he is the one who hears our cry in the middle of the night and comes to us with open arms to comfort us. He desires that we love, trusts and obey Him because it's in our heart to do so, not because we have to.

What we learn about Thanksgiving is that we should give God thanks for being the same God today as He was yesterday and will be tomorrow. We are never to forget from where God has brought us throughout the years. When we wake up, we should be singing His praises.

In the story of Jonah, it was His thankfulness that got him out the belly of the whale.

> "In my distress, I called to the Lord, and He answered me. From deep in the realm of the dead I called for help, and you listened to my cry" (2:1-2, NIV). "Those who cling to worthless idols turn away from God's love for them. But with shouts of grateful praise, will I sacrifice to you. What I have vowed I will make good. I will say, "Salvation comes from the Lord" (2:8-9, NIV).

Thanksgiving is what brings great things to our life, especially if we are in the midst of a difficult situation. If we want the miracles from God, the least we can do is to be thankful.

Chapter Thirty-Four

Believe It! To Receive It!

Before we came to Christ Jesus, He had already found and seen us in the mire of our lives. He also saw the good in us. God neither cares so much about our imperfections nor for our sins. God just wants us to come to Him and get clean up and sit at His table.

No Dummies Allowed

But the children of God are living in a world of confusion, and they are teaching their children about all the gods that the secular world worship, like the cellphone, video games, uncensored television programming, body piercing, and tattoos. "Do you not know that your bodies are temples of the Holy Spirit, who is in you, whom you have received from God? You are not your own; you were bought with a price. Therefore, honor God with your bodies" (1 Corinthians 6:19-20, NIV).

On the last Sunday service of 2014, I was at my former church in Eastport, and the guest pastor said something that stuck with me throughout the following year 2015. He said,

> "it is a dangerous thing to have God and not have faith. God is trying to bless us, but we get an attitude about it. Our doubt will make us dumb. Don't bring doubt into your future. Don't be dumb in the years to come. This is the season that God will bless those who are connected to Him. Don't listen to negativity. Don't let anyone speak negativity into your future. Don't let anyone stop us from receiving our victory. Be around the saints who believe."

I had determined in 2015 to move forward like a locomotive toward my goals. I had gotten close to God and was practicing what I was reading. I wasn't going to allow anyone from derailing me from God's goals and purpose.

At the beginning of 2016, I began my journey to author my first book and continued to have faith in God. God kept me during those difficult moments when I thought that financially it was impossible. God would come through every time, and I kept my hopes up high because I believed in the God of miracles. Toward the end of 2016, I graduated from the Eagles International Training Authors Institute (in Dallas Texas) with a Certificate of Completion and had authored my first book. I had applied for the 2017 EITI Flag course to train as a flagger and bought some beautiful praise and worship flags to bring back to Connecticut.

I was back in the northeast for ten months, and I was excited about telling my pastor everything I wanted to do in the church. I was ready to start my evangelistic ministry as well as start a Dance ministry at the church. I also wanted to tell him that I was going to take a Flag Course to teach those who were interested in flagging.

I had scheduled an appointment to meet with him and discuss my plans.

I arrived about ten minutes early and waited outside the office. He had his children in his office, and I could hear them talking because the door was opened. Another member came to his office, and they made him aware that I was waiting. I continue to wait for what seemed like thirty minutes, and then he came out and sat across from me. I greeted him, and he nodded his head. He had a rare look on his face that made me feel I was disturbing him. (my estimation)

I felt I had to make my presentation in haste. I got up and walked over to him to give him a signed copy of my book. He spoke to me in a rather harsh tone that was hurtful. Not once did he congratulate me on my book. He was offending as he mentioned the dance ministry. It was unfortunate I could not get anyone to volunteer to be in my dance ministry. I sat there and didn't say a word. After he was done berating me, I packed up my flags and said goodbye with a grin on my face. After that visit whenever I saw him, I would greet him and his family with a smile and a blessing. We must not feed into the enemy because we know his time is short.

There is supernatural warfare in the spiritual realm taking place as sure as you are reading this book. But the Bible assures us that we win if we keep our wits.

Choose Success

Every season should be a season for a great victory. There are residual blessings God promised us years ago, and they will come to pass. God is going to do things for us that people are going to say, Wow! We should be around people who have our best interest at heart and have a positive spirit to believe with us.

There are several types of people in the church I had the misfortune to come in contact with. The ones who have lost their faith and are walking around downtrodden. They look like they have been trampled but want to stay there. Then there are the ones who have become so bitter with their life that they want to make others around them just as miserable. These people neither believe in God the Father, the Son, nor the Holy Spirit. They believe in themselves, and they try to project that negative attitude onto others. How can there be people who serve in the church, pray in the church but don't have faith?

As for you and me, we are going to stay around positive people.

When we examine our spiritual life, are more likely to be reflecting Christ and following Him around to do His will or are we following the world and all its foibles? The answer should be a positively and unequivocally yes to Christ Jesus. We must stop with all the negativity and leave room for the positive things. Jesus always had a positive answer, and if we are going to reflect Him in our lives, we have to start thinking like Him. There were times that Jesus remained quiet and I believe that He could not speak anything negative toward another person. Jesus was honest but never negative. If we can begin to think in a positive way, I am confident that we can find better solutions. We need to change our mindset and think more in line with the word of God.

We need a revolution that will jump start changing the fundamental things from Satan's rule and sin to God's commands and salvation.

Pastors everywhere must start asking questions that will have a powerful influence on the mind of the hearer because questions force us to think. The mind has to believe what the word of God is saying to the people. So, we must prepare our minds for action and hope in Christ and the Cross. Let the Lord open our eyes and see the good in us and in others.

John Maxwell tells his audience,

> "Share our growth with somebody who is cheering us on, (stay away from negative people and haters). If they are happy [for you] do tell them and if they are not, drop them. Have good people around. People who are happy with our growth and commitment. Be grateful for those who help. Get with people that can multiply you. [And], add value to others." [31]

We must help and encourage each other and be a catalyst to greatness.

Every experience is a learning experience, and we will learn from our and others mistakes. Remind yourself what good things have happened in the past years. Positive questions will empower us. We are going to let our light shine in this dark world because this isn't the time to hide our lamps in the closet. Pastor Tony Evans from the Urban Alternative concurs,

> "Everyone has come out of the closet we might as well come out too. The Bible says, that when we come to Christ, we are transferred out of the kingdom of darkness

into the kingdom of His Son. We are now living in a different realm. The governing guides are given to us by His word. It is the job of God's people, God's church to be the immune system for the culture. Church members aren't here to attend church Sunday after Sunday and go home and ignore what is happening in and around our nation. We have a job to do for the kingdom. In the church, we learn to arm ourselves with the word of God and receive strength for our belief system to go out and share with boldness – whether saved or unsaved. We must give the lost world a glimpse of what we receive from God so that they will want more of what we possess and seek it for themselves." [32]

We will see the salvation of God in the lives of this lost generation if we don't lose faith and continue to press on. The word promises that "every knee will bow and every tongue will confess Jesus is Lord" (Philippians 2:9-11, NIV).

Where we have given up, God will give us hope. There is something that the Lord will put in us to ignite the fire to succeed in all we put our feet to do for the kingdom and in our lives. Our story will change from a history of failures to a story of success. Let the fire be in you. When there is a fire in you, then you will want more of God, more of the word, more church, and more midnight vigils.

Those who come to the midnight vigils come to seek more of God. Be on Fire for the Lord. Step out of your comfort zone and seek God like never before and when you do, He will lead you to His secret place. Come to church expecting something different. Forget that you are in the church but allow yourself to be transported to the mount where Jesus sat to speak to His disciples. After all, we are His disciples.

I believe that every yoke will be destroyed and many Christians who are spiritually dead will be plunged into a glorious revival. Church people must stop limiting God's power and allow Him to open up the windows of heaven and bless us. You and I will wait for the day when we will reap all the blessings God has in store for us for being a good and faithful servant (Matthew 25:23). Let you, and I be in the right place.

CHAPTER THIRTY-FIVE

REMEMBER ME, GOD

Tell God to remember you and what He had done for you and He will answer you. There is a time when we need to get God's attention for a very difficult situation that overwhelms us. We should not forget how He got us out of other troubles we have gotten into.

> "Remember me, LORD, when you show favor to your people, come to my aid when you save them, that I may enjoy the prosperity of your chosen ones, that I may share in the joy of your nation and join your inheritance in giving praise" (Psalm 1064-5, NIV).

Grant Us Favor

When we pray in faith-believing God will send angels on our behalf. Think of what we have done in His name and then tell God to cancel whatever problem we are experiencing. We must place our hope on Christ Jesus. In the story of Hannah, she calls on God in prayer and supplication to give her a child because she was barren.

> "In her deep anguish, Hannah prayed to the LORD, weeping bitterly. ¹¹ And she made a vow, saying, "LORD Almighty, if you will only look on your servant's misery and remember me, and not forget your servant but give her a son, then I will give him to the LORD for all the days of his life, and no razor will ever be used on his head." (I Samuel 1:10-11, NIV)

She prayed to God, "Oh Lord remember me," and the Lord remembers. The effective, fervent prayers of the righteous people are heard by God, and He dispatches angels to come to our assistance. When we put our hope in Christ just wait with confidence and expectation for the outcome. When it is in the will of God, it will happen. We must never forget that God is our only source and that everything we have comes from Him. Without God, in our lives, things become difficult and unbearable to handle. But with God in charge, we can rejoice and let Him handle everything we need help with.

Those who don't believe in God have to go through their struggles alone and face insurmountable obstacles. The Bible encourages us to know that whatever we bind on earth is bound in heaven and whatever we loose on earth is loosed in heaven. I pray for my church family that they will seek God and not allow this world to ruin them.

It's my observation that the more education we get, the more intellectual we become, the more we deviate from God's plan of redemption. We think that we can do without God. I know, I hear it all the time from my own youngest son who has a CNC Machine Technology Certificate. He reminds me that there are only a handful of people that can do what he does for this type of work. Hence, his intellect gets in the way of his need for God. He will tell me, "mom I don't want to hear about your God." I tell him, "He is our God, the Creator of the Universe and it's because of Him that you have your being."

The more educated, the more depraved this nation becomes. Everyone can see how God is being forced out of this nation, out of the universities, and in some cases out of the religious establishments like in the 'New Age' movement, and 'Scientology' to name a few.

Christians are not managing very well the moral dilemma facing the nation in this generation. The choices of the church of Christ will either hinder or enhance the nation. The church is allowing this nation to do things to shut out God. What this nation needs is the church to declare that Jesus Christ is God. They must stop being ashamed to admit that God is real. We need a church united that will declare that they love Jesus Christ. The Bible preaches that Jesus said, "And, I when I am lifted up from the earth, will draw all people to myself" (John 12:32, NIV).

But Satan has come as the angel of enlightenment with all the media gadgets that have the church people on a frenzy. The church members are buying the newest cell phones and the latest game box in the market for their children. They are substituting material things for the true joy, who is the Savior. None of those gadgets are going to give my brothers and sisters in Christ a ticket to heaven.

What should be more important to the believer, but eternity, and where they will spend it? Marcus Lamb founder of Day Star has this to say to us, "It's time to put the focus on Jesus Christ and preach Him."

I came to realized how much time I was spending on Facebook and decided to take a hiatus from it. I have nothing against the social media, and they have their usefulness, but they can be addicting. Social media allows us to see our family and friends and chat with them. And, it can also be useful for posting scripture and important health information and yes, every now and then we can post an event. But I have limited my time on Facebook and have even taken lengthy hiatuses from it. Facebook like all the other social media can become a distraction for the Christian because it leads to spending less time reading the Bible, and from spending quiet time with God. Facebook can even affect the time we need for evangelizing a lost soul.

We need to open our eyes and realize that we are in spiritual warfare. When the devil comes to entice us with all these social media apps, we must push back and tell the enemy, "get thee behind me Satan" (Matthew 16:23, NIV).

We are going to declare victory and take authority overall power of the enemy. The enemy isn't going to tell us what to do, but we are going to tell the enemy the devil, "go to hell." The next time you feel the urge to read the Bible, pray or just spent time with God alone but find yourself picking up your cell phone or start to search your social media don't go for it! But realize, it's the devil telling you what to do. "Endure suffering along with me, as a good soldier of Christ Jesus. Soldiers don't get tied up in the affairs of civilian life, for then they cannot please the officer who enlisted them" (2 Timothy 2:3-4, NIV). God called us to be His army, and the message from Him is to fight. The Apostle Paul wrote in the second letter to Timothy,

> "Preach the word; be prepared in season and out of season; correct, rebuke and encourage—with great patience and careful instruction. For the time will come when people will not put up with sound doctrine. Instead, to suit their own desires, they will gather around them a great number of teachers to say what their itching ears want to hear. They will turn their ears away from the truth and turn aside to myths. But you, keep your head in all situations, endure hardship, do the work of an evangelist, discharge all the duties of your ministry. ...I have fought the good fight, I have finished the race, I have kept the faith (2 Timothy 4:2-5, 7, NIV).

You and I must fight the good fight because we know God has our back and we are running to finish the race set before us. It is a good thing that you and I are here for such a time as this (Esther 4:14, NIV). It is God who grants us favor, who protects us, who loves us, and who cares for us. I believe God will empower His chosen priesthood to touch the lives of all those He sends to us.

Nothing Is Impossible

It's almost the middle of 2015, and I am preparing to move back to the northeast and regretting it because I really liked living in the Southwest. I didn't want to leave the church, the pastors and my newfound friends. I looked back at what I had accomplished, how many people I had ministered to, and thought about those that I will miss. I have shared anecdotes of my experience with church people who have hurt me with their negative behavior and attitude. But let me share with you a story of two families who broke my heart in a different way.

The first family whose story I am about to share with you I had met in my cell group. They had attended the group a few times until they moved away to another town miles away. But we maintained the friendship since we attended the same church.

Several months later I receive a letter from them inviting me to a secret meeting at their home. I wasn't the only one invited but a few from their new cell group. They wrote in the letter that I wasn't to tell anyone about this meeting. The meeting was scheduled for after one of the Sunday services, and they offered to serve lunch.

They were people in the house who I didn't know, but we introduced ourselves because the host and hostess were busy with the lunch preparations. We all went into the living room after the introductions and the feasting. The husband was quiet she was doing all the talking. She began by telling us that she had received a revelation that 'Armageddon' was soon to happen. She said, "we have been offered a bunker at a friend's yard who lives two towns over, and we are thinking about going there with whoever wants to come with us." She continued to share the reason for choosing us, in particular, to come to this meeting, "we were supernaturally chosen because we are educated and intelligent people and others will listen to us." I couldn't believe what I was hearing, but I kept my composure and asked questions relevant to their plans and if they had discussed this with their cell group leader and the pastor.

Some of the other members talked about ministering to the lost souls before hiding out in some bunker. We discussed the importance of sharing this information with people who need to be evangelized and baptized. After more discussion on the topic of salvation one person who came with his wife asked, "Can I get baptized." I thought to myself, he must really believe that the end is near and wants to get right with God. I must say that it is a good tactic to have us if get someone to repent and give his/ her life to Christ in that instant. But that wasn't the case. The host filled a children's pool with water, and the wife got some towels, and the rest of us there sang praise songs.

I went home feeling somewhat disturbed and concern about this couple who I had come to truly adored. They didn't appear to be happy with the outcome of the meeting. They were expecting everyone to be on aboard with them and no one committed to doing anything. (My estimation.)

The following Sunday I saw him (he was ushering), and I greeted him, he appeared odd. He told me, "I don't care if no one believes we received the revelation." I became concerned for him and his family due to his odd behavior toward me. I was worried. That Sunday I spoke to one of the members I had met at his home and asked him for the cell group leader's name and phone number. I just had to speak with the cell group leader about this couple. I was able to speak with the cell group leader a week later and told him everything. The couple stopped coming to church. I stayed in touch with the couple by phone and email but she stopped taking my phone calls, and her email was no longer available. My heart was broken because there was nothing else I could do for them but connect them to those who would be available for them. I was moving back to the northeast.

We must realize that there are people in the church that are weak and vulnerable. Some will cry out to God for help, but they will not go to the church family for fear that they will be ridiculed and gossiped about. They have probably had the experience and choose to remain in their mess. But I know that they can't do it on their own strength. It takes those of us who are stronger mentally, emotionally and physically in the church to assist them without prejudices. We must remember when we were in our mess. Perhaps it was a different scenario, but we needed someone to reach out to us.

The other couple I met and spent some time with lived in deplorable conditions and they had several small children. I would see them in church on Sundays and noticed how disheveled the mother and children looked. I had been attending church for two years, Sunday after Sunday, I never saw the mother wear anything but same oversize sweats, and the same dirty sneakers. Her hair was always unruly (like she just had gotten up from bed). One Sunday after service I stopped her and asked the usual questions after my introduction. "How are you and the family?" The following time I was bolder and asked her if she didn't mind me coming over and spend some time with her and the children sort of like to give her a break. She had four and was expecting another one, (they were close in age). She agreed, and I didn't hesitate to come over. When I went to their home, I was appalled at the way she and her family lived. There were garbage and clothes on the floor and everywhere around the apartment. The walls had brown roach stains all around the ceiling and the corners. The roaches had made her home their home. There were roaches crawling around in the kitchen. These critters knew they were home, and they were not going anywhere. I offered to help her clean up and organize the apartment for, and she allowed me. So, the following week I came ready to clean house. I brought all my cleaning supplies and started to clean. She wasn't there, and neither were the children, but the mother (who lived with her) opened the door. I cleaned and organized the best I could. I brought bins to organize the children's clothing. They had no kitchen table. I went to the church's community closet and asked if they would find her a dining table for the children to place their food plates on instead of on the floor. The community closet got them a kitchen table. The person who delivered the table to her home happened to have been her cell group leader. He and I talked about their situation, and he told me that they have been trying to work with this family for a long time but they keep very much to themselves, and the husband would not say anything in the cell group about their plight.

I felt relieved that someone else knew about their situation and would follow-up with them once I left.

I saw her in church several Sundays later after that talk I had with her cell group leader, and she acted differently with me. She didn't want to stop to say hello to me anymore. I knew then that I wasn't wanted in her home anymore. My heart was broken because I was trying to help her and her family change their situation. I involved her group leader to work close with the family. That was the best I could do.

I share all this to bring awareness that in our church there are hurting people. People who are misled. People who are disabled. The church is like a hospital that helps bring healing and assistance to those who need it.

Stay focus on things you can change. If it's a difficult task take the issue head-on with God before you. "Nothing is impossible with God "(Matthew 19:26, NIV). This is not a cliché; this is the fact, a Biblical fact.

Some members are lost in the church, and they are trying to navigate through life without a compass. They need the assistance of those who are grounded in the word to help bring them through. It doesn't mean that we are better than they are because we are not. The Scriptures reminds us that there is no one good, not one. That without God we are nothing and we can't do anything.

CHAPTER THIRTY-SIX

THERE IS NO ONE GOOD, BUT JESUS

When Jesus Christ isn't the foundation of the message, the church is weakened and eventually crumbles. It's time for the church leaders to tell the truth or hang up their priestly garments. How did the Christians lose their validity? How did the culture influence the Christians? I tell you that it happened because they got complacent. All it took was for the devil to give them what they liked most and he pulled them in. Those are the same members who come to the church and don't greet the members.

I have noticed that the new Christians don't carry a Bible to the church which could indicate that they don't care about reading the Scriptures or are ashamed to be recognized as church attendees. (My estimation.) For me, to carry my Bible to church means that I am going to read it in church during service. I carry the Bible with pride because it's God's word written inside. I'm not ashamed to carry my Bible to church. My neighbors know that I go to church on Sundays not just because I carry my Bible but because I invite them to church.

> "There is no one righteous, not even one; there is no one who understands; there is no one who seeks God. All have turned away, they have together become worthless; there is no one who does good, not even one." (Romans 3:9-12, NIV).

Pastors Face Challenges

Everything else is sinking sand unless the Lord builds the church (Matthew 7:24-27). Christ is the head of the church, and He deserves all the accolades and respect. What is the sense of going to church on Sundays if God is not preached? What is the sense of attending Bible study if God isn't in the lesson plan? What is the sense of going to Sunday School if God isn't taught?

The church is built by the Lord and His laws. The church must remain the true foundation of society, or we will return to being barbarians. (My estimation.)

What I see happening is a difference between what the church leader is teaching and what the church members are receiving. The church members may have a doctrine that is custom-fitted that is unlike that of the church leader's teaching.

Let me explain it this way, the pastor may say to the church give your neighbor to your right a "high five," and the person standing next to you or me may turn to the person on the left because they choose not to give you or me a high five. Then when the pastor repeats himself and tells the congregation to greet the person on the left the person goes forward, and you and me are standing with no one to give a high five to. That member has chosen to follow their own doctrine because they choose not to be neighborly to you or me. So, the same will be for when the pastor tells the congregation to love one another; they will choose to love only those they want and forget about the rest. Equally the same, when the church leader tells the church about going out to evangelize the lost souls, they instead hear "stay home" on that day. Those same people become a hindrance to the church spiritual growth.

"Woe to you, teachers of the law and Pharisees, you hypocrites! You shut the door of the kingdom of heaven in people's faces. You yourselves do not enter, nor will you let those enter who are trying to" (Matthew 23:13, NIV).

The pastors are facing a tremendous challenge with the new

so-call Christians. Because the members have shut their ears to the truth, and they serve as a deterrent to the other members around them, just as the Pharisees were doing in the New Testament. Those members continue to attend church, but their interest is not in the kingdom but to distract those around them.

There's no doubt in my mind that there are many members who have been delivered, who are saved and sanctified. But there are those who continue to behave like heathens and need deliverance. I have heard pastors tell the church to stop listening to worldly music and to stop watching the soap operas. To keep themselves from entertaining vulgar jokes, but they do what they want to do. We should not burden the pastor with our attitude but assist the pastor. Pastors are not perfect, and they don't profess to be so. They are servants of God but with a lot more responsibility then the members of the church. I have seen pastors do some silly things on the pulpit, but I never thought I would see one look so frustrated that I thought he would walk off and go home.

There has to be more than some pastors that are frustrated with their members because of their blatant disregard for Biblical doctrine. Those members have rebelled against God, and they are disobedient to the pastors. It appears that the spirit of Jezebel is in the church of today. Those members don't want God and are not believing the Bible.

There has to be something terribly wrong with the Christians of today when they are questioning the Scriptures. The Scriptures should encourage them to want to change. They attend church and pretend to listen to the preacher, but there are no visible signs that they are following Christ Jesus. They are what the Scriptures call double-minded people (James 1:8).

It was during a normal Sunday morning service. The praise and worship team were outstanding, and the reading of the word was a blessing to my ears. The only difference that I noticed was that not too many members had come to church that day. When the pastor came to the altar, he didn't pray his usual prayer but began to rant about people doing picnics during church service and pulling half the church with them. I saw signs of a very frustrated and discouraged minister. I felt sad for him. He was having difficulty accepting that he knew his members were at a (member of his own family) picnic. According to the comments he was making he didn't want to have service that day. That is how frustrated he was.

I heard Pastor Paul Sheppard on one occasion share with the church that doing the work God wouldn't be in vain,

> "I have faith at any age. What the church needs are people with a spirit of Caleb. As we get older, we adjust, and we oath to know where we are in life. We must remain significant even when we age. Caleb walked with God. Concentrate on what God has ordained us to do. Do the things that count for God." [33]

Caleb was with Joshua from when he was forty years old, and they journeyed together through the desert those forty years. Caleb trusted God all those years and believed that God would give him and the Israelite the 'Land of Promise.' Caleb never stopped believing, and he went to Joshua to claim the land. Joshua gave Caleb the land that had been promised to him. Caleb never stopped believing God for keeping him all those years and for giving him the victory. "So here I am today, eighty-five years old! I am still as strong today as the day Moses sent me out; I'm just as vigorous to go out to battle now as I was then. Now give me this hill country that the LORD promised me that day." (Joshua 14:10-12, NIV).

I believe that everyone at one time or another have doubted this whole issue of Christianity. From the disciples who walked with God, Jesus Christ in the flesh, and all those who followed after His Resurrection, like Thomas. We are no exception. But I also believe that if we have doubts, then we have nothing to give us the hope to survive in such a cruel and unkind world. If we have doubt, we can't receive from God everything He has promised us in the Scripture.

In Jeremiah 29:11, (NIV) He promises us, "For I know the

plans I have for you," declares the Lord, "plans to prosper you and not to harm you, plans to give you hope and a future." I am a witness to what God can and will do for those who believe in Him and continue to please Him. He will bless you. I guaranteed it. The true God followers will not get frustrated and stay in a right relationship with God.

Discipling Is A Challenge

Pastors may have to go back to the old school basics of evangelizing new converts sort like what the Salvation Army started doing back in the late 19th century. I want to share how the Salvation Army began and the reason for their existence,

> "The Salvation Army is a Protestant Christian church and international charitable organization structure in the quasi-military fashion. Their mission statement reads: The Salvation Army, an international movement, is an evangelical part of the universal Christian church. Its message is based on the Bible. Its ministry is motivated by the love of God. Its mission is to preach the gospel of Jesus Christ and to meet human needs in His name without discrimination. ...The Army was founded in 1865 in London by one-time Methodist circuit-preacher William Booth and his wife Catherine as the East London Christian Mission and can trace its origin to the Blind Beggar tavern. ...William Booth's early motivation for The Salvation Army was to convert poor Londoners such as prostitutes, gamblers, and alcoholics to Christianity. ...William Booth described the organization's approach: The three 'S's best expressed the way in which the Army administered to the 'down and outs': first soup, second, soap, and finally salvation. ...The familiar use of the bell ringers to solicit donations." [34]

Most everyone in the community knows about the Salvation Army, they know the name of the General and they know to get soup, soap, and salvation. If you ask any homeless person if they have heard about the Salvation Army, they will without question give you the address and tell you what they offer. The Salvation Army supply to people in need, as mentioned before, "soup, soap, and salvation. Their intentions are in the right place, and they value themselves on doing good where it is needed. Mind you that no one is perfect, and there are many negative faults in everyone. The Salvation Army has endured and they ought to be commended.

We must start with building God's house and then stop making excuses about being true Christians but stand up for our faith. There will be challenges in every sphere of life and ministry is not an exception. Pastors will have to take the good with the bad and depend on God's grace and strength to keep them from losing their sanity. But if they happen to get lost in their circumstance, at least, they will know that God will remember them.

CHAPTER THIRTY-SEVEN

GET RIGHT WITH GOD

When I offend God with a minor sin infraction, like having a negative thought, I immediately repent and ask God for forgiveness. In my early days before my conversion, I did things that I didn't think sinful and offensive. I know now the difference in how offensive it's to God and to me as well. How then can people continue to offend God and not think anything of it? I wonder how many people would invite God to take part in their sinful behaviors. For instance, invite Him into the tattoo parlor when they are marking their bodies (private parts or any other part for that matter.) Who would ask Him to share a cigarette and have a drink? How many female members would invite God to a store to help them pick out a provocative outfit to wear for church on Sunday? How ridiculous of us to think that a holy and perfect God would go against His principles. This is what the church family want to believe when they outright sin. They choose to believe that God is all right with their sins.

Do Not Be Left Behind

I have news for you; He is not all right with your ungodly behaviors and attitudes. The Scriptures have laws after laws on how followers of Jesus Christ are to behave and what is expected of them. I know that for the most part people follow the Ten Commandments found in the book of Exodus 20:1-17.

- I am the LORD your God.
- You shall have no other gods before me.
- You shall not make for yourself an image in the form of anything in heaven above or on the earth beneath or

in the waters below. You shall not bow down to them or worship them; for I Am the LORD your God.

- You shall not misuse the name of the LORD your God, for the LORD will not hold anyone guiltless who misuses his name.
- Remember the Sabbath day by keeping it holy.
- Honor your father and your mother.
- You shall not commit adultery.
- You shall not steal.
- You shall not give false testimony against your neighbor.
- You shall not covet your neighbor's house

God is looking for people to live right and stop offending Him. I may sound naïve, but I never thought I would see the church turn against God during my time. I know that the church has always been rebellious and the 21st century is no different from any other era in time when the church has turned its back on God.

But you and I will continue to put forth all that we can muster to finish this journey that God has called us for. We will be the difference makers in our church, in our family, and in the community. We will stay the course to bring the gospel of Jesus Christ to fruition. Then we will sit back and watch how God will do something great in our lives. You and I have been called for such a time as this (Esther 4:14).

If we dedicate ourselves to follow what God puts before us, we will get right with God. To get right with God we start with a 21 day fast, and schedule a daily prayer time. You decide how you are going to consecrate. See how much better things will appear in your life and how much more you can accomplish for others. Talk to your pastor and serve as an encourager instead of being a burden to him/her. I believe God for a new season for the pastors as well as for us.

After we consecrate ourselves God is going to tell us where we are going and what to do. He will take people out of our life that is dragging us down, and he will connect us with successful people that are willing to join hands. There will be no more I when God draws us nearer to Him. He will bring those we are to disciple. We must follow God and bear our own cross without complaining.

When the year 2016 rolled around there was a thickness in the church atmosphere that I could cut it with a knife. All I heard from the people in the church were negative statements against the new President. That is when it was made obvious to me that the church had taken a turn for the worse. From the pastor down to the members they were afraid of their future and the future of their loved ones. It made me think how they were putting their faith in the government. I couldn't believe what my ears were hearing from the pulpit, "Satan put that President in office." "Get ready to say "yessa massa" (slave words for yes sir master). I found it so appalling that a pastor could put such fear in the hearts of his members. I wonder what other pastors must have thought in their churches. He was speaking against his blessings and the blessings of the members by preaching gloom and doom into the atmosphere. I went home that afternoon and canceled every negative thing he spoke into the atmosphere, and I turned everything around. I asked God to forgive him for his foolishness.

We can't live in fear but in the expectation that God will do everything as long as we have faith and hope in him. The pastor should preach on God's goodness and provisions at times when the government is unstable. That is the time to pray for God to show up and help the church when they are in trouble.

The pastor and the church have the blessing in their mouth and should release it to God for He is ready to help us. God will show up when we believe who He is and He rewards those who diligently seek Him (Hebrews 11:6).

It's at uncertain times that we must ask God, Lord what am I supposed to be doing? These are the times to run to God and do what He has called you to do. We must run toward the purpose God has given each and every one of us and then wait on His timing because the kingdom can't be built in our way. God wants people who are obedient and who are serious about doing the work he/she has been called to do.

God can't use those in the church who are having a difficult time changing their behaviors.

I recall one Sunday morning the pastor out of frustration asking the following question, "do you serve God or Satan? And he went on to share his thoughts, "Satan has his plan when you don't pray and don't read the Bible. … And, when you are behaving negative and mean."

We are living in an era where people are sinning and not allowing God to deliver them from their sins. The Bible passages mention that in the end days there will be the hardening of the hearts (2 Timothy 3:1-4).

Some of the members are not getting delivered because they have a hardened heart. They have one choice to get delivered, and that is through the spilled Blood of Christ Jesus. When they confess their sins, the Lord will fix them before they die in their sins. The church needs to reestablish their relationship with God because we are living in the end times.

I watched one of the "Left Behind" movie series, and it was sad to watch those family members who stayed behind because they were left with a great loss and uncertainty for the future as they watched everyone around them disappearing and the chaos in the streets. I pray to God almost every day to help me get it right with Him that I do not get left behind.

Spirit of God Come

I have mentioned before the church is a hospital where people come to get healed from all of their infirmities. Where God must get rid of everything that has contaminated us, including the toxic idols in our lives. The Lord is trying to help us clean ourselves up before we can help clean others from their own dirt. In this hospital, people go from being worldly sick to holy healed. These are the things that will help build them up: daily reverence the name of Jesus, daily prayer and reading the Scriptures. You and I need the power of God through the Holy Spirit to be able to face the challenges life throws at us. The Holy Spirit promises to lead and guide us. The Holy Spirit will help us set up a standard in our house. The Holy Spirit will convict us to live a decent and moral life. Everyone that professes Jesus Christ as Lord and Savior should have the Spirit of God.

We must know that God will walk with us once we recognize Him as the King of kings and Lord of lords. And, that through the Holy Spirit we may have a discerning spirit to know the difference between what is godly and what is demonic in the home, church, job, and the environment.

Round Up Those Loose Demons In the Church

When we get up in the mornings, it gets the devil angry because he knows that we are up to do kingdom work. The chaos in the church today isn't about the people but about the demons that are in the church.

I have witnessed several demonic manifestations in my lifetime but not like the one I witnessed in one of the churches I attended. The incident I want to share with you had to do with a female who walked into the church (for the first time) on a Wednesday evening right before the start of Bible study. I walked into the sanctuary as it began to play out. I saw this over-weight female trying to hit one of the male members in the face. I was shocked because it took place in God's house. The male member is trying to grab her because she wanted to hit the pastor's wife. She managed to slip away and run to the front of the church where other male members are trying to catch her. She eludes them and runs to the back of the room where eventually she was surrounded by about four male members who were able to subdue. The female deacons were reminding the men to be careful about how they were restraining her since she was after all a female. But because she was under demonic possession, she was fighting to get up, and it took another two males to hold her down. The female was subdued, and older of the female deacons began to talk to the demon to release the woman, but he was mocking all those around her. She started to spit out some yellow phlegm unto the floor and burping as the members were praying. The female was lying on the floor still held down by three of the males now and the pastor. One male who was not a member of the church but only visits several times with a female member approached the area where the female was being held down. He told the demons, "I command you to come out of her in the name of Jesus" and the demon looked at him and told him (loud so all can hear), "who are you to tell me what to do you serve me." At that point, the male exited the sanctuary and the church and was never seen back in the church at least while I was attending there.

We have to be very careful in situations like that because the devil will expose whoever belongs to him in front of the congregation. The church must know whom they are serving, God or Satan, because you will be exposed. I would rather be exposed as God's elect than the devil's slave.

The church leaders and the members must take very seriously what people are doing to each other in the church because one of them is a demon. The devil finds anyone vulnerable enough to disrupt the peace and create discord in church.

The Doubt demon is enemy number one for a Christian believer. The doubt demon will infiltrate our prayer time and cause us to think that God isn't listening to our prayer. The demon will lie and tell us that the prayer will not be answered. The doubt demon will sabotage our faith and cause it to dwindle little by little, especially when we are waiting and we don't see anything happening to change whatever situation we prayed about. We want things to happen right there and then for us. God doesn't work that way. It's on His time.

Always pray in the expectation that God will answer you and don't concern yourself about it anymore. You must have faith that it will come to pass and never lose hope. Of course, there will be prayers that God will not answer if they go against His principles. So, think what you want to pray for before you go to God. And, pray specific prayers and straight to the point. I have been blessed immeasurable because I have asked God in prayer for what I want in specific terms. I know to go to God in prayer in faith-believing and with boldness. Joyce Meyers once said, "when you pray send your prayers up like laser beams not like match lit fire."

Just like you mortify the flesh every day mortify doubt right along with it because both can be manipulated by demons.

The Toxic relationship demon is enemy number two for a Christian believer. In my experience, those people that were close to me were the worst because they were always so negative about everything and all they did was whine about one thing or another. They were very discouraging, to say the least. We can still love them but from afar. There are some people God had me separate from because they were not supportive of God's purpose for my life. These are people who have no aspiration and envy those who do. They expect us to stay where they are, in nowhere land. They are people who never call but are quick to judge you if you neglect to call them and always want to make you feel guilty. God expects from His children to do extraordinary well not to settle for a mediocre life.

Christians are to be around those who support what God is doing in their lives and help move them along. That is why it's important that we ask God to give us a discerning spirit to know which relationships are good for us and which are not. We must never forget whom we serve and that we are to encourage one another. Remember that we are made in His image, and that should mean a whole lot to us.

The Distraction demons are the number three enemy of a Christian Believer. Unfortunate, during my ministry I had been distracted after my conversion on two separate occasions, (when I went to the Catholic church and when I got married and changed churches). My second distraction occurred when I widowed, and I make mention of it in an earlier chapter. Satan and his demons are very subtle when they move in to distract us from our walk with God.

When we are overconfident, that is when pride can sneak right in and cause us to focus more on the self than on God. We become tolerant of secular things because the pressure is on to side with or face repercussions. It's a distraction if we allow medical problems to consume us physically, mentally, and emotionally to discourage us from attending church. Medical problems can cause church members to stop reading the Bible and praying, even when we know that God is our healer and provider. There will be times that God will not heal us, but we must have faith that He is still in control of all situations and He has His reasons. We are never to question God's decision. Can we pray that He will change His mind? Sure! Will He answer our prayers? Sure? We just have to believe in Him. But never allow stress or despair to distract you from seeking God. And, whatever you do never stop obeying God and believing in the truth that is found in Christ Jesus.

The demon of Indifference is the number four enemy of a Christian believer. Jesus requested that we love one another because "when we were still sinners Jesus loved us."

If you don't love, don't think you are going to heaven. There are too many people very mistaken about that and continue to behave callously in the church. How in the world can they think they are going to heaven when they don't love their own church family? Christ Jesus made a command that we love one another. Jesus loved us and died for us even while we were wicked and undeserving of such a sacrifice. We aren't perfect people we are far from it, but all we are called to do is to love and be patient with one another. God knows that without love there is only evil, but because He is the God of love and we claim to be His children, we must have love in our heart for everyone, even those who hate us.

In his book, "People of The Lie: The Hope For Healing Human Evil," Scott Peck shares this insight of what it actually would take to conquer evil, and Jesus Christ said it first over Two Thousand years ago,

> "It is in the struggle between good and evil that life has its meaning – and in the hope that goodness can succeed. That hope is our answer: goodness can succeed. Evil can be defeated by goodness. When we translate this, we realize what we dimly have always known: evil can be conquered only by love. So, the methodology of our assault…on evil must be love. …I can't be any more specific about the methodology of love than to quote these words of an old priest that spend many years in the battle, "There are dozens of ways to deal with evil and several ways to conquer it. All of them are a facet of the truth that the ultimate, the only way to conquer evil is to let it be smothered within a willing human being. When it's absorbed like blood there in a sponge or spears to one's heart, it loses its power and goes no further." [35]

The only way that we can rend evil from our hearts is through replacing it with love. Evil can't thrive in a church full of love. The challenge we have ahead of us is to embrace those who are different from us and love them as Jesus would, with a surpassing love.

CHAPTER THIRTY-EIGHT

SALVATION IS IMMINENT

Rumor has it that the church is in danger because the members don't want to go through the process of being delivered from their present sins, because they don't have the patience. Biblical history has shown us that God allows His children to go through some trials and tribulations that we may need more of Him. God knows that this present-day church doesn't love His Son, Jesus. He knows that they have lost their passion for Christendom. The church has become a place to meet up with people and socialize. Some just go through the formality of praise and worship others don't even bother to try. There are still a few members in the church who say like King David, "One thing I ask from the Lord, this only do I seek: that I may dwell in the house of the LORD all the days of my life. To gaze on the beauty of the LORD and seek Him in His temple" (Psalm 27:4, NIV).

Radical Transformation

Salvation is individual, is what I tell everyone I talk to. You are the only one that should be concern about your salvation, and so you seek God for yourself and not worry about anyone else at the moment. You will have plenty of time to go out and save others. I go church nowadays in the expectation that I am going to receive my blessing. I go to praise and worship God and to give Him my best, and I do this all by myself. If no one else wants to praise Him, they lose their blessings, and that is on them. But you make sure that you get yours. If anyone should be concern about the church members erratic behavior is the leadership of the church. The church members need a radical transformation of the heart and a spiritual revival to awaken what is dead in them. We are the children of the most high God, and we are to stay encouraged, keeping a positive outlook in a negative world.

We will continue to be people of faith and learn to encourage ourselves even if no one else will. We must be the people that keep hope alive for the next generation because they are looking to us and we can't let them down. In this present day our young people are living in two different worlds due to all the social media they are being exposed to, and they need the church to help them stay grounded. You and I must keep them interested in the things of God since the secular world is trying to claim them for Satan.

Let us be real here for a moment and look around your church and tell me what you see with your young people today. Our Christian sons and daughters are hanging out with ungodly friends and family members and have lost respect for the authority figure in their life. The young church girls are showing their body with the latest fashions that leave nothing for the imagination while the wolves are figuring out when to bounce on them. It's the responsibility of the adults in the church to put structure and set Biblical standards on the children and young adults.

I believe the adults in the church need to take a stance and tell the devil you can't have our children and take action. Keep in mind that the church is dealing with demons and it's only through the power of the Holy Spirit that they can be rebuked. Fasting and prayer are what is needed beforehand to prepare for the battle. It's an epidemic that is affecting the church members in every state in the nation, and the pastors are very much aware of it.

I heard Bishop Hezekiah Walker preach one evening about the condition of the church and the battles that face its members nowadays. He didn't mince words that night. He began by telling the church how God desired to bless them but that they need to get right with God. He also said,

"If your heart is not right, and your attitude is bad and nasty, and you act like a hypocrite; you talk about your brothers and sisters in church after seating next to them in church then it is obvious that you are definitely not seeking the kingdom of God. You are living the life of those serving the devil. We must be careful how we act because out of the heart comes the truth. We can dance and shout, but we need the truth of God in our heart." [36]

As I continued to write, I heard this thought come to mind that echo these words, nothing has changed in over Two Thousand years you are wasting your time. I understand that the more things change, the more they stay the same but if we have to try every Thousand years then so be it.

We Need A Fifth, 'Great Awakening'

In the Old Testament alone the children of God had to be taught harsh lessons several times for their disobedience and rebelliousness toward God. In the book of Exodus after they left Egypt and were in the desert, they complained and built idols even when God had shown them supernatural signs. "Then the LORD said to Moses, "How long will you refuse to keep my commands and my instructions" (Exodus 16:28, NIV). Then again in the book of Numbers, they rebelled again, "But the whole assembly talked about stoning them. Then the glory of the LORD appeared at the tent of meeting to all the Israelites. The LORD said to Moses, "How long will these people treat me with contempt? How long will they refuse to believe in me, in spite of all the signs I have performed among them" (Numbers 14:10-11, NIV)? In the book of Deuteronomy 9:7, (NIV) "Remember this and never forget how you aroused the anger of the LORD your God in the wilderness. From the day you left Egypt until you arrived here, you have been rebellious against the LORD." Hosea repeats the contempt they have for the Lord, their God, "Woe to them because they have strayed from me! Destruction to them, because they have rebelled against me. I long to redeem them but they speak about me falsely (Hosea 7:13). In the book of Zephaniah 2:1-3, (NIV) God lets the righteous and unrighteous know His plan, "Gather together, gather yourselves together, you shameful nation, before the decree takes effect and that day passes like windblown chaff, before the LORD's fierce anger comes upon you, before the day of the LORD's wrath comes upon you. Seek the LORD, all you humble of the land, you who do what he commands. Seek righteousness, seek humility; perhaps you will be sheltered on the day of the LORD's anger."

They rebelled against God so much that he had to do what He told them He would do. In the books of the Prophets, they are being exiled from their precious land to Babylonia a place synonymous with sin and pride. A place where they become slaves because they took the freedom God had given them to defile God and turn their backs on Him. God continues to be angry with His children and through the Prophet Ezekiel he repeats what he is going to do because of their rebelliousness, "But they rebelled against me and would not listen to me; they did not get rid of the vile images they had set their eyes on, nor did they forsake the idols of Egypt. So, I said I would pour out my wrath on them and spend my anger against them in Egypt (Ezekiel 20:8).

Paul gives a brief history of what happened to the Israelites for their disobedience to deter the new Christians from committing the same mistake against God. This is his reminder to them,

> "For I do not want you to be ignorant of the fact, brothers and sisters, that our ancestors were all under the cloud and that they all passed through the sea. They were all baptized into Moses in the cloud and in the sea. They all ate the same spiritual food and drank the same spiritual drink; for they drank from the spiritual rock that accompanied them, and that rock was Christ. Nevertheless, God was not pleased with most of them; their bodies were scattered in the wilderness.

Now, these things occurred as examples to keep us from setting our hearts on evil things as they did. Do not be idolaters, as some of them were; as it is written: "The people sat down to eat and drink and got up to indulge in revelry." We should not commit sexual immorality, as some of them did—and in one day twenty-three thousand of them died. We should not test Christ as some of them did—and were killed by snakes. And do not grumble, as some of them did—and were killed by the destroying angel. These things happened to them as examples and were written down as warnings for us, on whom the culmination of the ages has come. So, if you think you are standing firm, be careful that you don't fall (1 Corinthians 10:1-12, NIV)!

The United States by itself has had its share of God's wrath in the past as well as spiritual awakenings and revivals. We must continue to pray to God for another spiritual awakening in our churches and in the nation.

In the Old Testament, they had many spiritual revivals, but they would go back to forgetting their covenant with God, and then they would have to go through yet another spiritual revival. In the book of 2 Kings 23, King Josiah sets off a revival after he found the Book of the Law. He told everyone about the covenant his ancestors had neglected but that he would follow the covenant and so would his people.

"Then the king called together all the elders of Judah and Jerusalem. He went up to the temple of the LORD with the people of Judah, the inhabitants of Jerusalem, the priests, and the prophets—all the people from the least to the greatest. He read in their hearing all the words of the Book of the Covenant, which had been found in the temple of the LORD. The king stood by the pillar and renewed the covenant in the presence of the LORD— to follow the LORD and keep his commands, statutes, and decrees with all his heart and all his soul, thus confirming the words of the covenant written in this book. Then all the people pledged themselves to the covenant." (NIV)

We will keep doing spiritual revivals until Christ returns and we will not get tired. For the sake of the next generation, we must do it. According to Wikipedia, a revival is described as such,

> "revival" to refer to an evangelistic meeting or series of meetings… Revivals are seen as the restoration of the church itself to a vital and fervent relationship with God after a period of moral decline. Mass conversions of non-believers are viewed by church leaders as having positive moral effects." [37]

According to the data, I collected there have been four distinctive 'Great Awakenings' aka revivals. Revivals began to break out in the United States as early as the 18th century, in 1727, 1792 and in the 19th century, 1830, 1857 and 1882. More revivals occurred in the 20th century that includes those of the 1904–1905 Welsh Revival, and the Azusa Street Revival of 1906. Many of the men associated with these revivals were Solomon Stoddard, Jonathan Edwards, George Whitefield, Dwight L. Moody, Billy Sunday, and an African American named William J. Seymour, the "Azusa Street Revival" pastor. I want to share a brief insight look into the revivals of the 20th century in the United States.

According to Patrick's Morley, he found that,

> "At the turn of the 20th century, the mood of the country was changing. Outside the church, it was the era of radio, movies, and the "Jazz Age." World War I led to a moral letdown and the Roaring Twenties. When that era ended abruptly, on October 29, 1929, followed by the Great Depression, there was surprisingly little

interest in a spiritual revival. ...Inside the church, a half-century-long battle raged between evangelicalism and theological liberalism which had penetrated major denominations... in Pennsylvania, in late 1904 a revival broke out. By 1905, local revivals blazed in places like Brooklyn, Michigan, Denver, Schenectady, Nebraska, North and South Carolina, Georgia, Taylor University, Yale University, and Asbury College in Wilmore, Kentucky. Billy Sunday, who became a key figure about this time. The Azusa Street Revival, 1906. In 1906, William J. Seymour, an African-American Holiness pastor blind in one eye, went to Los Angeles as a candidate for a pastoral job. The Promise Keepers Revival, the most publicized of the mid-1990s Revivals, began in 1991 when 4,200 men descended on the University of Colorado to be challenged to live up to their faith. [38]

America is due for another 'Great Awakening' in the 21st century.

We live in Satan's territory, and we have to fight to stay free of him. But there should be 'no worries' because we have the most powerful defender, the Messiah, Christ Jesus. You and I have already won the battle because Christ defeated Satan.

Our problem is that we keep forgetting that one important fact, that Jesus defeated Satan at the Cross at Calvary. God gave us the victory. God tells us that if we fight, we will win. It looks like we are losing because there is so much sin in the church and the church refuses to believe that we are out of God's will. The same God who delivered Israel time and time again from their enemy is our God. We need to think back at a time when God rescued us from a battle, we thought we were losing and how He brought us out of it. God can do it again because He is the God of second chances. We have the victory, but we just refuse to believe it.

I believe and live it. I know that God has already won the battle for us and all we have to do is walk in it and take back our church, and the young people from the enemy.

The church has to realize that God is a government of one God. He doesn't need our assistance only our obedience. God will expose those people who are a hindrance in the church, and the pastor will have to deal with them. If they insist on living ungodly lives, then they must move on but not in the church. Pastors are going to have to stop trying to hold on to that tithe and offering because it is not worth keeping on a demon at the expense of the other members who want to live right.

It's time that people make up their mind to live by the will of God and get delivered from every hindering demon. Especially that spirit of indifference, as one pastor from South Carolina shared,

> "Some of us walk into the church and don't say hello to each other. We are not being honest with ourselves and our sins. The heart of the people is deceitful.
>
> …people have heart issues, and they need to be cleansed, consecrate themselves.
>
> …God has called us to be obedient and follow His commands, love one another."

Every morning I wake up and pray the following, "empty me of me God that I will not offend anyone with my flesh." I am not perfect, but I want to do things right and have others see Christ Jesus in me. "Not I who lives, but Christ…" (Galatians 2:20, NIV).

When I listen to pastors whose spirit is aligned with God, I do an inventory of my life and tell myself; I better get it together. It's like God is telling me through the word to take heed or else.

The Bible is a book of facts, and that is all the pastor has to preach to us, the facts, anything else that is added will tend to lose the members interest. The church should never stop speaking the truth, especially to the children. The Bible is still clear on this command, "Train up a child in the way they should go" (Proverbs 22:6, NIV).

Speak It Into the Atmosphere

The church is and always will be the pillar of righteousness in any community and we the members must always be separated from the things that will pollute us in this pagan society. The devil knows that his days are numbered, and when he sees that God's time is nearer, he goes after man to create havoc in their lives. Man will turn away from God in the last days and sin will continue to plague society, and the church is no exception. But God will not stand for the lawless. But He will save the righteous. You and I will be in that number with the righteous.

The devil is mad at any church that puts God first and put their own issues aside to praise Him. While we are acting petty toward one another, and creating division, the devil is coming against our children. He is coming against them with a vengeance to stop a generation from believing in God.

Church members have to let go of the ungodly things and just continue to serve God by following His commands. They need to love one another and break the walls of separation and stop fighting over stuff that makes no sense. We must pray over our children and grandchildren because the devil wants them.

There is something wrong with this culture when parents are too interested in buying their children the latest cell phone or game box and are not a concern for their souls. Brothers and sisters take heed that you will not regret it later. Pray for your family with boldness and in expectation. Just ask God.

The church is somewhat ignorant about obtaining God's blessings when all they have to do is speak it into the atmosphere. Many people in the church don't believe in the supernatural. Some think that it has to do with witchcraft. Remember that God is a Supernatural Being and thus everything about Him is supernatural.

But the church refuses to use those supernatural powers to obtain things from God. The church has had this gift since before Moses. God told Moses to use his staff to bring about the plagues, to open the Red Sea, to bring forth water from the rock. Also, when they were in the desert, and God sent manna from heaven, and that was supernatural. Now fast forward, the feeding of the five thousand, the raising of the dead, the miraculous healing of people, and the resurrection of the Messiah, Jesus.

So, let us think for a moment when have you asked God for something and it has not materialized. I mean something that you know that only He could have made it happened because when you asked you had hope and faith connected to that prayer request. Nothing has changed. God is the same yesterday, today, and tomorrow. When we ask God for things, we don't realize that it's already done. Church people are their own worst enemy when they refuse to walk in the supernatural.

To believe in the supernatural, we first have to believe that we are the chosen children of God and that God is not a figment of our imagination. God is real. We are hypocrites when we say to each other in church, "believe to receive." We say it, but we don't believe it.

During an evening service at my Southwest church, the pastor called the congregation to the front of the altar to pray. He told the church to come and in faith-believing that God would answer their prayers. I went to the front in faith-believing and prayed something like this, "God I want those men who stole my money to pay it back. I want my money. They own me that money it's mine." I prayed that prayer in faith-believing that God was going to do it.

Around that time, I wasn't doing well financially. I couldn't find a job and was living on my Retirement Pension. I had pawn most of my jewelry to buy groceries and other much-needed things. Several months had gone since that service, and I had forgotten the prayer. I received a slip from the Post Office informing me that I had a certified letter. I went to the Post Office and picked up my letter. It was from my lawyer whom I had forgotten about. When I opened that envelope, there was a check for $9,998 and some change. I started to jump up and down in the Post Office and praised God for hearing and answering my prayer. The other customers in the Post Office stared oddly at me and possibly thought for sure I had lost my mind. I could go on telling you about all of my supernaturally answered prayers, but you get the idea.

All you have to do is believe and trust God to bring your prayer to fruition. It's no secret that God has given us the authority to do the supernatural. However, how can you pray in the supernatural when you don't even think it's real. Believing in the supernatural is like having faith the size of a 'mustard seed.' You and I can move mountains when we have faith.

There was a movie that came out in 2015, called, "Little Boy." It's a story about a boy 's love for his father and the faith he had to bring him back home from the war using magic powers. During a certain scene, he believed that his powers had made a mountain move. He believed it, and the mountain moved but not because of his make-believe magic powers but because there had been an earthquake that made the ground shift that made it appear as if the mountain had moved.

God is our earthquake and when we believe He will shift some things to bring about our request because we believe that He can do it.

Do what I do. Pray and speak it into the atmosphere and believe in faith-believing that it will come to pass. The power of God is in us, and He is the God of the supernatural. In the book Matthew 14:29-33, Peter walked on water with Christ Jesus, and when he took his eyes off of Jesus, he began to drown. That is what happens to us when we don't believe that Jesus is a supernatural being. We must believe in Him, or we might as well walk away from the church forever. If we are not going to believe the Scriptures then why bother coming to church. Do you not believe that the Messiah turned water into wine or do you think that these are stories for our entertainment?

Because I serve a supernatural and powerful God, I can ask and get what I want that is within His will. I know the victory I have in Jesus.

Remember the all-time favorite praise song, "In the Name of Jesus." It's one of my favorites because I believe what I am singing:

> "In the Name of Jesus,
> in the name of Jesus,
> we have the victory
> Satan you have to flee
> Oh, Oh, tell me who can stand before us…" [39]

Victory is ours is the song message. When we sing praises to the Lord, He inhabits those praises, and we are saturated with His presence. There is nothing I can't ask from Him that He will not give me (Psalm 22:3). Whenever you are going through struggles, troubles, and problems, never stop seeking God and giving Him the praise. Trust God and live in victory.

Daniel and his friends were sold out to God, and God showed up in the fiery furnace (Daniel 3:8-25).

Again, I say to you stop looking at the Scriptures as a form of entertainment. Those are real incidents documented not only in the Scriptures of the Bible but recorded in history by the secular historians of that era.

The Spirit of Jezebel Must Go

The church has turned from God because they believe the lies of the secular world. The secular world believes that God isn't real and that the Bible was written by men to control the people. I know that God is real. I have experienced what believing in God has done in my life. I believe that Jesus is real and that He sacrificed His life for you and me.

Don't give up believing in the Messiah, Jesus. Believe that He loves us and is able to do anything for us. Let us stand firm and believe that Jesus is with us all the time.

I believe that we are living in the end times, but that will not detour me from living my life serving the church until God either calls me home or I get caught up in the rapture.

But for many church members, God and eternity are far from their minds because they have been contaminated with the spirit of Jezebel.

I read this article written by Michael Brady that describes the spirit of Jezebel as thus,

> "Without question, the nastiest, evil, most disgusting, cunning, and seductive spirit in Satan's hierarchy has to be what many call, the Jezebel spirit.
>
> This evil spirit has been responsible for not only tearing down churches, pastors, and different Christian ministries, …This is a "type" of evil spirit in Satan's kingdom. There is only one devil, one Satan, but there are many spirits that would be considered a Jezebel type spirit, as they all have a particular type of personality and a specific way in which they like to operate.
>
> The reason many deliverance ministers have used the term, "Jezebel spirit," is because of the nature of its personality and the way it operates once it sets up shop within someone. The word "Jezebel" is coming from the OT story of Queen Jezebel back in the days of Elijah. She was a ruling queen back at that time, and she had cold-bloodedly killed many of God's prophets back at the time she was ruling. For those of you who have been hit and slimed by this evil spirit, or have encountered it in some way, you will know what I am going to talk about in this article. It is without question, one of the most evil and vile things I have ever come across in my life. Like Satan, this type of spirit is simply pure evil." [40]

There is something very wrong when the church no longer gets excited about being in the presence of the Savior. When they don't care to praise and worship Him in the church. It's just not Christian behavior. People should come into church singing and praising with a grateful spirit for having been kept by God all week long and having enjoyed all His benefits. The only one who will not join in praise and worship is a demon. The Jezebel demon.

My brothers and sister must examine themselves to know what type of spirit is operating in them. Or should I say what type of demon?

Come Into The Light

That spirit of Jezebel is determined to keep the church from following Jesus. This demon is determined to stop the saints from sharing the good news of the gospel because it knows that the time of its demise is near.

Therefore, having knowledge of the scheme of the adversary we should defend with boldness and authority what we believe. This isn't the time to hold back what we know about Christ Jesus. It's the time to spread the light until someone turns to the Savior.

"So clean house! Make a clean sweep of malice and pretense, envy and hurtful talk. You've had a taste of God. Now, like infants at the breast, drink deep of God's pure kindness. Then you'll grow up mature and whole in God" (1 Peter 2, MSG).

Most of the Christians in church God has kept from childhood, and some He has saved from dying in their sins; so, we know that He can break yokes and deliver us. We must not allow the hindering spirits of fear, doubt, and distraction to hold us back or hold back our loved ones from coming into the light.

I've listened to a program called "Unshackled on WIHS 104.5 FM radio for many years. Lately, I've searched the homepage for certain episodes depending on the subject matter. I tend to listen to the program when I have my dinner. The program is pre-recorded by actors in a live studio at The Pacific Gardens Mission in Chicago

Illinois. Each episode brings a true story of deliverance, salvation, restoration, and redemption. The stories are about people who have either wondered into the Pacific Garden shelter or have sent in their story to be broadcast on the radio. These are people from all walks of life and ethnicity. What I like about the program is how all these individuals come to the saving grace of Jesus Christ sooner or later, and it fills me with such joy.

One story in specific resonated powerfully with me due to having had similar experiences. It was the story of Diane Joy Truitt. The story dealt with confusion, drugs, theft, divorced parents, feeling unloved, neglected and rejected (episodes 3507 & 3508). Diane has since moved on in her life and authored several books. I took this excerpt from one of her books that speaks to God's love for His children as she experienced it. 'Note from the Author,' from her book, "God Is Always Close,"

"The sole purpose for telling my story is so that you will witness for yourself that God's love, protection, and guidance indeed exists. He does this for every individual; no one is exempt from God's devotion, and no one is exempt from His presence. He is always close by. God promises to standby. [41]

> "I am with you always, even unto the end of the world"
> (Matthew 28:20, NIV).

It's December 2016, and 2017 is just a few days away. It dawned on me that in 1987, thirty years ago I was converted to Christianity. I had repented of my past sins and received Christ Jesus into my life. Those years have been filled with a mixture of pain and joy, struggles and peace, doubts and assurance, shame and forgiveness. But I will not complain. The Bible tells me about the Savior and His life as the Messiah and what He went through for you and me. The Messiah who was born in a manger homeless and naked to die on a Cross for your sins and mine. He was to be the "Light of the World." He was born to die a cruel death for you and me and all who receive Him, that our sins will be forgiven by the Father in heaven.

We must always remember the birth of Christ Jesus, His resurrection and His much-anticipated return. Christ is coming back for His church. A church "without spot or blemish."

Since the fall-out in the "Garden of Eden" we have been connected to the beginning in the book of Genesis. God foreknew and preordained you and me for this time in history to challenge the world and share the Gospels to those in darkness. We have been called to boldly share the gospel of Christ to the world "by the word of our mouth and word of our testimony."

God has equipped me with the word for the past thirty years to be able to go out and share what I know. God will give me the grace to talk to kings and princes of His love and mercy. If we all come together boldly to share His good news millions of lost souls will be won for God's kingdom. Remember Jesus is not coming back until a good portion of people have received Him as Lord and Savior.

Nothing we do in this world is without struggles. I will not lie to you and tell you that it will all be 'peaches and cream' while serving in the kingdom but I can assure you that it will all be worth it. Saying yes to Christ Jesus is saying yes to the struggles and sufferings that will follow those who serve God. And, we will have encounters with Satan on occasions but nothing we can't handle when we put God before us. He is our battle fighter, and He never loses a fight.

Never forget that demons feed on your fear so when you tell them to go back to 'hell' in the name of Jesus; they have no choice in the matter.

"And the Gates of Hell Will Not Prevail…"

Realize this, Satan can only bind you if you give him the power, so don't ever relinquish that power. It's obvious that Satan will do anything to distract the church from moving forward with God's plan by causing them to stumble aimlessly in this culture.

Again, I tell you, Satan knows our weaknesses, and the one weakness humans have is vanity. We all want to look beautiful and pretty and attractive, and he uses that for his advantage to distract us from our goals and purpose in the kingdom of God. This old adversary, Satan goes back to the beginning. He was an angel in heaven but was dismissed from heaven because he wanted to be like God and God doesn't share His glory with anyone.

Many of the early saints were faced with the same dilemma we are faced with today. Satan is relentless in his quest to deceive God's people and stop God's plans.

Never forget why you were chosen by God and be proud that He did. We are special to Him, and He knows the gifts we possess because He gave them to us. We are to use our gifts to encourage this lost generation to follow Christ Jesus.

The Apostle Paul said, "I consider that our present sufferings are not worth comparing with the glory that will be revealed in us" (Romans 8:18, NIV). So, count it all joy no matter what we go through. A perfect example is when Paul and Silas are in the prison cell, and they began to sing praises to God regardless of their present situation because of their assurance in their God. Praising God is essential. He will know our reverence toward Him.

A young pastor (whose church I had frequent several times) put it in this content,

> "To deny God praise is to deny that He is in the presence
> of our situation. Our praise tells God that He is able.
> Praise is the execution of willingness to bless us. ... Give
> God severe praise in a severe moment."

I have learned to praise God during my worse moments and it works for me because His presence permeates the atmosphere and all the negativity has to leave. Let us purpose in our hearts to live for Jesus and do the work we have been called to do for the glory of God.

You and I must continue to maintain the joy of being saved. I thank God for setting you and me free that we may purpose in our heart to help others be set free and lead them to Jesus.

When we look over our life, we can see how far God has brought us and from where. We should be thankful that we didn't die in our sins. God is sovereign, and His word is true.

> "This is the kind of life you've been invited into, the kind of life Christ lived. He suffered everything that came his way so you would know that it could be done, and also know how to do it, step-by-step. He never did one thing wrong, Not once said anything amiss. They called him every name in the book, and he said nothing back. He suffered in silence, content to let God set things right. He used his servant body to carry our sins to the Cross so we could be rid of sin, free to live the right way. His wounds became your healing. You were lost sheep with no idea who you were or where you were going. Now you're named and kept for good by the Shepherd of your souls" (1 Peter 2:21-25, NIV).

There is still a remnant of believers in Christ Jesus who must stand up and take the baton and keep going as others have done before us. You and I would not be here if it were not for them who didn't give up. We must cry out to God to move in this nation because he has all the power in the whole universe. This nation needs a measure of revival. "The prayer of a righteous person is powerful and effective" (James 5:16, NIV). Jesus said that whatever we ask Him is as if we are asking the Father.

This nation and our lives are in a gigantic mess. We are to pour out our hearts to God in prayer that He will heal our land and our lives and turn us back from living like heathens. "If my people who are called by my name…" (2 Chronicles 7:14, NIV).

Now is the time to grab hold of our bootstraps and pray like never before, trusting and believing God for a miracle. Faith begins in the mouth to speak into existence what we want to happen in our churches. And, wait on God to open the windows of heaven and rain on us the revival that is long overdue. While we wait, we will recommit ourselves to God.

The church leaders are encouraged to address the privileges some members have taken that have corrupted a good portion of the church. One rotten apple in the bunch rots the rest. Every member must be treated the same with the utmost respect and without favoritism which lends to everyone feeling appreciated and thus putting the spirit of jealousy and discord to death. Every member is valuable to the church, and they have gifts and talents given by God to be utilized for service in the kingdom. No one should be overlooked, and everyone as long as their health allows should take some part in church activities and events to encourage camaraderie.

I pray that the church will no longer be a yesterday church but that it will head toward a new future where God's love will permeate every church member and will steer us all the way to heaven bound.

The word of the Lord reminds us of God's love for us and His desire for us to be more like Him. "And we all, who with unveiled faces contemplate the Lord's glory, are being transformed into his image with ever-increasing glory, which comes from the Lord, who is the Spirit" (2 Corinthians 3:18, NIV).

Prayers are necessary to be in communion with God. We must seek him and must make sacrifices to be in His presence always. We must condition ourselves to turn off the TV and pray. We must shut-off the game and pray. Take time during our busy schedule to pray. We need to be in daily consecration.

It's time for the spirit of ignorance and apathy in the church to be evicted. No more being an army of silent soldiers. It's time to come out of the trenches and combat hand to hand. We must inform the people about this lie perpetuated by the secular world about the separation of church and state because it has created too much confusion among both the secular and the Christian folks.

In the movie, "God is Not Dead 2", the character Tom Endler (Jesse Metcalf), plays the lawyer for the defendant. He comes back at the end of the movie with a very compelling argument that raises the truth about "the separation of church and state." The attorney for the defendant is facing the jury and gives his opening statement,

> "I have here a copy of the Constitution of the United States of America and its Bill of Rights arguably the two most important documents in the history of our great nation… You know what you won't find in it, that no matter how hard you look, the phrase 'separation of church and state.' That right it's not in there, it has never been because that phrase comes from a letter written by Thomas Jefferson… Jefferson was writing to a Baptist congregation assuring them that they will always have the right to believe as they wish free of government interference. But lately, that phrase has been taken out of context and twisted…to mean the exact opposite." [42]

Jesus didn't die for us so that we stop believing in Him and start believing the lies fabricated by the secular world. The Bible is the only truth, and that is the fact.

Jesus death was not in vain. There have been way too many people saved because of His name, and there are still plenty of other souls who need saving. Pastors must get off their bottom and take the gospels to the streets where it belongs. God is still in control.

I will not allow what happened to me in my past to interfere with my future walk with God. And, I refuse to let the scars of yesteryears to change who I truly am in Christ. I will continue to do right before God and walk in His shadow daily.

As I conclude my story, I must confess that God has put me in the right place, and at the right time with the right people. God has given me something to do, and I am enjoying every minute of it. The favor of God is on me, and it will never leave me. Put your hands to do something, it will keep your focus on more positive things in life.

In the church of today as in yesteryears, members have experienced much pain and isolation caused by the church family.

The true believer will be tested during his/her walk-in Christendom. If they are able to weather the storms in the church, then they will have won their crown in heaven. They will have proven to be loyal. No matter how bad you and I have been mistreated and wounded the Risen King is our healer, and He will break the yoke and shackle of anger and bitterness and put goodness and love in us. There is no one good, but Christ Jesus, and with the help of the Holy Spirit, we can strive to be more like Him.

Victory is guaranteed if we just let go and let God take over. I believe we have done enough damage in trying to do things on our own strength instead of letting God be in charge of our lives. Don't argue with God He is creating a masterpiece out your broken life. So, we need to step aside in order that God may bless us after He has pulled some things out that don't belong in our lives.

"And I also say unto thee, that thou art Peter, and upon this rock, I will build my church; and the gates of hell shall not prevail against it. And I will give unto thee the keys of the kingdom of heaven: and whatsoever thou shalt bind on earth shall be bound in heaven: and whatsoever thou shalt loose on earth shall be loosed in heaven" (Matthew 16:18-19).

"Welcome to the living Stone, the source of life. The workmen took one look and threw it out; God set it in the place of honor. Present yourselves as building stones for the construction of a sanctuary vibrant with life, in which you'll serve as holy priests offering Christ-approved lives up to God. The Scriptures provide precedent: Look! I'm setting a stone in Zion, a cornerstone in the place of honor. Whoever trusts in this stone as a foundation will never have cause to regret it. To you who trust him, he's a Stone to be proud of, but to those who refuse to trust him, The stone the workmen threw out is now the chief foundation stone. For the untrusting it's. . . a stone to trip over, a boulder blocking the way. They trip and fall because they refuse to obey, just as predicted. But you are the ones chosen by God, chosen for the high calling of priestly work, chosen to be a holy people, God's instruments to do his work and speak out for him, to tell others of the night-and-day difference he made for you—from nothing to something, from rejected to accepted. Friends, this world is not your home, so don't make yourselves cozy in it. Don't indulge your ego at the expense of your soul. Live an exemplary life among the natives so that your actions will refute their prejudices. Then they'll be won over to God's side and be there to join in the celebration when he arrives. Make the Master proud of you by being good citizens. Respect the authorities, whatever their level; they are God's emissaries for keeping order. It is God's will that by doing good, you might cure the ignorance of the fools who think you're a danger to society. Exercise your freedom by serving God, not by breaking the rules. Treat everyone you meet with dignity. Love your spiritual family. Revere God. Respect the government.

1 Peter 2:1-17 *(MSG)*

Author's Note

It's through the media that Satan has been able to entice the church family. But it's also through the media that Christians can gain insight and perspective into God's world and mysteries. Through the real-life experiences of people like you and me. The secular world has told the Christians that God is dead and that Jesus was only a prophet and a myth. But the true believer, the one who has not fallen prey to Satan's lies know that God is real, and the Scriptures are the truth. Satan is very cunning, and he introduces his plan of destruction in a subtle way; through the comedies, we watch in the television or in the theaters, to the sports events, and the talk shows.

It was Monday night prayer at church, and there was a small group of members in attendance, as usual. I shared that people, especially Christians are doubting the Scriptures because they believe the lies of the culture. The lies are spread to make the church appear to be 'bigots and deplorable because we will not accept their views. They want the church to consider tolerating whatever is introduced in the culture of the day and to be "politically correct." My thought was why not introduce the Christians to real-life stories of God's miracles and saving grace through the media. Use the same methods that the enemy is implementing to entice the church into sinning.

One of the movies I mentioned was, "Badge of Faith" a real-life story of faith and courage against all the odds. I also mention and encouraged them to read "Pilgrims Progress" an allegorical book based on the many complexities that Christians encounter in their Christian walk.

These are tools to get them to see real people going through real struggles but finding God's grace and mercy through it all. Using the media in no way takes away the truth from the Bible, the inspired word of God it just enhances the reality of who God is in the modern world. But that wasn't received very well by a few members. One of the older season female member made a comment, "let us discern what is of God and what is not." I thought to myself, that is being closed minded. We are living in a time that we must figure out a way to encourage people to seek the truth about the Scripture, Christ Jesus, and God. For some people who have been hurt in the church, it's not easy convincing them to return just because and for the non-believer it gets even more complicated. We need to give them something that will be substantiated that God is truly real. Real life modern stories about real people. Show them that the Savior is whom He says He is through the experience of those who have seen Him and experienced His miracles in the 21st Century. These are the signs and wonders the Scripture speaks about for the modern world and the 'end times.'

In the book of Acts, Paul travels to Greece to share the gospel of Christ Jesus, and he is met with many challenges. But he wasn't discouraged because he used their own words to disciple them.

"Paul then stood up in the meeting of the Areopagus and said: "People of Athens! I see that in every way you are very religious. For as I walked around and looked carefully at your objects of worship, I even found an altar with this inscription: TO AN UNKNOWN GOD. So, you are ignorant of the very thing you worship—and this is what I am going to proclaim to you." (Acts 17:22-23, NIV.)

All I am saying is that besides using the scriptures from the Holy Bible, we use the culture's own words to disciple them. Use the tools, the talents and the gifts that God has given us to reach the culture.

In his book, "The Case for A Creator," Lee Strobel a former self-proclaimed Atheist goes on a journey to discredit the existence of God. He interviews many people in the field of science, Astronomy, Cosmology, Biophysics, Biochemistry, including Physicist, Mathematicians, and countless others. To his surprise, most of these scientists (most of who **were** Atheist) he interviewed all have concluded that the universe, including earth, was created by a Master

Designer. God is real. That God created the universe and that He is without a reasonable doubt the designer of the galaxy, the planets, and the humans. Darwinism has been blown out of the water, and there is no evidence that suggests his theory is reliable. I say all this to say that God is very real and thus proved that the Scriptures are the truth and nothing but the truth.

I want to thank Mr. Lee Strobel for an amazing job in writing his book on The Case For A Creator to encourage people to come into the light and knowledge of our Creator from a scientific view. It's not to say that the Bible isn't a book of enlightenment because it is that and more. But some believers have become intellects and because of the culture have begun to question the Scriptures. I believe, in my opinion, that reading a book such as this one alongside the Bible would not be such a bad idea. I can appreciated Mr. Strobel for taking on such a feat to prove to the world, especially the church in this case, that God is not a figment of the Christian's imagination. I would admonish the church of Christ to rethink their loyalty to the God of the universe and recommit themselves to take very seriously who God is and why He is. They are to stop playing church and consider their ungodly behavior before a true and living God. Let me leave you with this excerpt from Lee Strobel to contemplate on as you decide to get right with God.

> "...the convincing evidence establishes the essential reliability of the New Testament, demonstrates that fulfillment of ancient prophecies in the life of Jesus of Nazareth against all the odds, and supports Jesus' resurrection as being an actual event that occurred in time and space. Indeed, this return from the dead is an unprecedented and supernatural feat that authenticated his claim to being the one-and-only Son of God. To me, the range, the variety, the depth, and the breathtaking persuasive power of evidence from both science and history affirmed the credibility of Christianity to the degree that my doubts were simply washed

away. ...Unlike Darwinism, where my faith would have to swim upstream against the strong current of evidence flowing the other way, putting my trust in the God of the Bible was nothing less than the most rational and natural decision I could make. ...I see faith as being a reasonable step in the same direction that the evidence is pointing. In other words, faith goes beyond merely acknowledging that the facts of science and history point to God. It's responding to those facts by investing trust in God."[43]

This is another form of media that will bring insight and revelation to a modern world where seeing is believing. Here we have it the truth in black and white what else do we need to know. The Scriptures in the Bible are accurate real-life events that occurred in history. God is very much alive and the Messiah, Jesus sits at the right hand of the Father in heaven. They are both observing what you and I are doing so get it right because the 'crown of life' awaits us.

We are God's royal messengers – we must travel to bring the word to others and faithfully deliver God's message to the lost – we have God's authority to speak in public. God will be with us always. It is foolish to refuse to do what God has called us to do because society deems it not being 'Politically Correct.'

"Political Correctness, [is] a term used to refer to language that seems intended to give the least amount of offense, especially when describing groups identified by external markers such as race, gender, culture, or sexual orientation. The concept has been discussed, disputed, criticized, and satirized by commentators from across the political spectrum. The term has often been used derisively to ridicule the notion that altering language usage can change the public's perceptions and beliefs as well as influence outcomes. The term first appeared in Marxist-Leninist vocabulary following

336

the Russian Revolution of 1917. At that time it was used to describe adherence to the policies and principles of the Communist Party of the Soviet Union (that is, the party line)." [44]

Political Correctness can go straight to Hades as far as I'm concern because it does nothing to enhance the kingdom of God. The only thing political correctness is good for is for teaching our young people to engage in the things of the secular world. To engage in such things as sexual immorality, marking their bodies with tattoos, body piercing; watching uncensored movies and television programs, and wearing tight clothes and leggings to the church that leaves nothing to the imagination. The church becomes helpless slaves to sin.

In my frustration, I cried out to God about the condition of our nation, the United States of America, and what was going to happen to my children and their families if this nation continued on the path of moral decline. And, as usual, God always responds to me through the Scriptures. I read from Philippians 2:12-18 and this was the revelation I received from God. We are neither to complain about one another nor argue among each other. We are to live clean, innocent lives as children of God. We are to hold firmly to the word of life. That we have the privilege of sharing the gospel and we are to share it with boldness. We are to let everyone know that Christ Jesus is real. That those who have been redeemed should help others receive salvation, and we are not to keep it to ourselves. The church is to let everyone know that the truth brings freedom from darkness, falsehood, and sin.

My inspiration for writing this book came from a desire for every Christian to live right before God. I desire that they will have their names written in the book of life and not have to face eternal condemnation.

It wasn't much longer when I got this hunger to write the book. It took me six years to decide to sit down to write. It was a struggle because 'life happens,' in the interim but I was determined to write it. By writing this book, I envision change to take place in the church where members would treat one another with love and respect. My story will inspire people to stop living a double life. Instead, they should seek to be holy as God is holy. And, last but not least, for the people to take responsibility for their actions for the sake of the next generation.

The adults of this nation, especially the church members, have the responsibility for leaving a legacy to the next generation. What will that legacy be?

I can only speak for myself when I say that I will stay focus and complete the task that God had assigned to me. I will not be afraid because I'm standing on God's promises. I believe God for a saved and sanctified family.

Thank God for the strength and the wisdom I needed to complete this book.

My hope is that this book will be read in Bible study groups, and in Sunday school classes. I would also want this book to be used as a teaching tool on college campuses and universities.

It's my deep concern that Christians, as well as unbelievers, understand that genuine transformation is expected of all who say they are servants of the Lord. We must depend on Christ Jesus who is the gatekeeper. He has the key to open and close heaven's gate to us. If you don't love, then you are not a child of the "Father who is in heaven."

As I mentioned before sharing certain movies and television programs will help us minister mainly to the youth of this nation and some more hard-headed adults (I say this with all due respects.)

I would use movies like Sheffey, Left Behind, God's Not Dead I & II, Badge of Faith and countless others that will reflect the real battles we face between good and evil, and how good always prevails. For example, if you were a fan of 'Star Trek' in the 60s most of the episodes, if not all dealt with good versus evil and how good always prevailed over evil. Why do you suppose that was? Because the majority of the people want to believe that good is always the right thing. They know that there is too much evil in the world and their desire is for evil to be gone, to disappear forever.

That is why we must with all diligence seek to be in intercession for our family, our church family and the nation. Let us be more empathic with everyone and love as Christ loves. Our prayer must be that there should not be any kind of phoniness in the church but total submission to God. That total submission is a pre-requisite to being in the kingdom and no 'half-stepping' allowed. We must gain insight into our sins and learn to deal with them in a much healthier manner. We must stop creating bad situations in our lives and in our environments because everything from God is good.

In my thirty years, I don't think I had taken eternity serious as I determined in 2017. I made up my mind to live a godly life with the expectations of eternity. I live life as if Christ is coming today. I rejoice, pray, give thanks, and think happy thoughts. I ask God daily to guard my heart and give me peace. I ignore the rudeness and show the love of the Living Christ to everyone. 'Teach me your ways', Lord Jesus.

I want to display all of these virtues: Be true to God's word. Respect and honor others. Do what is morally right in God's eyes. Live a pure life. Live life according to God's will. Let the light of Christ shine that others will see Him in me.

We must serve God voluntarily not grudgingly.
Always depend on God to fix your mess.
Mortify the flesh daily.
This earth is not our home – it is a temporary dwelling.
God bless you.

NOTES

1   M. S. Peck, People of the Lie: The Hope for Healing Human Evil. (New York. Simon & Schuster, 1983), 255.

2   R. C. Sproul, Conscience. Renewing Your Mind, Ligonier Ministries. Lecture. (9/15/2017). Retrieved from https://renewingyourmind.org/

3   Sproul, Conscience.

4   Jakes, T. D. I Need to Know My Purpose. Sermon. Cornerstone Church, San Antonio, (10/24/2014).

5   Hagee, John. Prophecy For Tomorrow: The Anti-Christ Is Here. Sermon. Cornerstone Church, San Antonio, (10/12/2014).

6   The Encounter God Worship & Film Channel. Sheffey. Inspirational Film. Published (3/9/2018). Retrieved from YouTube. https://youtu.be/lfnf1l4gzps.

7   Christus Rex. Jim Caviezel Testimony. Interview. Published (Mar 25, 2016). Retrieved from YouTube. https://www.youtube.com/watch?v=0Ejaw0F8-sY&t=1s

8   Wikipedia contributors. Star Trek. The Arena. In Wikipedia, The Free Encyclopedia. Retrieved (2/3/2018). from https://en.wikipedia.org/wiki/Arena_(Star_Trek:_The_Original_Series)

9   Wikipedia contributors. St. Maximilian Maria Kolbe was a Polish Conventual Franciscan friar. From Wikipedia, The Free Encyclopedia. Retrieved 6/15/2018. https://en.wikipedia.org/wiki/Maximilian_Kolbe

10 Bible Study.Org. The Meaning of Numbers: The Number 8. Retrieved (3/21/2018) from http://www.biblestudy.org/bibleref/meaning-of-numbers-in-bible/8.html

11 John Bunyan. Pilgrim's Progress. (New York, Barnes & Noble Classic, 2005). 28.

12 G. H. Chesterton, Heretics. (Freeport, New York, 1970 Reprinted), 32.

13 Wikipedia contributors. Patron Saints Festivals. The Free Encyclopedia. Retrieved (4/3/2018) from https://en.wikipedia.org/wiki/Fiesta_patronal

14 Focus – Fellowship of Catholic University Students Jim Caviezel "Paul The Apostle of Christ." Retrieved (4/5/2018). from YouTube. https://youtu.be/e9z-dMQjRBE

15 Wikipedia contributors. Generation X. The Free Encyclopedia. Retrieved (5/10/2018) from https://en.wikipedia.org/wiki/Generation_X

16 Wikipedia contributors. Millennials. The Free Encyclopedia. Retrieved (5/10/2018) from https://en.wikipedia.org/wiki/Millennials

17 Janet Meyers Everts. The Apostle Paul And His Times: Christian History Timeline. Christianity Today. Retrieved (5/24/2018) from https://www.christianitytoday.com/history/issues/issue-47/apostle-paul-and-his-times-christian-history-timeline.html

18 The Encounter God Worship & Film Channel. Sheffey.

19 Bunyan. Pilgrim's Progress. 142.

20 Five Things You Should Know About Stress: Everyone feels stressed from time to time. National Institute of Mental Health. Retrieved (6/9/18) from https://www.nimh.nih.gov/health/publications/stress/index.shtml

21 Compelling Truth. Religiosity. Retrieved (6/20/2018) from https://www.compellingtruth.org/religiosity.html

22 Christianity Today. Brother Lawrence Practitioner of God's Presence. Retrieved (6/20/2018) from https://www.christianitytoday.com/history/people/innertravelers/brother-lawrence.html

23 Blu Greenberg. My Jewish Learning. Jews Hang a Mezuzah on the Doorpost. A Mezuzah declares that the people who dwell here live Jewish lives. Retrieved from https://www.myjewishlearning.com/article/mezuzah/

24 The Jesus Question. WWJD, Part 3: The Bracelets and Ensuring Graze. Posted January 16, 2012. Retrieved from https://thejesusquestion.org/2012/01/16/wwjd-part-3-the-bracelets-and-ensuing-craze/

25 Goodreads: Christian Quotes: Gandi. Retrieved from https://www.goodreads.com/quotes/tag/christians

26 N. C. Mullen. My Redeemer Lives. Word Records, 2000. Accessed (6/25/2018). Retrieved from http://www.metrolyrics.com/my-redeemer-lives-lyrics-nicole-c-mullen.html

27 Eddie James. House of Prayer. Shift (Awakening, 2014. Accessed (6/25/2018)). Retrieved from http://www.metrolyrics.com/house-of-prayer-lyrics-eddie-james.html

28 Alex Campos. Taller Del Maestro (Master's Workshop). CanZion Group LP, 2003. Accessed (6/25/2018). Retrieved from https://www.letras.com/alex-campos/450619/

29 Christianbook.com. War Room. YouTube. Published (6/29/2015). Retrieved from https://youtu.be/2DbRwcrhiLA

30 Sharon Nesbitt. "Rhua" (Holy Spirit). Sermon. Eagles International Training Institute Summit. Dallas, (10/27/2016).

31 Philip Kosloski. Aleteia: Catholic News. A Powerful Exhortation from FDR in a WWII Bible Given to Soldiers. Published November 11, 2017. Retrieved from https://aleteia.org/2017/11/11/a-powerful-exhortation-from-fdr-in-a-wwii-bible-given-to-soldiers/

32 John Maxwell (Producer). 2018. Leadership Training: Go Get It. Webinar. Accessed from http://www.johnmaxwell.com/

33 Tony Evan. The Kingdom Agenda. The Urban Alternative. WFIF Radio 1500 AM. Accessed (4/10/16).

34 Paul Sheppard. For Lovers Only. Sermon. Cornerstone Church, San Antonio, (3/24/2013).

35 Peck. People of the Lie. 268-269.

36 Hezekiah Walker. Wait on the Lord. Sermon. The Cathedral of the Holy Spirit Church. Bridgeport, (8/20/16).

37 Wikipedia contributors. Salvation Army. The Free Encyclopedia. Retrieved from https://en.wikipedia.org/wiki/The_Salvation_Army

38 Wikipedia contributors. Awakenings in the United States. In Wikipedia. The Free Encyclopedia. Retrieved from https://en.wikipedia.org/wiki/Christian_revival

39 In the Name of Jesus. Hymnary. Org. Song. Retrieved from https://hymnary.org/text/in_the_name_of_jesus_in_the_name_of_jesu

40 Pat Morley, (Founder & Co-CEO of Man in the Mirror). A Brief History of Spiritual Revival and Awakening In America. (6/30/2015). Retrieved from http://patrickmorley.com/blog/2015/6/23/a-brief-history-of-spiritual-revival-and-awakening-in-america

41 Michael Brady. Jezebel Spirit and How It Operates: How To Handle A Jezebel Spirit. accessed 8/6/18. Retrieved from https://www.bible-knowledge.com/the-jezebel-spirit-and-how-it-operates/

42 Diane Joy Truitt. Unshackled Program, Episodes #3507 & #3508. Pacific Garden Mission. Chicago. Accessed 5/20/2018. Pureflix.com. God Is Not Dead 2. Retrieved from https://pureflix.com/videos/253290022484/watch?recommended=r:home/exclusively-on-pure-flix

43 Lee Strobel. The Case for a Creator. (Grand Rapids, Zondervan, 2004). 285-286

44 Encyclopedia Britannica. Political Correctness. Accessed 9/25/18. Retrieved from https://www.britannica.com/

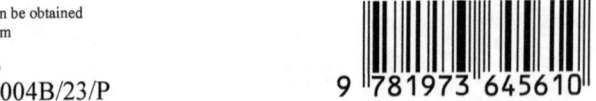